Best Possible Odds

Contemporary Treatment Strategies for Gambling Disorders

William G. McCown
Linda L. Chamberlain

John Wiley & Sons, Inc.

New York • Chichester • Weinheim • Brisbane • Singapore • Toronto

This publication is designed to provide accurate and authoritative information in regard to the subject matter covered. It is sold with the understanding that the publisher is not engaged in rendering professional services. If legal, accounting, medical, psychological or any other expert assistance is required, the services of a competent professional person should be sought.

Library of Congress Cataloging-in-Publication Data:

Chamberlain, Linda L.
    Best possible odds : contemporary treatment strategies for gambling
    disorders / Linda L. Chamberlain and William G. McCown.
        p.   cm.
    Includes bibliographical references and index.
    ISBN 0-471-18969-3 (alk. paper)
    1. Compulsive gambling.   2. Compulsive gamblers.   3. Impulse
    control disorders.   I. McCown, William George.   II. Title.
    RC569.5.G35C47   1999
    616.85′841—dc21   99-16055

10   9   8   7   6   5   4   3   2   1

In Memoriam:

Professor Hans Jurgen Eysenck (1916–1997)
Urbem latericium invenit, marmoream reliquit.

Foreword

A NOTE FROM A COMPULSIVE GAMBLER IN RECOVERY

MY NAME is "John" and I'm a compulsive gambler, an alcoholic, a cocaine addict, a nicotine addict, and a sex addict. I've been asked to read the manuscript for this book from the perspective of a recovering gambler. I don't know these two therapists personally, but wish I had met them when I started my pathway to Recovery. They and this book might have made things one hell of a lot easier.

I've been "wager-free," as these authors like to call it, since—well, let's put it this way: I was around to bet on all of Reggie Jackson's career, but not long enough to wager on Seattle Slew. Anonymity is important, so I apologize for this and subsequent vagueness.

Gamblers, even those of us who are in what we call Recovery, usually don't mince words. We are blunt, arrogant, narcissistic, and, usually, rude. So let me be blunt about this book, especially for those of you who will read no further. Every mental health professional, regardless of training, needs to read this book.

What makes me qualified to say this? Indulge me for a few minutes. I started gambling heavily in college, sometime before the late '60's. Friends said I majored in poker, although I was actually heavily involved in a real major in the physical sciences. I also drank a lot. Somehow, I managed to do well enough in college, despite the fact that I was constantly drunk. As part of the social climate following Sputnik, I received a scholarship to pursue "advanced professional training." I finished my doctoral work—again, I need to remain anonymous—at the same time that I became a genuine, shaking, hide-your-liquor-in-the-closet drunk.

One problem, my drinking, was obvious to those around me. The other problem remained secret for many more years. I wish someone around me had read a book similar to this one.

Gamblers hail from all lifestyles. Your surgeon could be a chronic gambler, betting on the results of your bypass. Your plumber could be betting with his assistant on where he will find the blocked line in your water system. Your estate planner might be up to her neck in gambling debts owed to all kinds of nasty underworld types, just like on television.

Compulsive gamblers are everywhere. Like people with other socially forbidden behaviors, we recognize each other through elaborate codes, nonverbal communications, and what frankly seems to be almost a sixth sense. Nevertheless, like many gamblers I know, I was a highly functioning and well regarded professional, despite the fact that I was stoned drunk.

Early in my professional life, I made a lot of money. My work was technical, tedious, and lucrative. For fun, I went to the races, played cards, and went to Mecca, otherwise known as Las Vegas, just about any chance I got.

As Chamberlain and McCown note, my behavior was typical of many gamblers. I changed my line of work to allow me to wager legally. I specialized in securing a type of scientific contracts for which I had to bid fiercely and fake out the competition. It was just one big poker game to me. In the good times, which were plentiful until the late 1960s, I thought I was God. Even drunk, I could still feel omnipotent when I landed "the big one." My boss was happy, even when I reeked of vomit.

Chamberlain and McCown do an outstanding job of nailing the deceptions that gamblers generate. I know because I lived them.

I stumbled into GA [Gamblers Anonymous] quite unintentionally. I had no thought of giving up my secret little "hobby." However, I had just lost a big government subcontract, probably because some higher-ups realized that I might be a real security risk. My "conversion" to GA was not the kind that's written up in the Hollywood tabloids. I was broke and trying to put together a payroll for my fledgling company. In my mind, I was a hero, despite the fact that I was robbing my workers to pay for my gambling losses. In desperation, I did what every gambler does: I tried to borrow more.

I desperately needed a loan to "float" the company until the next payment was received from my contractor. For very good reasons, I was turned down by my banker, who wanted an audit. It was obvious that somebody was stealing from the corporation and not doing a good job of hiding it.

My banker, a grouchy bastard, confronted me about these "loose books." For a few seconds, I envisioned a jail cell. To my banker, I muttered something about taking the last few hundred out of my account and trying to make the payroll at a harness track where I had heard races were fixed. At that moment, I hit the real bottom.

As fate or something higher would have it, my banker also had a gambling problem. He asked, matter-of-factly, whether I "gamble excessively," as he judiciously phrased it. I swore at him, but then listened to him further, since he was my only hope. Incredibly, he next made an offer that no one could make today.

"I think you have the same problem I have. We're both compulsive gamblers. It's a disease. If you'll go to Gamblers Anonymous with me for a month, I'll loan you enough to make your next two payrolls. And I'll give you the loan today. But you have to come with me to meetings."

I protested that I was a recovering alcoholic and GA couldn't address my real problems. After all, I'd already worked a program. But he was insistent. He took me to a meeting that afternoon. It was one of the few places you could find an afternoon meeting. I went through the "Twenty Questions" and realized that, in addition to being an alcoholic and a cocaine addict, I was also a compulsive gambler. As Chamberlain and McCown note in this book, gambling is often the hardest addiction for a person to acknowledge.

But the evidence was undeniable. In GA, they say the average compulsive gambler drags down two dozen people who are not gamblers. That was an understatement. Two wives, two bankruptcies, ruined relations with four children, and parents who died without my saying goodbye. Quite grudgingly and slowly, I began to admit my problem.

Chamberlain and McCown are to be lauded for their emphasis that a compulsive gambler (I know they don't like to use the term, but I do!) often has psychiatric problems. Along with my addictions, I was depressed and anxious, and I was increasingly tending toward agoraphobia. I became impotent with anyone who would be a potential long-term partner. Furthermore, I was becoming obsessed with pornography, strip shows, topless bars, and anything tawdry that kept me from intimacy.

For a while, I became addicted to sex with anonymous partners—often, people who were high on cocaine that I had bought for them. I was living a complete lie. Had someone in my Program discovered a book like this one, I might have been advised to get professional treatment for some of my problems. I would have been spared an extraordinary amount of suffering and at least one more suicide attempt.

In time, things started to come together. Eventually, my company was saved and placed on a firm financial footing. Part of the mystery of Recovery is the little coincidences that keep giving needed help. Many of us ascribe them to a caring Higher Force. Quite by accident, and in a most unlikely place that will have to remain anonymous, I found a responsible business partner.

I had relapses. I kept gambling in secret for quite a while, though at a lower intensity and reduced frequency. This book discusses the fact that relapse is almost ubiquitous. Readers should realize that such relapses do not mean the end of Recovery.

My process of "chasing" was not superdramatic, but I have my own ugly truth. It's been 20-plus years since I placed a bet, and around 30 years since I had my last drink. I go to CA, AA, and GA. I know the programs work; still, I fight the impulses. Maybe an inpatient program, or other suggestions such as relaxation training, would have helped.

I don't agree with everything in this book. As a gambler, I tend to be superstitious. GA worked for me and I believe it is probably the only way to learn honesty, the gambler's biggest problem. On the other hand, what is targeted here is a life beyond the last bet. That took me a long time to learn.

I can't make this point strongly enough: Every so-called mental health professional should read this book. If someone I knew had had the awareness that these two therapists show, maybe, just maybe, I would have been confronted earlier. Would it have helped? Only God knows. I like to believe it would have turned me around sooner.

"JOHN"

New York, New York
April 1999

Acknowledgments

WE WISH to thank all of our clients for their courage, vision, and tenacity. For their decision to seek help, they are the true teachers and heroes. We cannot repay them, but we hope to pass on what we have learned from them.

Collectively, we owe a tremendous debt to the staff at John Wiley & Sons, Inc., especially Kelly Franklin. Her patience, editorial prowess, and general positive outlook in the face of our constant procrastination and delays are greatly appreciated.

Most of the ideas regarding nonlinear dynamic change were generated from our collaboration with Michael Bütz and our involvement with the Society for the Study of Chaos Theory in Psychological and Life Sciences. A central thesis of this book is that addiction or recovery from addiction is essentially a nonlinear process. Michael's clinical creativity, enthusiasm, and argumentative brilliance constantly made us rethink all of our assumptions. Michael epitomizes a "Renaissance therapist" who exhibits skill, cultural sensitivity, and flexibility in his clinical and scientific work.

Bob Abouee helped by providing constant humor. We will always appreciate the depth of his smile.

William McCown would like to thank a number of people. Dr. Judith Johnson, a longtime collaborator, suggested much of the newer research contained here. Her influence will always be part of my life, despite distances and circumstances. *"Non curo. Si metrum non habet, non est poema."*

The clinical experiences of Drs. Sean Austin and Alan Summers have been invaluable. Dean Tom Rakes at Northeast Louisiana University deserves special credit for his enthusiastic endorsement of applied scholarship. A Faculty Enhancement Grant from Northeast Louisiana University made much of this research possible, as did the willingness and enthusiasm of many graduate students. Jerry Garcia's ephemeral guitar enhanced the creativity in our laboratory and also generated the flippancy that allowed us to procrastinate unmercifully. Finally, Renee Fleming's and Elizabeth Futral's matchless sopranos made the sweltering, insufferable Louisiana bayou nights a mystical experience in which to ponder and write. Thanks, all.

Linda Chamberlain would like to thank the Colorado Council on Compulsive Gambling for their support. I am particularly indebted to Nancy Lantz for her guidance and devotion to working with problem gamblers and to Dr. Robert Hunter for helping me get involved in this field and for his devotion to helping other professionals learn to work with this population. Thank you, David, for your unfailing encouragement. Finaly, thank you, Bill, for all we shared along the way.

W.G. McC.
L.L.C.

Contents

CHAPTER 1

An Introduction to Gambling and Gambling Disorders

The problem with gambling is that no one can consistently win, but everyone's certain that they will.
—"Pittsburg Phil," early twentieth-century race track legend

DIANNE[1] IS a 47-year-old physician. Despite a very successful practice in internal medicine, she is always "running out of money." Recently, she has begun to drink excessively and is often hung over during the morning medical rounds. Her only social life revolves around daily visits to a casino to play blackjack, a game that she believes she can eventually learn to beat. During the past two years, Dianne has lost over $87,000 while gambling, including $20,000 that she lost during a two-week junket to Las Vegas. Despite these losses, Dianne does not see her gambling as problematic. "The only problem I have is when I lose," she says matter-of-factly.

Bob, 25, is a part-time bartender and a graduate student in English. As part of his bartending chores, he channels illegal bets from bar patrons to his boss and his boss's associates. He simply writes down a patron's code name and wagered amount; at the end of each day, someone comes by to collect the sheet. He knows that his boss is heavily involved in under-world activities, but Bob has begun gambling himself. He already owes several thousand dollars to his boss's "business partner" for wagers on

---

[1] Each case presented herein has identifying details removed. Case material was peer-reviewed to ensure adequate confidentiality. Chapters were peer-reviewed for both clinical relevance and scientific accuracy. Thanks are due to Dr. Ross Keiser, who coordinated these reviews, as well as to the anonymous reviewers, whose comments were greatly appreciated.

the recent collegiate basketball tournament finals. His boss tells him that he can "work off the debt" by agreeing to sell shipments of cocaine. Bob is desperate and, despite the danger, agrees to this arrangement. Although he would very much like to quit gambling, he admits that it is "tremendous fun" and that he constantly thinks about winning "the really big one that would let me break out of here."

Nate is a 16-year-old suburban high school student who buys lottery tickets from his older brother's friends. He has no consistent income, but he still manages to buy ten or more tickets each day, often at the inflated prices that accompany these secondhand transactions. He also bets liberally on sporting events and is usually heavily in debt. To finance these wagers, he often engages in "theft to order"—soliciting a buyer for merchandise that is not yet stolen. Despite his young age, Nate has shoplifted thousands of dollars' worth of computers, audio equipment, cameras, and other high-ticket items. He would like to quit "wasting my money" because he knows he will eventually be caught. "I want to be a chemist someday," he notes. "I don't know too many chemists who have gone to good schools and have a shoplifting history." However, when he does not gamble, he becomes cranky, nervous, and agitated. For a while, he became interested in computers, but he quit because "I was developing an Internet addiction."

Dianne, Bob, and Nate share two things: (1) they have problems with gambling, and (2) their cases had poor outcomes. They were improperly diagnosed and treated by various mental health professionals. Their gambling problems were never addressed or appropriately treated. As a result, they experienced financial devastation, legal problems, elevated psychiatric symptoms, and, too often, complete personal disruption. One client almost succeeded in a serious suicidal attempt. We believe there was a strong probability that these clients' behaviors could have been changed by adequate and appropriate therapeutic interventions. Unfortunately, clinicians treating these cases knew almost nothing about problem gambling behavior.

The primary purpose of this book is to provide clinicians with an understanding of the variety of gambling disorders. Problematic gambling behavior is at epidemic proportions, and this growth will continue (Volberg, 1996; Volberg, Dickerson, Ladouceur, & Abbott, 1996). Available theory and research on gambling are often deficient (Gowen & Speyer, 1995; Griffiths, 1996b; McCormick, 1994; Murray, 1993). Furthermore, inadequate resources are now devoted to the prevention of problem gambling behaviors (Goodman, 1995; McCabe, 1992). We believe that this lack of prevention may incur massive social costs for future generations.

The goals of this book are modest. Our purpose is to highlight the problems, possible causes, and treatment options for people who exhibit excessive gambling-related behaviors. A book cannot make its readers into experts. This process occurs through training, supervision, scholarship, and experience. Nor do we attempt a comprehensive review of gambling literature, theory, or treatments. Instead, we present clinical strategies that have worked for our colleagues and for us. Few treatments in the gambling literature meet the rigid standards that would qualify them as "scientific." Far more research is needed.

We have attempted to remain impartial about the expansion of wagering opportunities, which is occurring at an almost logarithmic pace (Marvel, 1994; Moody, 1995). The expansion is propelled by economic, moral, and political decisions that are beyond the scope of this book. The Internet has carried the problem worldwide (Galston & Wasserman, 1996). We feel that it is vital for clinicians to concentrate on what they do best—changing behavior. Discussions for which they are less prepared only distract from the seriousness of the clinical problem.

GAMBLING THROUGHOUT HISTORY

The word *gamble* has at least two important meanings. According to *Cambridge International Dictionary* (1999), its primary meaning is "to play games of chance for money or other reward." A secondary meaning is "to take a risk in order to gain an advantage." The etiology of the word *gamble* is unclear. It probably relates to the Old English word *gamenian*, meaning "to play," from which we derive the present-day word *gambol* (frolic) (Onions, 1966). It may also be distantly related to the Old French word *gambet*, which evolved into the current term gambit, meaning "a maneuver or action intended to gain an advantage." The irony is that people who develop a problem with gambling-related behaviors view their actions as gaining a financial advantage, while the rest of the world simply sees them wagering unsuccessfully.

Data indicate that most people in the world have gambled (Herman, 1967; Kusyszyn, 1972), even when gambling opportunities were scarcer than they are today (Lesieur, 1994). The great majority of people who gamble do not lose control of their behaviors. Like alcohol use, for most people, gambling is a pleasant pastime, a benign amusement. Yet, for a small subset of people, gambling is a serious behavioral disorder that is associated with depression, anxiety, substance abuse, theft, family disruption, and suicide. These people are labeled as "pathological gamblers" in the *Diagnostic and Statistical Manual of Mental Disorders*, Fourth Edition (*DSM-IV*; APA, 1994). From a psychological perspective, they have failed at self-regulation (Baumeister, Heatherton, & Tice, 1994).

Griffiths (1996a) provides an excellent historical review of the concept of the pathological gambler. Its evolutionary nature is not unlike that of alcoholism. Most national surveys about gambling behavior have concluded that, in almost every culture, there are more gamblers than nongamblers. Furthermore, although most gamblers can control their gambling behavior, a small minority, probably 3% to 5%, will inevitably be labeled as suffering from pathological gambling. Some people in this group eventually seek clinical intervention, but knowledge of how to undertake successful treatment is still scant (Murray, 1993).

Despite its importance, the development of pathological gambling behavior is controversial and poorly understood (Brister & Brister, 1987; Griffiths, 1996a; Hollander & Wong, 1995). Clinical research regarding appropriate treatments of gambling disorders is scant, partly because of inattention and partly because of a lack of funding (Ladouceur, 1996). Society is slowly beginning to realize that, for an important minority of people, gambling can be as disruptive as any other addiction (Walters, 1994). This disruption affects individual gamblers, their families, and, often, their entire social systems (Hraba & Lee, 1995).

Some of the current alarmist headlines cast gambling as a new behavior, almost like a mutant virus that suddenly finds an environmental niche (e.g., Gallo, 1994). Coverage in the popular press frequently vacillates between condemning the apparent gambling "epidemic" as an intrinsic evil and praising the gaming industry for solving the economic problems of large urban areas and rural poor communities. Not surprisingly, the truth is far from both extremes. Gambling has been a ubiquitous phenomenon throughout history (Eisenbuch, 1977). Indeed, according to some authors, gambling is older than money itself (Kusyszyn, 1978). Although it is problematic for some people, its roots are deep in our past.

Gambling may actually predate history by many millions of years. Palmer and Palmer (2000), in an evolutionary behaviorist perspective, argue that analogues of human gambling can be found in the decision-making processes of animals trying to pass their genes on to future generations. They develop mating strategies that are beneficial and give them a reproductive advantage, compared with others of their species. Usually, these strategies involve mating with the strongest or most likely fertile partner that is available. Occasionally, though, animals "gamble" with their genetic lineage by mating with an atypical partner that has traits not usually classified as ideal. In a sense, they are gambling on a "long shot"; their mate has genetic characteristics that might be adaptable in conditions of marked environmental change. This "long-shot mating" may make genetic variability much more probable, enabling the species to adapt to dramatic new conditions that may suddenly emerge.

GAMBLING IN ANCIENT AND MEDIEVAL HISTORY

Regardless of their evolutionary roots, games of chance have been developed throughout human civilization. Early humans apparently used the process of chance to select individuals for certain tasks, provide entertainment, exchange property, or settle disputes (Kusyszyn, 1977). Cartons made of bones, found in prehistoric caves, apparently represented the modern-day equivalent of dice. By the time of the ancient Egyptians, a popular game involved participants' guessing the number of fingers upheld by a priest or other important figure. Often, life or death decisions were based on the outcome of this simple, childhood game. The ancient Greeks developed similar games that were played with another primitive form of dice.

One of the early uses of the printing press was to make specially marked playing cards. With the invention of movable type, developed in China fifteen hundred years before it appeared in Europe, entirely new games of chance and gambling opportunities were created. This tradition spread rapidly to the Arab world, where it remained despite antagonism from Islam. Professional bookmakers—persons who collect and make wagers for a living—arose during this period (King, 1969).

Games of chance were particularly popular in more advanced cultures, such as the early Jewish nations, where gambling was used in an attempt to link the physical and spiritual worlds. Early Hebrew scripture refers to this form of gambling as the "casting of lots"—small, flattened stones that were tossed much like dice (Baly, 1978). The direction that these stones pointed out, once they hit a diagram or the bare earth, indicated the winner of the decision in question. Casting of lots was used in assigning land among tribes (Num. 2:55; Josh. 18:10), in the selection of men for expeditions or battles (Judg. 1:1–3; 20:9), and even in the detection of guilty parties (Josh. 7:14; 1 Sam. 14:40–42). The role of chance was also used in selecting the first Jewish king (1 Sam. 10:20–21), and in determining the role of priests in temple worship (Luke 1:5–9). According to scripture (Matt. 27:35), Roman soldiers cast lots for the clothing of Jesus Christ during his execution.

The Roman civilization, especially during early Christian times and onward, seems to have been especially interested in gambling. Prior to this, Julius Caesar, in 49 B.C., is supposed to have cast lots to determine whether he should attack across the Rubicon and march on to Rome. He did, and the civil war with Pompeii then followed. The expression "The die is cast" (*Alea iacta est*), attributed to Caesar as head of his rebellious army, indicates the seriousness afforded to casting a die. Similarly, the expression "crossing the Rubicon" now indicates an irrevocable commitment.

In Rome, the Coliseum is a monument to how the ancients cherished the sport of chariot racing. A remnant of these competitions survives in our present-day sport of harness racing. (Wagering on horses ridden by jockeys seems to have been a later variation.) The Coliseum also provided the wagering public with opportunities to bet on the outcome of bloody gladiatorial conflicts.

The history of gambling indicates that it coexists quite well with monotheism. During the Dark Ages, games of chance were popular in Hebrew, Islamic, and Christian communities. This may seem to be contradictory to the traditions of the great religions, inasmuch as most sacred writings are, at best, ambivalent about gambling. Yet religion may foster wagering because it may encourage belief in luck (David, 1998), and few religious people or communities want to believe that life's misfortunes are due to their own inadequacies or are deserved. Belief in luck postulates that a force outside of Providence helps to shape our destinies (Curtain & Bernardo, 1997). While this may be psychologically necessary, it also may foster problem gambling. Social history repeatedly shows that wagering is much more common when people believe that luck is an important determinant of their behavior (O'Brien, 1998).[2]

Not surprisingly, because of (or despite) religion, gambling flourished during most periods of Western history (Deutsch, 1990). Until the Crusades, gambling was probably as common in Islamic societies as it was in Christian Europe. Games of chance were everywhere in medieval life (Brenner, 1990). Peasants and Bedouins wagered on the weather, the yields of neighbors' crops, and the dates when babies would be born. Tribal or community festivals were especially celebrated with wagering (F. Rosenthal, 1997). Gambling was one of the few recreational and intellectual activities available, and almost every faction of society pursued it with vigor.

Following the Crusades, gambling became even more common in Europe. Most wagering was heartily proscribed by Islamic cultures as a "Christian vice" during this period (F. Rosenthal, 1997), but Europe's economic and political ascendancy witnessed the rise of the first independent bookmaker (Marx, 1952). Landed classes could place bets with someone other than their friends. Much of the early postal traffic involved correspondence regarding such bets. There is some evidence that ruinous debt acquisition from gambling became common during this period. Nobles wagered high stakes on animal fights, natural events, races of all sorts, and card games (Ashton, 1969).

---

[2] More specifically, believers in a corporeal deity may be faced with the dilemma of reconciling their theologies of a benevolent and caring Being with evidence that their lives are unsatisfactory. Rather than believe that their lack of fortune is due to God's activities and will, such people will frequently turn to "fate" as an explanatory concept. This allows for reduction of the cognitive dissonance associated with the contradictory claims that God is loving and infinitely wise, but "He has not blessed me." Rather than believe that "God forgot me" or "I deserve my negative lot in life," it is often psychologically easier to believe that a proportion of success in life is independent of God's direct intervention. Luck or Fate may help explain Job's eternal query: Why is the world often kinder to evil people than to those who do good?

Gambling among the artisan and peasant classes became more common only with the rise of surplus production (Chinn, 1991). Farmers with small excess could risk it all for the opportunity to receive much more than they ever could produce by themselves. The advent of a currency-based, rather than bartering-based, economic structure encouraged personal speculation. The lack of life opportunities afforded to people during this period added urgency to these wagers. By the time of the Renaissance, peasants and artisans frequently gambled in taverns, towns, and even in churches, with a zest that would shock even present-day observers. For many people, then as today, gambling was perceived as one of the only chances for bettering one's station in life. Superstition, irrationality, and the absence of education fostered these beliefs.

With the rise of capitalism and peasants' migration to cities, gambling became even more common (Geha, 1970). During this period, society witnessed its first large-scale problem of chronic gambling by many citizens. Alcoholism and gambling became common addictions during this period of social change. Working-class people often gambled much more than they could afford to lose. The results were predictably disastrous. Many people were incarcerated for debts incurred in games of chance. Such wagering was often fueled by cheap alcohol and fetid social conditions and fostered by professional bookmakers (Munting, 1996).

By the colorful time of Samuel Pepys, the famous diarist (b. 1633), Londoners were wagering on practically anything—the outcome of the disastrous war with the Dutch, the mortality of the Plague, and even the damage estimates of the Great Fire of 1666. They were also wagering on who would make the life-threatening trip across the ocean to the New World (Ashton, 1969). Undoubtedly, they would have wagered on who would survive such an arduous journey had they any way of receiving accurate feedback.

GAMBLING IN NORTH AMERICA

When settlers arrived in the Americas, they had almost as many betting opportunities as in the Old World (Fenster, 1994). In the New World, gambling has a long and uneven history, not unlike that of Europe. Games of chance were common among the early colonists. The American Revolution was financed, in part, through lottery proceeds (Pavalko, 1999). Not surprisingly, Americans have long had a fascination with horse racing, and they adapted this sport to the frontier and rural environments. Wagering between local settlers or farmers was quite common in America during the eighteenth and nineteenth centuries. In many communities, as in preindustrial Europe, few other leisure activities were available (Burnham, 1994). Native Americans of various tribes had long had friendly wagers, but the vigor with which the new arrivals gambled was often shocking to the indigenous peoples.

The American prohibition against gambling, from which we are now emerging, arose in the last quarter of the nineteenth century (Valverde, 1998). In part, this was a reaction to consistent illegal tampering of state-run lotteries and other games of chance. However, the gradual trend toward outlawing gambling of all types was also a response to the social mores and general prohibition sentiment of the United States during this period of early Modernism (Bergler, 1957). Most racetracks closed down, raising the ire of the newly wealthy, who regarded this "sport of kings" as part of their acquired cultural "heritage." State-run and private lotteries ceased. With the return of Fundamentalism to the American religious community, even card playing became socially unacceptable (Fenster, 1994).

Despite admirable intentions, gambling was never eliminated; it simply went underground (Livingston, 1974). Some evidence suggests that gambling actually increased during this period. It became the "bread and butter" of a variety of criminal societies. Most new immigrant and minority communities offered access to a variety of daily wagering opportunities. These included "punch boards" and "pull tabs," as well as early precursors to the pin-ball game. "Respectable" citizens found other wagering opportunities, mostly within their own social groups, and the newly expanding moneyed classes enjoyed the opulence associated with gambling in Europe, Cuba, or Mexico (O'Brien, 1998).

Gambling became immensely popular during another period of moral legislation—Prohibition. Many "speakeasies" or clandestine bars or taverns had open gambling behind their closed doors. Persons who sold liquor were also able to take wagers (Pavalko, 1999). Many people who had never been in contact with gamblers soon found themselves in situations that made gambling not only respectable, but fashionable. Prohibition merely encouraged the appetite of a prosperous nation for additional forbidden activities. Outside of illegal restaurants and bars, both alcohol and gambling could be paid for by credit, usually with usurious interest rates.

Gambling declined during the Great Depression. However, this economic calamity became the next theater for its eventual expansion and explosion. The relegalization of gambling in the United States began in earnest in 1931 in Nevada, when Governor Frederick Balzar signed Assemblyman Phil Tobin's "Wide-open gambling" law. The law all but acknowledged that illegal gambling had been ongoing for years. Gambling had long been popular in Nevada and was hardly underground (Marx, 1952). This was especially true during Prohibition, which was expected to end shortly. Tobin's sentiment was simple and has been echoed repeatedly throughout this century: If gambling already exists unchecked, then why not regulate it and cash in on it for the good of everyone?

Tobin's actions were largely a concession to the economic realities of the Great Depression and to the downturn in mineral wealth that Nevada was experiencing (Lorenz, n.d.). However, Nevada had the forethought to capitalize on the new economic clout of the growing West Coast, with its comparatively looser moral structure. People had long traveled past the state line of Nevada to "sin." Tobin reasoned—correctly or not—that illegal gambling only encouraged additional criminal behavior. Unfortunately, open gambling made matters worse.

The history of gambling in America has been intimately connected with the rise of organized crime. Nevada proved an excellent opportunity for this relationship to continue. Many of the major casinos of the 1940s and 1950s were paid for by illegally obtained funding, such as drug money or pension funds from unions. Skimming from casinos was considered a part of appropriate business practice. Las Vegas, particularly, became a kind of ersatz capital for organized crime. However, most American and international patrons forgot this as they embraced the glamorous image that Las Vegas was promoting for itself. Organized crime remains intimately involved with both legal and quasi-legal gambling, despite the best attempts of regulators (Sternlieb & Hughs, 1985).

In 1963, the fiscally and morally conservative state of New Hampshire legalized the first statewide lottery. This was largely an attempt to prevent any increase in taxes. Slowly, other states followed. In 1998, 36 states had legalized lotteries, despite controversy regarding their economic impact and some evidence that legal lotteries disproportionately transfer wealth away from poorer communities. However, the rise in legal lotteries, with a variety of gaming opportunities, hastened the decline of the community institutions of "numbers' rackets." These petty wagering activities were connected with the results at local racetracks, and usually supported organized crime.

In 1978, casino gambling was legalized in New Jersey. This came at a midpoint of a long recession and general economic disaster in the area. After a rough financial start, it appears that this industry has stabilized. By 1979, more than $17 billion was legally gambled in the United States. Regulators in Atlantic City were initially more cautious in their support. For example, they did not legalize off-track wagering and sports gambling, as Las Vegas did. Missing little time, organized crime began exploiting this market. Illegal sports betting increased substantially, especially on the East Coast.

In 1988, the Federal Indian Gambling Regulatory Act legalized casino gambling on Native American land. By the end of the decade, Americans had wagered $247 billion legally, up 1,450% from the previous decade

(Simurda, 1994), despite a severe economic downturn in Nevada and a major recession at the start of the decade. In 1995, this number had more than doubled to a record of $482 billion legally wagered (Schlichter & Valente, 1996).

By 1998, ten states had "general" casinos, and casinos were operating on Native American land in 24 states (Munting, 1996). Thirty-six states had lotteries, and six had legalized video poker or other noncasino electronic games. Pari-mutuel wagering—usually on horses, but also on dogs and in Jai Alai frontons—was available in some form in 34 states and was clearly tolerated in several more. Only two states, Utah and Hawaii, do not have some legalized form of gambling within their state borders. Even in these states, many bars, lounges, bowling alleys, truck stops, and restaurants have illegally run video games available for payoffs if the client is a "regular."

The Electronic Revolution and Gambling[3]

The electronic revolution brought on by the personal computer has had a substantial impact on types and perhaps on frequency of gambling. Initially, the computer gave gamblers in select events, such as horse races, an advantage over other betters. People with access to computer technology could employ multiple regression algorithms, which would give them a slight edge over other pundits. This advantage quickly declined when personal computers became more universal.

During the early 1980s, entrepreneurs with their own personal computers could establish their own bookmaking services, with bets placed anonymously. A humble Apple II or Commodore 64 could be programmed to answer telephone calls without human intervention. (The authors witnessed this process on several occasions and at several college campuses.) By the mid-1980s, it was not uncommon to find university students running such enterprises out of their dorm rooms or even via university computing facilities! Most major campuses had several "agents" who would set up accounts from credit cards, and credit wins or debit losses anonymously and automatically (Layden, 1995). Anecdotal accounts from people whom we now treat suggest that many of these entrepreneurs developed gambling-related problems themselves.

The wager of choice in the youth-oriented market of the 1980s was in the rapidly expanding sports betting market, especially for college and professional sports (Williams, 1999). This change from the traditional

---

[3] Much of this section is an oral history of gambling in the 1980s, chronicled by anonymous recovering gamblers. We especially thank Lloyd L. for his assistance.

emphasis on horse racing was boosted in part by the proliferation of sports through cable television and satellite transmission. It became commonplace for local or network television sports commentators to discuss the gambling point spread—a concession to the ubiquitousness of sports wagering. For a brief time, organized crime appeared slow to react to these changes; most traditional bookmakers were reticent to handle such unconventional "traffic." Again, this opened the door for students and other inventive techies to market a perceived vice to a new social niche. However, once organized crime saw the enormous profit potential, the "amateurs" were squeezed out, often by violent means.

During the 1980s, computer technology ushered in another revolution. The slot machine, invented in 1887 by Charles Fey, had made gambling popular for common, low-stakes players. The innards of the machine were previously composed of a variety of mechanical springs, wheels, and notches acting as stopping points for specific payoffs (O'Brien, 1998). Pull the lever and the slot reels turn, landing on a fairly random basis. By 1980, a microprocessor controlling these components stopped them randomly, within the limits of the payoff desired by the casino. This greatly reduced the cost of slot machines; expanded their availability, and allowed very rapid play.

Although slot machines brought in countless millions, they attracted only players who had few expectations. The "low stakes" slots were of little interest to serious players. The practical limitations on the physics of the pull-lever machines kept their potential combinations to usually fewer than 8,000—hardly enough to allow them to pay out the huge dollar amounts that the public demanded.

Today, multimillion-dollar jackpots, available on "fruit machines" (Griffiths, 1994), have heightened interest in slot machine wagering. This change was made possible by additional innovations in computer technology (Daniels, 1994). By 1984, most slot machines were "virtual reels" (programmed images). Unlimited numbers of reels, each with an unlimited number of stops, were possible. Computer chips could be programmed to make jackpot payoffs much scarcer than previously, which made tremendous jackpots possible. This added interest to fruit gambling, a type of gambling behavior that may have its own potential problems. A new market of older, lower-stakes players began to be courted, and many of them lost control of their gambling behavior.

The cost of machines kept dropping, which helped both the legal and illegal marketers. The authors once saw an illegal homemade slot machine, constructed from an old computer and scraps from a defunct jukebox. This machine took in over a $1,000 a day from bar patrons but cost less than $400 to put together.

At present, wagering opportunities for anyone with a credit card are only a telephone call away. The Internet proliferates with gambling sites, located in countries with liberal gambling laws or on Native American land (G. Johnson, 1996). Despite the attempts of legislators to curb these wagering possibilities, both offshore toll-free numbers and Internet gambling services seem likely to thrive in the foreseeable future (Impco, 1996). Abolishing or limiting the transmission of dollars over the Internet will not be easy. Even if such gambling were prohibited, it would undoubtedly continue to thrive with secretive numbers, not unlike the private bulletin boards that dominated cyberspace before the Internet.[4] "Cyberbets" will be as easy to access as Internet pornography or bootlegged software.

HOW SIGNIFICANT ARE GAMBLING PROBLEMS?

Gambling is not new, but some persons have significant problems associated with gambling. How widespread and significant these problems are remains unknown, in part because of the difficulty in studying the phenomenon and in part because of scant attention afforded it by the scientific community.

The acquisition, development, and maintenance of pathological gambling are areas in continual dispute. One reason may be that pathological gambling was only recognized as a bona fide mental disorder in the Third Edition of the *Diagnostic and Statistical Manual of Mental Disorders* (*DSM-III*; APA, 1980). A second reason is the dearth of research. There are over 1,000 times as many articles on schizophrenia, which affects only one percent of the population, as there are on gambling disorders, which are at least three times as prevalent.

The data we have indicate that gambling is a major problem for a subset of persons. For example, Abbott and Volberb (1994) summarized major findings of a 1991 national survey of problem and pathological gambling among 4,053 adults in New Zealand, and compared these findings with those of epidemiological studies from the United States and Canada. Lifetime pathological gambling prevalence estimates ranged from 0.1% to 2.7%, and current estimates ranged from 0.6% to 1.2%. Shaffer and Hall (1996) estimated that about 1% of the adult population and 3% of the adolescent population have current chronic gambling problems.

---

[4] One of the authors was told by a therapy client (whose details have been removed to exclude identification) that the state-of-the-art for gambling is computerized software that calls into a private 800 number via a modem. The computer at the other end is a powerful laptop; its location changes by the hour. It seems unlikely that law enforcers will be able to stop this degree of technology.

Volberg (1996) examined the results of prevalence studies of problem and pathological gambling that have been carried out in 15 U.S. jurisdictions since 1980. Problem and pathological gamblers in the general population were significantly more likely than nongamblers to be male, under age 30, non-Caucasian, and unmarried. Furthermore, they started gambling at a significantly earlier age. There are critical challenges in conducting surveys of gambling and problem gambling in the general population, but this approach remains an important and cost-effective method for obtaining information about gambling that is unavailable from other sources.

Other researchers are less clear about the seriousness of the problem. The prevalence of pathological gambling refers to the percentage of cases of pathological gambling occurring in a community at a given time. When prevalence studies were conducted in different principalities throughout the world, none of them was found to conform to this definition of prevalence. The major error, in all but the most recent surveys conducted, has been identified as the use of questions that ask whether gambling-related problems *have ever occurred* rather than whether they *are currently occurring*. This error will lead to an overestimation of the prevalence of pathological gambling in society.

Perhaps the best generalizations regarding gambling in the United States can be made from the meta-analytic review by Shaffer and Hall (1996), which reached four conclusions:

1. Adult *prevalence* rates of pathological gambling increased from 1977 to 1997.
2. No regional differences in gambling disorder prevalence in North America can be found.
3. Adolescents gamble abundantly and tend to gamble on noncasino games.
4. Adults are gambling more on casino games and the lottery.

Beyond mere numbers, researchers must pay attention to the severity of the problem afforded by gambling. It is clearly a social problem with a potentially vast impact. Blaszczynski and Silove (1997) provided evidence that pathological gamblers are at high risk for committing criminal offenses in order to maintain their habitual gambling behaviors. The average gambler who enters inpatient treatment is approximately $80,000 in debt and has lost almost everything he or she owns. Gambling problems correlate with substance abuse, depression, anxiety, suicide, antisocial behavior, joblessness, divorce, and family dysfunction (Vitaro et al., 1998. Not surprisingly, children of persons with gambling problems are at high risk for anxiety, somatization disorders, depression, substance abuse, low academic achievement, and personality disorders (Maurer, 1994).

Perhaps the most fear-inspiring aspect of gambling disorders is that they are increasing at an apparently rapid rate among the young (Winters, Stinchfield, & Kim, 1995). Indeed, one of the authors treated a nine-year-old child who gambled away not only lunch money, but also household furnishings and money stolen from his mother's purse. The object of the wagers usually was the outcome of pick-up basketball games played in inner-city playgrounds by older youths.

Prevalence studies support this. For example, Schaffer and Hall (1996) reviewed published and unpublished studies that estimate the prevalence of adolescent gambling problems in the United States. Data from more than 7,500 adolescents, aged 13 to 20 years, were included. In addition to comparing the conceptual and methodological differences among these studies, the article employed a meta-analytic strategy to synthesize prevalence estimates from the existing studies. This analysis revealed that, within a 95% confidence interval, between 9.9% and 14.2% of adolescents are at risk for developing or returning to serious gambling problems. Similarly, between 4.4% and 7.4% of adolescents exhibit seriously adverse compulsive or pathological patterns of gambling.

GAMBLING AS AN ADDICTIVE PSYCHIATRIC DISORDER

Although we have made frequent reference to problem gambling, we have not defined it yet. This is analogous to society's response to gambling as a disorder. Despite data to the contrary (e.g., Galdston, 1968), The American Psychiatric Association did not formally recognize pathological gambling as a genuine psychiatric disorder until 1980. Freud (1929/1950) had studied problem gambling, but he was rather pessimistic about its prognosis.

The most current definition of "pathological gambling" appears in *DSM-IV*, published in 1990. The American Psychiatric Association defines pathological gambling as a progressive psychological disorder characterized by emotional dependence, loss of control, and accompanying negative consequences in the gamblers' school, social, or vocational life. Other common names for pathological gambling are *compulsive gambling* and *addictive gambling*.

More specifically, in *DSM-IV*, Pathological Gambling (312.31) is defined as an Axis I disorder of persistent and recurrent maladaptive behaviors. To receive the diagnosis, the patient must demonstrate five of the following:

1. Preoccupation with gambling.
2. Need to gamble with increasing amounts of money to achieve heightened arousal.

3. Repeated unsuccessful efforts to control, cut back, or stop gambling.
4. Restlessness or irritability when attempting to cut down or reduce gambling.
5. Gambling as a way of escaping from dysphoric moods.
6. Returning after a losing day, to "get even."
7. Lying to family and others about extent of involvement with gambling.
8. Commission of illegal acts to finance gambling.
9. Jeopardization of a significant relationship or of an education or career opportunity from gambling.
10. Reliance on others to provide money to help the financial status caused by gambling.

The sole exclusion criterion is that gambling behavior is not due to bipolar disorders.

The argument concerning whether gambling is an "addiction" is unnecessarily controversial and at times defies common sense (Kusyszyn, 1980). For example, several years ago, a popular advice columnist ran an article from a physician stating that gambling "could not possibly" be addictive. By definition, according to this person, actions such as gambling, shoplifting, and excessive sexual behaviors do not involve substance ingestion and therefore are not addictions. Instead, the physician argued, they are usually manifestations of manic depressive illness. (Interestingly, mania is an exclusion diagnosis for gambling disorders. If this were true, then gambling patients would almost all be controlled with lithium, which is not the case.)

Unfortunately, this is an outmoded yet still popular view. In part, the *DSM-IV* supports it. Gambling is not classified as an addictive disorder because the latter term is reserved for behaviors associated with specific abused substances. Instead, it is characterized as a *disorder of impulse control.* Gambling is placed in the same category as fire setting, hair pulling, and explosive temperament, rather than alcohol abuse and cocaine use, despite the fact that the dynamics of gambling include preoccupation, loss of control, tolerance, withdrawal, and other aspects that make it indistinguishable from a classic addiction (Lesieur, 1989).

Our bias in this volume will become more obvious throughout, but we choose to be explicit here. We believe that this pseudo-distinction between chemical ingestion and behaviors not directly caused by chemical ingestion, as a criterion for addiction, conflicts with current definitions of the concept of addiction. For example, L'Abate's (1994) definition, which has been highly instrumental in influencing the World Health Organization, defines addiction as involving compulsive use of a substance over time, despite suffering social and/or health consequences; an overwhelming preoccupation with obtaining sufficient supply; and a re-laxation after use. Peele (1990), a persistent critic of many aspects of ad-diction treatment and diagnoses, defines addiction as a preoccupation with one person or activity as the sole potentially desirable reinforcer.

Our philosophy is that there is no real distinction between disorders classified in the *DSM-IV* as substance abuse disorders and many of those classified as disorders of impulse control. Gambling, simply, is one of many nonpharmacological addictions. Others include workaholism, In-ternet addiction, and incessant watching of rock videos. Hundreds of oth-ers could be named.

The *DSM-IV* (1994) notes the first symptom of Pathological Gambling as follows:

> is preoccupied with gambling (e.g., preoccupied with reliving past gam-bling experiences, handicapping, or planning the next venture, or thinking of ways to get money with which to gamble). (p. 618)

The example—preoccupation with past experiences—implies that patho-logical gamblers, like drug addicts, are seeking to recreate a prior sensa-tion. It is our experience that gamblers are preoccupied with future expectations, not past experiences. That is part of what differentiates pathological gambling from drug addictions. Gamblers are addicted to fantasy and "what if." They are generally more consumed with imagin-ing the next big win than reliving a past success.

Difficulty in understanding the concept of a nonpharmacological ad-diction has been pronounced, especially among biologically oriented re-searchers, who lean toward a simplistic view of biological processes. J. Johnson and McCown (1993) have noted that there was once an over-whelming sentiment that each substance of abuse involved only one spe-cific neurotransmitter. For example, LSD binds to serotonergic receptors and therefore has its properties because it more efficiently mimics nat-ural neurotransmitters. Because there was not a specific gambling recep-tor, the behavior was denied the label "addictive."

Allied to this sentiment was a strong but highly erroneous belief that drugs that did not produce gross symptoms of physical withdrawal were not addictive, in any but a trivial "psychological state" (White, 1998). In-deed, great distinction was made between drugs that were "genuinely physically addictive" and those that were only "psychologically addic-tive," primarily because they had strong reinforcing properties. The com-parative clean bill of health afforded cocaine in the 1970s illustrates how disastrous such thinking was to public health.

Since that myopic period, there has been ample evidence that the body may be addicted to behaviors through its own neurochemical and

Table 1.1
Commonalities between Pharmacological Addictions and Gambling

Symptom or Behavior	Alcohol and Other Drugs	Problem Gambling
Cravings	Yes	Yes
Denial of problem's severity or existence	Yes	Yes
Disruption of families	Yes	Yes
Effects on specific neurotransmitters	Yes	Unknown
High relapse rate	Yes	Yes
Loss of control	Yes	Yes
Lying (to family, friends) to support use	Yes	Yes
Preoccupation with use	Yes	Yes
Progressive	Yes	Yes
Tolerance developed	Yes	Yes
Used as means of escaping problems	Yes	Yes
Withdrawal symptoms common	Yes	Yes

neurohormonal processes. This will be discussed in detail in later chapters. We do not believe that it is helpful for either researchers or clinicians to draw a distinction between disorders that are supposedly chemically based and those that are not. Addiction has common features, regardless of whether a specific substance is involved. Table 1.1 illustrates the commonalities of so-called "addictions" and nonpharmacological behaviors that have an addictive quality.

Apply the concept of addiction to the following case study to see how it applies to excessive gambling.

Rena Lopez

This young woman was introduced to casino gambling through her boyfriend and pursued it vigorously after her boyfriend broke off their relationship. She stated that playing slot machines made her think less about her boyfriend and provided for her a thrill that was otherwise missing in her life.

Rena lived about 100 miles from a casino. Initially, during the week, she confined herself to a local version of video poker, with limited stakes and no immediate paybacks. Although she spent most of her spare time in the video poker arcades, this was not enough stimulation. She moved to another state where a variety of gambling opportunities were available on casino-based boats. Although she had a well paying job as a pharmacist, she supplemented her income with prostitution or theft. She sought treatment—only after being arrested for theft—and was initially successful with abstinence from gambling behaviors. During her initial phases of abstinence, she was angry, depressed, and highly sensitive to stimuli similar to gambling objects, and she drank heavily. She described this period—lasting about three weeks—as her "withdrawal."

Following the death of her mother, she began playing video poker in earnest, and then branched out to other slot games. She dropped out of treatment after informing the therapist that she was going to move to another area of the country where "there's more action in the casinos." By this time she had lost her pharmacist's license and was living in a cheap motel. Her primary means of support was work as a prostitute in an escort agency.

Apart from the use of any specific substance, Rena's behavior is indistinguishable from that of any alcoholic or drug user whom we have treated.

The present authors might disagree about a number of ideas regarding the etiology and treatment of gambling behaviors, but we are unified in the sentiment that gambling can be pathological and still have dynamics identical to those of pharmacologically mediated addictions. The attempt by the writers of *DSM-IV* to place nonpharmacological addictions in a separate class is both scientifically inaccurate and therapeutically inadequate for the client or patient. It has often resulted in clients' being denied reimbursement by third parties for what are, in many cases, life-threatening disorders. This is particularly true for patheological gamblers who are one of the highest risk groups for suicide.

THE PURPOSES AND DIRECTION OF THIS BOOK

This book will not make anyone an expert in the treatment of gambling disorders. As we stated previously, only experience and supervision will succeed in this area. We do not expect all experts in the field of gambling to agree with our treatments or beliefs. At heart, we are eclectic—we do what works. We employ techniques as diverse as Gamblers Anonymous, aversion therapy, desensitization, family therapy, and other forms of treatment inspired by the new field of chaos theory.

We argue that a scientific eclecticism is necessary as well as desirable. For years, practitioners were taught that the word *eclectic* had somewhat nasty connotations, and that true therapists should understand something from one orientation and stick to it. In other words, the behavior in question was forced into the theoretical mold of the practitioner. Perhaps the relatively unsuccessful state of psychotherapy exemplifies the effect of forcing people into therapeutic or theoretical systems.

Our bias is reversed. We believe that because human behavior is infinitely complex, it is often necessary to view it from several different vantages (Bütz, Chamberlain, & McCown, 1997). The same behavior can and should be viewed from psychodynamic, biological, behavioral, and cognitive perspectives. Theories regarding gambling and chronic gamblers are not true or false; they are simply useful or not, depending on whether they help or hinder the therapeutic goals at hand. Rather than use the term *eclecticism,* we prefer the one popularized by William James and John Dewey: *pragmatism.* Consequently, a view expressed in this volume will be that a grand theory of gambling disorders is perhaps as impossible as a grand theory of human behavior. Just as we see light sometimes as waves and sometimes as particles, we will see gambling, variably, as a learned disorder, a family pathology, a psychodynamic need to fail, and a deficit in learned behavior. The overriding principle is that theoretical flexibility is necessary if the client is to receive the needed treatment.

Does this mean that we abandon empiricism in favor of an unverifiable mishmash of "anything goes?" No. Experimental paradigms will frequently be used throughout this volume to suggest the origin, maintenance, and dynamics of problem gambling. Often, though, these will be simply heuristic. No model, laboratory, or other source can predict more than half the behavior it specifies in advance. We construct our models by operationalizing them to specific behaviors that we feel are relatively predictable—another evidence of the immense task of the behavioral scientist and practitioner.

For those who read further, this approach will translate into a frustrating lack of solid rules. Is gambling a symptom of a deeper disorder? Sometimes yes and sometimes no. Can people with problem gambling ever return to social gambling? Sometimes yes and sometimes no. Is gambling a function of opportunity? Of personality? Of deviancy? Of psychopathologies? Yes and no. It depends on the client and the level of behavior that is examined. There is no guru, no single method, and no ultimate teacher. Finally, there is no substitution for both clinical experience and multifaceted theoretical exposure. We do not pretend to synthesize the relatively minute literature on problem gambling, but we hope to present enough of it to enable clinicians to become more critical thinkers. Our fondest hopes are that this guck, our stew-without-a-recipe, raises questions more than it provides answers, and that it will soon be obsolete, having been supplanted by more and better research, more refined theories, and better clinical methods.

- To outline briefly: Chapter 2 presents a number of traditional accounts of gambling behaviors and illustrates the problem in particular cases. At the risk of offering an exercise in academic excess, we describe various paradigms of classifications of gambling disorders. However, as J. Johnson and McCown (1993) have noted, paradigms may be the most important variable in the treatment of addiction.

- Chapter 3 illustrates experimental/laboratory data relevant to understanding the behavior of gamblers and the acquisition of chronic gambling behaviors.
- Chapter 4 is much more phenomenological; the case material highlights the developmental process of dysfunctional gambling.
- Chapter 5 discusses some of the basics of treating gamblers in the "luxury" of an inpatient setting.
- Chapter 6 probes different strategies that are imposed on clients who are treated on an outpatient basis.
- Chapter 7 highlights a variety of therapeutic techniques that are useful as adjunctive therapies for either inpatients or outpatients.
- Chapters 8 through 10 are more controversial. We highlight the uses of psychological testing and other psychometric instruments in treatment planning and assessment. We devote chapters to the use of family therapy and to the brain-behavioral relationship with gambling disorders. We also discuss high-risk populations—persons who have often been ignored in the comparatively new field of gambling research, but who are more likely to develop gambling disorders. We also present a new theory of addictive behavior, changes, and relapse, based on chaos theory.
- Chapter 11, an epilogue, looks toward future research and interventions.

CHAPTER 2

Paradigms of Problem Gambling Behavior

Tell me what you think about gamblers and I'll tell you what type of agency you work for. . . . And I'll bet on it . . . .
— Anonymous Client, after multiple treatment failures

AN INTRODUCTION TO PARADIGMS[1]

Although therapists often are quick to cite their allegiance to particular schools of thought or theoretical orientations, they are less clear when questions arise concerning metamodels of abnormal behavior, which they endorse. Yet the recognition of implicit and explicit metamodels of behavior is fundamental to successful therapists, especially when they are attempting to change behaviors that society stigmatizes (J. Johnson & McCown, 1993).

We believe that it is highly necessary for anyone working in the field of addictions to understand the impact of their diverse models on their clinical conceptualizations and interventions (McGurrin, 1992). In this chapter, we label these metamodels as "paradigms," to borrow a felicitous phrase from Thomas Kuhn (1963). Paradigms of behavior help determine how a client's presenting problem is conceived. They do this by elucidating what the problem is, what may have caused it, what can be done to solve it, and how successful the solution might be. They also act as heuristics, enabling us to make sense of large amounts of data very quickly (Wong & Weiner, 1981).

---

[1] This chapter was coauthored with Greg Stolcis, MSW, PhD. The content does not necessarily reflect the official opinion of Dr. Stolcis's employer, the Commonwealth of Virginia, Department of Mental Health, Mental Retardation, and Substance Abuse.

PARADIGMS AND ADDICTIONS

Paradigms, according to the classic exposition by Kuhn (1963), are competing ways of organizing data within a general framework to solve a specific set of problems. Paradigms emerge when a scientific discipline has reached some conceptual agreement regarding the basic underlying assumptions that are necessary for continued progress of a theory. Progress takes place when explanatory concepts basic to the theory are increasingly able to illuminate a wider variety of phenomena. The illumination, in turn, serves to strengthen belief in the adequacy of the paradigm. In a sense, paradigms become self-reinforcing. As we will see below, this is a major deficit in this way of organizing behavioral theories.

Theories in psychotherapy are lower-level constructs that help explain how models work. A collection of common models with similar domains becomes a paradigm. The boundaries between these constructs are often fuzzy; they may overlap from time to time. Most postmodern philosophers of science believe that scientific paradigms are neither "true" nor "false," but vary according to their usefulness in helping us understand the phenomena in question. [A more traditional view, advanced by Karl Popper in 1934, states that understanding necessarily involves the ability for prediction and control. However, see Bütz et al. (1997) for an alternative discussion of the role of prediction in validation of psychological theories.] In the areas of psychotherapy, counseling, and behavioral change, it is probably impossible to evoke such a positivistic standard. Contemporary science understands that it is quite permissible to view the world through multiple exclusionary paradigms (Costello, 1993). The Newtonian paradigm of physics works very well for most things in our solar system, but a more difficult and cumbersome paradigm is needed to explain a few anomalies—hence Einstein. However, Newton was sufficient to enable us to invent the automobile, the assembly line, and the airplane, which are among the most important contributions of the twentieth century. Only under special conditions do we need a more complex set of explanations or a broader theory.

Science itself is simply one of a number of competing metaparadigms of the world. Alternative possibilities include the religious, the mystical, the aesthetic, and an infinite number of other approaches (Keeney & Ross, 1985). The usefulness of the scientific metaparadigm is that it helps us by ruling out rival hypotheses through a number of rigorous and public methods (Kaufman, 1994). The most sophisticated approach, naturally, is the one involving true experimentation. However, the complexity and ethics involved in human behavior make it unlikely that we will ever have a science of behavior that can match the strength found in the traditional "hard sciences" (Casti, 1992). One reason, among the many often covered in Introduction to Psychology courses, is that many experiments that we might want to do to boost the utility of our model are untenable or unethical. Moreover, as Butz (1997) has noted, large portions of human behavior may simply be unamenable to the techniques of the "technological sciences"—chemistry, physics, and the like. We may, after all, possess a transcendental free will (Butz, 1992).

PARADIGMS AND PROBLEM GAMBLING

As is true with other addictions (J. Johnson & McCown, 1997), several implicit or explicit paradigms have guided thinking about gambling behavior. Some of the more common paradigms are described below. They are not the only ones that are relevant for gambling or for the more general field of addictions. They are simply useful heuristics for categorizing approaches to behavior that are common among a variety of practitioners (McGurrin, 1992). They may appear somewhat arbitrary to some observers, especially to eclectic practitioners who have treated a variety of people with problem gambling behaviors (Brenner, 1990).

At this point, readers may be tempted to ask: "Do paradigms really matter?" If they are fictitious and somewhat artificial constructs, then why are they important? In addition, if they are important for specific types of psychotherapy, is there any empirical evidence to suggest that paradigms actually matter in the treatment of gambling (London, 1986)?

For the specific treatment of gambling-related problems, the answer is, yes and no. For many types of psychological problems, evidence is inconsistent at best (Goldfried, 1980). However, for the broader field of addictions therapy and counseling, there is some convincing evidence that paradigms do indeed matter. McCown and Keiser (2000) have examined paradigms in addictions research and their impact on practitioners. Based on previous work, they constructed a dimensional (i.e., continuous scores) instrument to assess diverse factors associated with paradigms in addiction. This instrument, named the Dimensional Addictions Paradigms Assessment (DAPA), consists of five correlated (oblique) scales derived from factor-analytic studies of addiction treatment.

The DAPA was able to predict about 43% of the variance in addictions counseling sessions content. Traditional personality factors, such as extraversion, neuroticism, conscientiousness, openness, and agreeableness, accounted for only about 16% of the variance in sessions content. Moreover, clients who had a concordant treatment paradigm with their therapists showed the most improvement, although the statistical effect size was only moderate. A study such as this needs to be replicated, and, for our purposes, replication should involve gambling addictions counseling. Yet, this preliminary evidence suggests the importance of realizing that the client's worldview or paradigm can often conflict with the therapist's. Minimal change can be expected when paradigms of the therapist and the client are in conflict. That is why it is important to articulate those involved in beliefs regarding the acquisition, maintenance, and treatment of problem gambling behaviors.

THE MORAL PARADIGM

The moral paradigm can be summed up by saying, "Gambling is evil. That's all there is to it." Gambling as a moral issue has a lengthy history. Moral condemnation has accompanied gambling at least since Biblical times, despite ample reference to the fact that gambling was common in Hebrew societies. As we indicated in Chapter 1, during the eighteenth century, there were practically no restrictions on gambling in North America and Great Britain. Subsequently, with the alcohol abstinence movement in America, gambling began to evoke moral sanctions. The culmination was the era of "gambling prohibition," which demonstrated, if anything, that the length to which Americans would go to wager was a twin to how far they would go to imbibe in alcohol (Pavalko, 1999).

The moral paradigm suggests that pathological gamblers are responsible for their first and subsequent experiences. They are either morally weak or seduced by the glamour of a dangerous pastime. The increasing numbers of persons on the conservative right who wish to restrict gambling adhere to a moral paradigm. So do the numbers of liberals who wish to ban gambling because they view it as a regressive tax that disproportionately burdens the poor and socially vulnerable (Livingston, 1974), or as so dangerous that it should be banned for the common good. (McGowan, 1994). Both groups—despite entirely different ideologies—argue that gambling is "evil."

The moral model is also the dominant force in advocacy circles, such as those associated with numerous lobbyists. An implicit belief among these groups is that mere exposure to and availability of the opportunity for gambling is a sufficient precipitate to the acquisition of adaptive behavior (O'Brien, 1998). Similar views are strongly held by a number of grass-roots and well-organized substance abuse prevention organizations. These sentiments are not too far removed from the "Just Say No" programs of the 1980s and the "DARE" efforts during the 1990s. Both lack any serious empirical support for their efficaciousness, yet they continue to promote their methods.

An outgrowth of this view and of the consequent major strength of the moral model has been an emphasis on prevention. This is often overlooked by people who view the gambling problem in a more sophisticated light than is offered by those who promote or demand abstinence. In some societies, under some conditions, moral sanctions may have a major influence in the prevention of addiction. Draconian measures reduced substance abuse and illegal gambling in China and Iran. In other societies, or among certain subgroups, moral sanctioning may do little or nothing to discourage specific targeted behaviors. It may even encourage people to try behaviors considered "forbidden." This is a very complex issue, involving cultural and individual factors, religious and moral beliefs, and unpredictable changes in social components.

A less positive corollary of the moral model is the dangerous potential for addiction dissemination that accompanies its endorsement. According to the moral model, when self-control fails, the individual can fall prey to powerful drives that are subjectively deemed to be beyond personal control. The work of Marlatt and his colleagues (e.g., Marlatt, 1998) has illustrated the importance of considering the ability to feel competent in resisting an addiction as an essential component of recovery. This ability is also a seminal factor in prevention. When people are convinced that a situation is so overpowering that addiction is inevitable, they will tend to behave accordingly. Thus, gambling addiction may become a self-fulfilling prophecy, alongside many "psychological" problems (Gross, 1978; Wachtel, 1997).

The second problem with the moral model is the fact that it promotes harsh moral judgment on the part of the "therapist" or other change agent (who may be a neighborhood elder, religious leader, or stern physician instead of a mental health practitioner). Although therapists often choose not to believe it, they make moral judgments about their clients quite frequently (Egan, 1975). They view some behaviors as evil, others as good (Welt & Herron, 1990). There are no well-controlled studies highlighting therapists' beliefs regarding morality and behavioral change, but we can speculate, based on a wealth of data from social psychology and clinical studies, that client change is unlikely when the therapist feels that the client is "bad" rather than "sick" (Eysenck, 1993). A therapeutic alliance will not be possible, nor will a dialogue encouraging the client to discuss the "immoral" behaviors in question (Ferrari, Johnson, & McCown, 1995). Finally, behaviors that are complex and multidetermined are simply labeled as occurring due to a moral defect, when probing their origins may be more appropriate and beneficial. This level of primitive thinking hardly fits the data or clinical experiences of people who work with the complexities of addictions or other so-called "moral" deficits in their clients (Lykken, 1995).

It may seem that we have little use for the moral paradigm. In general, this is true; in our experience, labeling a behavior as "evil" increases its frequency (Brister, 1987; Costello, 1993). Little is gained by further stigmatizing a problem behavioral constellation, as has been shown with other drugs (Cooper, 1983). Yet, in our experience, the moral paradigm may be *occasionally* appropriate for specific domains of society (cf. Howard & Myers, 1990). For example, fundamentalist Christians may relate well to the paradigm that labels gambling as "bad." Some casual surfing on the Internet will produce numerous homepages where people disclose how Jesus, Yahweh, or Allah saved them from the sin of gambling. They ascribe the change to their repentance for abject evil.

As therapists, it is usually not helpful for us to view clients pejoratively. Most people who eventually seek therapy for gambling problems have already been to agencies that employ the moral model. They may have tried religion and found that it did not work for them. They may also have faced condemnation by their families and friends, or other social restraints intended to restrict the range of deviant behavior in society (Scheff, 1981). Quite often, their deviancy has an official label because they ran afoul of the criminal justice system. For them, the utility of the moral model has been exhausted. By seeking professional or peer help, a gambler indicates a need to move beyond the moral model or any existing community healing institutions that may operate successfully with others (Horowitz, 1998).

Frequently, a task of therapy will be to convince the client and his or her family system to move beyond the moral model (McCown & Johnson, 1993). As we argue in later chapters, this move is often necessary to allow a restoration of hope and a chance for a return to normal functioning. However, it may not be possible, or culturally acceptable, or even ethical to do this (Brehm & Brehm, 1981). If the client's belief system refuses to reject the moral model, the therapist may be required to suspend his or her beliefs and enter the client's phenomenological worldview to effect behavioral change. Therapists who cannot do this should admit their weaknesses and seek supervision regarding these issues. Because many therapists (especially psychologists) appear to hold moral and religious beliefs that are much more liberal than those of their clients (McCown & Keiser, 2000), this problem may be more profound than is typically assumed, especially among the "morally neutral" professional mental health practitioners emerging from present-day graduate programs.

THE DISEASE PARADIGM OF GAMBLING

The second major paradigm commonly found among treatment providers is associated with the "disease concept" of gambling (McGuirrin, 1992). The fundamental tenet of the disease model is that gambling is an affliction that prevents its victims from conquering their otherwise controllable problem of excessive gambling. According to this model, not all problem gamblers are disease gamblers; in the latter category are only those who cannot consistently control their gambling (O'Brien, 1998). A second tenet of the disease model is that the disease is never cured. Persons are said to be in recovery when the disease is in remission. The third and final crux of disease adherents' beliefs is that gambling disorders are progressive. The person with the disease will get worse unless treated.

Typically, novice substance abuse counselors (unless they come from a Twelve Steps background) question whether the concepts of addictions in general, and of dysfunctional gambling in particular, are "really diseases" (Zucker, 1987). It is probably more useful to avoid semantic interpretations and admit that the notion of "disease" is highly fuzzy. Since about the fifth century B.C., disease has implied impairment of the normal state of living, identifiable by specific signs that affect the performance of vital functions. Hippocrates postulated that diseases had somatogenetic, or physical, causes. He rejected the notion that diseases, especially psychiatric disturbances, were punishments from the gods.

Arguably, Emil Kraepelin (1856–1926) was responsible for the disease concept of mental illness that became accepted among physicians. Alcoholism has been the prototype of an addictive disorder within the disease model (Valverde, 1998). The view of alcohol abuse and dependence as a disease, rather than a moral weakness, became "official" in the mid-1950s, with the endorsement of the American Psychiatric Association. This delay is remarkable inasmuch as the father of psychiatry, Benjamin Rush, almost two centuries earlier, had labeled alcoholism as a disease. When effective treatments began to be realized (primarily through Alcoholics Anonymous), the medical community and the public began to view alcohol dependence and abuse as a disease. Ironically, the growth of effective treatments contributed greatly to the credibility of the disease concept.

The disease paradigm of alcohol is extraordinarily widely accepted (White, 1998). The disease model of chronic gambling problems—also known as compulsive gambling—is the paradigm endorsed by persons who are involved in Gamblers Anonymous. Unlike alcoholism, the disease model of gambling has actually been reified in the *DSM-IV* (APA, 1994) by inclusion of pathological gambling as a diagnosable psychiatric disorder. This contrasts with alcoholism, which is now a lay term and has been supplanted in the *DSM-IV* with "alcohol abuse" and "alcohol dependence."

There is no question that gambling fits historic and contemporary definitions of a disease. It has identifiable signs, and it interferes with vital functioning. Perhaps the most parsimonious definition of addiction and its relationship to disease has been postulated by Miller (1998), who sees addiction as a threefold process that is played out in spite of consequences.

The processes are: (1) preoccupation with compulsive use; (2) a chronic pattern of relapse; and (3) a loss of control. Miller believes that the loss of control, once established, exists for a lifetime. In other words, a gambler, alcoholic, or drug addict will not be able to indulge in the addiction as a recreation without experiencing a loss of control at some point following a resumption of the activity.

One advantage of labeling problem gambling as a disease is that this concept inspires hope and dignity. One of the brilliant contributions of the Twelve Steps and similar programs (e.g., Gamblers Anonymous, Alcoholics Anonymous, and Narcotics Anonymous) is that by labeling some behaviors as diseases they destigmatize them. In essence, they remove the shame from seeking treatment and from the previous behavior. The programs' perspective was recently voiced by a patient of ours:

> Gambling is like heart disease. You are born with risk factors. You live a certain type of life, which maybe makes your risk factors worse, but you don't really think they will apply to you. Then you learn you are a compulsive gambler, which is kind of like having a heart attack. You learn it's not your fault, but getting better is up to you. I had a heart attack one time. I did cardiac rehab. I have to change my behaviors for the rest of my life. I have a gambling problem. I have to go to GA. And I have to change my behaviors for the rest of my life. It's the same thing for any chronic disease.

Similar to the notions derived from Alcoholics Anonymous, the disease paradigm postulates that, for people with a "gambling disease," the outcome is progressively uncontrollable. Remission is possible only with complete abstinence. Not unlike the physical rehabilitation that is necessary with a chronic disease, the person with a gambling addiction completes the Twelve Steps to correct problems that were either the precursors or the results of the disease process. Practitioners interested in a fictional but extraordinarily accurate account of the progressive nature of gambling may want to read Nelson's (1998) recent novel *Compulsive,* which illustrates how the compulsive need to gamble becomes a progressive nightmare.

The disease paradigm is extraordinarily popular and is the dominant treatment paradigm in inpatient hospitalization programs, as we shall show in later chapters. The disease paradigm has become such a part of natural parlance that it resonates throughout North America, even among people who are unwilling to admit that they have the disease! However, one criticism has been raised: The reasoning is purportedly circular and explains nothing (Zucker & Gomberg, 1986). In essence, it seems to argue that people have this disease because they engage in a specific set of behaviors. Why do they engage in these behaviors? Because they have the disease. In other words, the labeling as a disease is tantamount to determining its etiology.

The disease model fails to explain, for example, why there is no "universal penetration rate"; in other words, why everyone who gambles does not become a compulsive gambler. A basic understanding of epidemiology can help to modify the disease model and make it more congruent with contemporary medical concepts. Yet, because it lacks predictive validity, the disease model is somewhat unsatisfying.

The disease paradigm, like the moral paradigm, has been criticized for its self-fulfilling nature (Marlatt, Baer, Donovan, & Kivlahan, 1988). When people relapse, which may be an inevitable aspect of recovery from any addiction or addiction-like behavior, they may believe that their "slip" initiates an inevitable downward slide until they "hit bottom" once more. By ascribing to gambling behavior a progressive process identical to that of a disease, the individual is stripped of the self-efficacy needed to enact behavioral change (Broucek, 1991; Walters, 1999).

Given these limits, is it useful to employ a disease paradigm? Perhaps the best answer is: Addictive gambling *may often be* very usefully labeled as a disease because it shares attributes with many diseases. Its etiologies are not well understood, but it has a common course of pathology, despite individual differences. In other words, it is a chronic disease with a clear pathological process that can be ordinally identified. This process can be halted and partly reversed with treatment. If it is not treated, addictive gambling has an end stage of financial devastation, anxiety, depression, and, frequently, suicide.

In our use of the disease concept, we retain the ability to view or classify gambling behaviors from other perspectives, if these perspectives have a clinical utility. The concept of flexible classification has gained more scientific credence with the advancement of a field of mathematics and engineering known as "fuzzy logic" (Kosko, 1990). This relatively new development argues that vagueness is a question of degree, a concept first suggested by Bertrand Russell (Casti, 1992). Gambling can be like a disease but also not like a disease, depending on the individual dynamics at hand. Fuzzy logic would suggest that any behavior can be characterized in an infinite number of ways, and the number of components or factors that we use to describe behaviors is a convenient fiction. The skein of neurons that we use to configure reality can be reconfigured, relatively easily, to view the same phenomenon from a different perspective (Pribram, 1991).

Arguments centering on whether gambling disorders or alcoholism are "really" diseases are therefore not useful. We leave the questions regarding reification to the philosophers of language. Sometimes the disease label and concept are useful, and sometimes they are not. Competent clinicians are able to judge them accordingly and employ them according to their utilitarianism. They may have to think "fuzzily" and flexibly, but flexibility in many domains should be a part of every clinician's abilities.

THE DISEASE OF GAMBLING: DIMENSIONAL VERSUS DICHOTOMOUS MODELS

One of the more contentious issues in psychiatric nomenclature has been whether diseases are best classified as dichotomous (either you have it or you don't) or continuous (you have it to some degree; Hurlburt, 1998). For a number of reasons, medical nomenclature has been constructed to reflect a dichotomous binomial distribution of psychiatric as well as other diseases. (For a discussion, see J. Johnson & McCown, 1993.) This division is appropriate for medical disorders such as cholera, where a clear pathogen results in a relatively unalterable course of events, but most diseases today are best characterized on a continuum (Miller, 1998). Consider the common problem of heart disease. A 90-year-old person who has a 99% occlusion obviously has a great deal of heart disease; but what about a 20-year-old person who has moderate hypertension and a 40% occlusion? Dichotomous distinctions break down at this point. Fuzzy logic shows us that this kind of breakdown occurs constantly.

Traditional statistics, which encompasses normal distributions as well as the modern science of fuzzy logic, illustrates that a person can have a little bit of a disease or a lot of it. Bifurcation of variables into binary characters simply does not occur with great frequency in nature.

In nature, most complex phenomena, especially complex mental phenomena, involve a number of causes (Miller, 1998). For example, the concept of pleasant weather may relate to appropriate temperature and expectancies regarding rain. These two relatively independent (orthogonal) concepts would be combined to help us understand the variations involved when people think of pleasant weather. By incorporating the two dimensions, we are better able to predict people's response to each day's weather. If we examined only one variable, we would not be able to see that a perfectly temperate day might be marred by excessive and unexpected rain. Traditional exploratory factor analysis with orthogonal rotations has attempted to identify the minimal number of mathematical entities, known as factors, and to show how they can account for the variation in behavior observed in normally distributed populations.

We prefer to employ the concept of a normally distributed model of gambling disorders. It reflects clinical reality much more appropriately. The person who has only four of the *DSM-IV* criteria may indeed have a problem, despite the fact that he or she has not matched the formal diagnoses. The severity of gambling behaviors may wane and ebb. The normal distribution can account for this better than the dichotomous distribution. This is, however, merely a heuristic model. Some researchers (e.g., Steel & Blaszczynski, 1996) have found four factors associated with gambling, which complicates model development even further.

THE DEVELOPMENTAL PARADIGM

Some experts conceptualize pathological gambling as a lifestyle that develops through a series of progressive stages. These occur to help individuals to ignore their personal inadequacies and low feelings of self-esteem. According to the late psychiatrist Robert Custer (Custer & Milt, 1985), who established the first clinic for treatment of pathological gambling in the United States, gambling can progress from a relatively harmless social avocation to a total life focus or lifestyle.

In the first stage of the development of the pathological gambler, the individual is simply a recreational player whose gambling occurs as harmless and light recreation. The person's behavior at this time is indistinguishable from the gambling patterns shown by ordinary people. They stop when they begin to lose or to exceed the amount of money (or time) they intended to allocate. When they feel playful or desire specific experiences, they may engage in gambling as a meaningful recreational activity.

Movement into the next stage signifies the beginning of pathological gambling. It occurs when the individual wins more than he or she reasonably believed possible. Often, what is experienced is a series of serendipitous *big wins*. The developing pathological gambler begins to self-identify (and be identified by the community of gamblers) as a "winner"—a person who has special talent or luck. During the early winning stage, the individual gains a degree of gambling skills. They enhance whatever luck is experienced, supplementing it with "knowledge" of the strategies involved in winning. They also often experience a "rush"; a feeling described as a tremendous high.

Inevitably, the good fortune does not last. The gambler, previously identified as a winner, begins to lose larger and larger amounts but keeps gambling in the erroneous belief that "If only I could win big again, all my troubles would be gone." The gambler may typically promise a spouse, or God, that he or she will stop after the next "big score." At this point, the individual begins to *chase,* wagering larger amounts so that the anticipated winnings will recover earlier losses. Desperation mounts as the individual is fully encased within an intensive and all-consuming enterprise of trying to stay even. Judgment becomes more reckless, and riskier wagers are made more routinely.

In the inevitably doomed search for another big win, a cycle becomes established in which the pathological gambler has periodic wins that maintain an unreasonable optimism. However, these gains never completely erase the debt. Gambling cannot pay forever, otherwise we would all be wealthy. In time, the gambler's psychological, financial, and, perhaps, physical resources are depleted. The pathological gambler may consider a drastic action: a crime, running away, or even suicide.

The similarities between substance abuse and pathological gambling are obvious: The individual continually seeks pleasure from behavior that possesses strong reward potential, especially in the short run, but is very destructive to both the individual and society in the long run (Griffiths, 1994).

An advantage of the developmental perspective is its presentation of gambling as a fairly normal behavior. Many people experiment with it and eventually find that it offers marginal pleasure. However, ideographic (individual) factors, based mostly on chance, combine to encourage gambling addiction.

The developmental model has possible heuristic use; it may indicate where prevention efforts will be maximally effective. Unfortunately, little is known about the developmental history of gambling, especially in children and adolescents, about whom preliminary data are just beginning to emerge (Derevensky, Gupta, & Cioppa, 1996). Consequently, we are vastly handicapped in our efforts to determine the extent to which alarm is warranted about the high amount of gambling among adolescents and preadolescents (Ladouceur, Dube, & Bujold, 1994).

SOCIOLOGICAL MODELS

Compared to substance abuse, comparatively little research has been undertaken regarding gambling (Murray, 1993). Perhaps this minimal attention indicates that gambling has not been considered sufficiently deviant by sociologists. Also, because much of sociology has traditionally focused on class variables, gambling, which affects every socioeconomic class, may have escaped interest (Walker, 1988).

Sociological explanations may be viewed as existing on both macro and micro levels. The tradition of micro sociological investigation suggests that community-based values or shared symbolic experiences determine the extent of gambling in a community. Addiction, from this perspective, is primarily a social construct; this theory tends to minimize the specific importance of substance versus nonsubstance dependence. The sociological process, rather than any addictive biological agent, is associated with the process of psychological dependence.

Perhaps the most important contribution of sociology to the study of gambling was *differential association theory*. This theoretical approach was formulated by Edwin H. Sutherland as an alternative to the prevalent beliefs of the criminology that dominated social theory during the 1930s. Sutherland (1947) believed that deviant behaviors did not result from either heredity or simple opportunity. These, especially opportunity, might be necessary, but they were not sufficient factors for the etiology and maintenance of deviancy. The presence of opportunity, Sutherland argued, does not, in itself, explain the existence of deviant or aberrant behavioral patterns.

Sutherland believed that socially proscribed behavior required specialized learning based on both abilities and inclinations, and that individuals acquired these from association with groups in their environments. The principle of differential association is that individuals will tend to commit criminal activities when their associations with groups that teach criminal abilities and favor criminal inclinations are more important than their associations with noncriminal groups. The importance of an association with a group is measured by the frequency, duration, priority, and intensity of that association.

Differential association theory was among the first sociological attempts to explain a form of deviant behavior in exclusively social, as compared to psychological, terms. Sutherland also suggested that this theory worked equally well for what he called "white collar crime," since among businesspeople there could also be a group attitude that was favorable to illegalities such as tax fraud, violations of safety standards, or embezzlement. Thus, the types of crimes committed will result more from the nature of the criminal group involvement than from the personality of the criminal. Applied to gambling, it is easy to see that opportunity alone is not sufficient to permit its problematic spread. Instead, an attitude favorable to gambling is necessary, and this attitude is acquired through group membership. Sutherland's work gives strong theoretical impetus for attendance at Gamblers Anonymous and other groups that advocate a negative association with gambling behaviors.

Macrosociology examines societal differences in gambling rates as a function of large cross-societal, sociological constructs. One finding (which still warrants further research) is that where gambling has long been institutionalized, fewer problems are usually associated with its occurrences. For example, McCown and Keiser (2000) reviewed community records and conducted interviews in various Southern communities in the United States; some had and some lacked histories of socially approved gambling. Among the types of gambling were local bingo halls, "bush tracks" (unregulated horse racetracks where betting was more informal than in regulated pari-mutuel settings), cock fighting arenas, and bars and taverns where gambling was unofficially encouraged.

McCown and Keiser then examined publicly available bankruptcy records, suicide rates, unemployment, alcohol abuse, and, where possible, diagnoses from state psychiatric facilities. Data indicated that where gambling occurred in a more socially regulated form, there were fewer problems of suicide, alcohol abuse, bankruptcy, and unemployment. Where gambling was vigorously proscribed by authorities, there tended to be less illegal gambling, but more severe gambling-related disorders.

Finally, where gambling occurred when alcohol was available and other family members were present, there were fewer problematic behaviors. Presumably, alcohol dampens some of the interest in gambling and reduces excessive problems. Many problem gamblers don't want their awareness to be dulled by alcohol. These findings suggest that socially regulated gambling—even in areas like the American South, where it is culturally frowned on—may be less harmful than minimally regulated gambling.

A similar finding has been reported for alcohol abuse (Valverde, 1998). Where alcohol consumption is encouraged at mealtimes and where public drunkenness is discouraged, there are generally low rates of problem drinking. The essential variable seems to be whether *excess* is tolerated. Where a behavior is allowed but excess is proscribed, problems seem to be fewer. Conversely, where a behavior is allowed by law but is heartily condemned socially, problems seem to mount. Complete prohibition of gambling would make problem gambling an irrelevant concern; however, a complete interdiction does not seem possible in the near future. With alcohol or with gambling, social constraints interact to encourage either moderation or excess.

Macro sociology has also focused on the correlation between gambling and such variables as poverty, race, age, gender, and social structure. Previous research in these areas was very crude but provided descriptions of some phenomena related to gambling problems. For example, it was revealed that gambling is popular among poor communities and that excess leisure time is associated with gambling abuse (Hraba & Lee, 1995). Regrettably, almost none of this literature has targeted high-risk populations.

THE PERSONALITY/VULNERABILITY PARADIGM

Individual differences in addiction remain widespread, especially among self-help groups. Several types of theories, none mutually exclusive, prescribe a role for personality and individual differences in addiction prominence, and thus are included in this paradigm.

Among the most obvious are biological deficit theories (Blum, Noble, Sparkes, Chen, & Cull, 1997), which assume that addictions such as gambling are caused by a defect in either neurological structure or functioning—or both. Biological variables are frequently described at the neurotransmitter level. Serotonin has long been implicated, but dopamine is increasingly being cited. The role of neuropsychological factors in encouraging restrained behavior is also stressed. Some theories suggest deficits in restraint as the cause of problem gambling behaviors. These deficits are related to orbito-frontal incapacity to modulate affect and to make appropriate decisions (Damasio, 1995).

Deficit coping theories suggest that personality-related defects in coping with stress are self-medicated by the excitement provided by gambling; in addition, the continued gambling avoids withdrawal symptoms (R.J. Rosenthal & Lesieur, 1992). This has been a very fruitful "subparadigm of research," and its explanatory power seems to be heightened by a capacity to link coping with biological variables (Eysenck, 1985; Smith & Darlington, 1996).

Deviance theories argue that "bad" personality factors, such as dysfunctional impulsivity, operate to prevent development of normal internal constraints against excessive gambling (e.g., Ciarrocchi, 1993). Again, there is ample evidence linking specific personality variables to potential risk factors for gambling (Blaszczynski & McConaghy, 1994; Blaszczynski, Steel, & McConaghy, 1997).

Each of these theories implies a concept of an "addictive personality." That concept has been severely criticized by some behavioral scientists, even though the intensity of addictive behaviors seems to be related to such constructs as sensation seeking, impulsivity, and antisocial tendencies (Blaszczynski et al., 1997). Perhaps the lack of enthusiasm for the construct derives from simplistic formulations of adoption promise arguments and method problems. One major problem in establishing a connection between identified personality traits and addiction lies in the retrospective nature of most of the research.

Regarding gambling, for example, prolonged and illegal contact with socially proscribed persons may lead to marked personality changes. A long history of financial losses would clearly lead to anxiety and depression (Blaszczynski & McConaghy, 1994). Thus, cause and effect have been confounded, although antisocial tendencies definitely place persons at risk for gambling disorders. Additionally, personality, as assessed during treatment, may not be a valid indicator. Persons with severe gambling problems may often be irritable, suspicious, and hostile, especially during initial phases of intervention.

Method problems aside, it is now evident that the existence of a single adaptive personality has not been demonstrated. More likely, there are multiple types of addictive personality factors, driven by numerous biological and learning processes (Zuckerman, 1999). These may include attention deficit disorder (Specker, Carlson, Christenson, & Marcotte, 1995), and depression may also be implicated (Becona, Lorenzo, Del Carmen, & Fuentes, 1996). Finally, anxiety may be important. Gamblers with higher capacities to experience this behavioral state or trait may magnify the negative effects of losing. When that happens, the process of chasing (described later) often follows. However, generalization regarding the role of personality and vulnerability is limited by the fact that variables related to causal direction have probably not been sufficiently explored.

EVOLUTIONARY THEORY AS A PARADIGM

The behavioral sciences have recently embraced evolutionary theory. Abnormal behavior is seen as having deep roots in the genetic past, where it may have had a functional aspect (Palmer & Palmer, 2000). Phenomena as diverse as borderline personality, schizophrenia, and depression may all have causes in the shared past of our species. For example, the propensity for abused children to develop borderline personalities may have evolved from the desirability of having such children impulsively attach themselves to neighboring groups rather than risk reproduction within the abusive kin group.

Gambling, according to the evolutionary perspective, is actually a phylogenetically old behavior. Palmer and Palmer (2000) note that as animals come into increasing contact with carnivores, they have to "gamble" for their survival more frequently. This may be best illustrated with an example from a herd of zebras, crossing a dry plain to obtain necessary water. Although each individual animal appears to be acting as part of an undifferentiated herd, behavioral ecologists are quick to point out the tremendous individual variations in the animals' behavior choices. Some may bravely run to the front of the pack, thereby maximizing their opportunity for access to water. However, these animals also maximize the chance that they will be eaten by a predator waiting in the grasses nearby.

Other zebras evoke a different strategy, because of genes, experience, or both. They travel in the middle of the herd. Their evolutionary strategy is to minimize their exposure to predators by remaining where they have moderate warning of potential threats. But they sacrifice the opportunity to obtain water first. Clustered in the rear may be animals with still another strategy. They travel with the slower, older, younger, or lamer members of the pack. If attacked, they have a marked advantage because predators are likely to chase their slower peers.

Each of these strategies represents a gamble; a course of action is followed to maximize reward—in this case, survival. Gambling increased dramatically in the human evolutionary transition from dense-forest dwellers to aggressive meat eaters and food gatherers. Success with this primitive form of gambling determined the ultimate survival of the human's genetic line. When a particular prey was discovered, the hunter had to decide whether to pursue this potentially enticing meal or to pass up this opportunity for abundant food in favor of ensuring safety. Humans evolved more or less successfully, so a quite high degree of speculation was successfully carried out while our species was making the transition from trees to savannas.

Palmer and Palmer (2000) note that many of the behaviors related to present-day gambling are probably deeply rooted in the early biological experiences of our evolutionary descendants. Often, these nomads had to choose their courses of action under conditions of uncertainty. Imagine a tribal chief who, in consultation with the tribe elders, had to decide whether to maximize food capacity by crossing a dangerous mountain ridge. The alternative—to stay put and enjoy a greater degree of safety from natural predators—meant there would be much less food. At that point, dice or their primitive equivalent might have been cast to ask the gods to intervene in the decision.[2]

Natural selection may have encouraged a variety of behaviors that are considered impulsive. Given the potentially ever-changing environmental situations, natural selection would have favored the survival of communities where some people were risk takers and others were much more conservative regarding risk assessment. This mixture allows for rapid adaptation to newly emerging environmental conditions (Geary, 1998). Readers interested in this topic will find fascinating and almost exotic accounts of competing survival strategies in several of the books of the Old Testament.

The evolutionary perspective suggests that there should be variable gambling behavior among people in the community, to ensure optimal selection in a potentially changing environment. This perspective may also explain some of the conditions of people who act under uncertainty. For example, social psychology has long noted that, under conditions where support for a belief is minimal, people will tend to endorse the belief even more strongly. This phenomenon, called *cognitive dissonance*, has generated a tremendous amount of research. Similarly, people who come close to winning a hand of cards, or a bet on the slots or the races, frequently increase their confidence in future wagering. The evolutionary basis for this phenomenon may have been allocation of resources under conditions of uncertainty.

Evolutionary theory implies that gambling may be both universal and "hard wired" in our biology. Certain social conditions may encourage high-risk behaviors, such as wars. People who excel in some social

---

[2] The inevitability of losing is based on two facts. In casino-type games, the house has the odds for everything except blackjack. A very talented and patient player may probably make the equivalent of a minimum wage by mastering very sophisticated card-counting techniques. In horse racing and other pari-mutuel wagering, a gambler is betting against odds set not by the house or the game itself, but by other gamblers. This is essentially an "efficient marketplace." The crowd odds represent all of the information that is publicly known and cannot be improved. Sports betting, where handicap lines are set by the house (in legal betting) or by a bookmaker (in illegal betting), now represents efficient marketplaces, in part because of the availability of personal computers. Exceptions to efficient marketplaces do exist. However, they represent such rare betting opportunities that a professional gambler inevitably makes less than minimum wage.

environments because they take excessive personal risk may be more socially dysfunctional in other environments. The evolutionary perspective may help to guide social policy by encouraging appropriate discussion of how society can prevent the behavioral tendencies of a subgroup from developing into fully dysfunctional behavior that may have immense personal and social consequences. It may also help us emphasize alternative behaviors for high-risk and recovering people.

THE EPIDEMIOLOGICAL PARADIGM OF PROBLEM AND PATHOLOGICAL GAMBLING

Epidemiology is the study of diseases and their processes, including their sources and the risk factors for their development (Westphal & Rush, 1996). Epidemiology has been an underrated but immensely successful part of the vast health improvement strategies of the twentieth century. For example, the great advances in eliminating or controlling diseases such as bubonic plague, dengue fever, and malaria are due in large part to the prevention that epidemiological studies allow us to perform.

The hallmark or central tenet of epidemiology is that the disease manifestations or symptoms are a function of interaction among the host, the environment, and the biological and/or psychological specifics of the disease. Epidemiology has been useful to illuminate pathological mechanisms, to estimate public health impact for social intervention, and to design and evaluate treatment programs. In discussing epidemiology, two words—*prevalence* and *incidence*—must be understood. The prevalence of a disease is the proportion of individuals in a population who have the disease The incidence of a disease is the number of new cases registered in a specific period of time—say, one year.

The epidemiology of pathological gambling is important to analyze because both the environment and the host may have substantially changed in recent years. As we stated above, gambling is now ubiquitous. Forty-eight states in America have some form of legalized gambling, and illegal gambling is only a phone call or an Internet visit away. Sports have become a worldwide obsession, and clever strategies encourage frequent bets on a variety of contests. In other words, the environment has become supportive of the potential disease entry routes. There are more "infectious agents" out there.

Furthermore, the host may have changed. Nelson (1998) argued that there is a general increase in intelligence; there may also be a general increase in impulsive behaviors. Since the 1960s, behavior that was once considered taboo and restricted has been socially approved. Indeed, society is attempting a noble experiment. Many of the constraints on risk factors or behaviors—for example, tight and extended family units, poverty, and religious affiliation—are weakening. As one of our patients stated, "Lot of money, no faith, no family; why not gamble?" These are risk factors that did not occur earlier in human history to any large degree.

Of concern to us is the development of rapid-play video-mediated gambling, such as video poker. There is also some concern that exposure to nongambling video games may be a risk factor for future use of video poker and other video-mediated gambling (Griffiths, 1994). One author, while wandering through a large, bargain department store, saw a stack of "gameboys" in the toy department. On closer inspection, they proved to be handheld video poker games for "ages 6 and up." Children are being introduced and taught to gamble in sophisticated ways at much earlier ages. Anecdotal accounts suggest that adolescent gambling in games rooms and pinball halls has been ongoing since these devices were invented (Griffiths, 1993). They may serve as a gateway to other types of gambling in the way that marijuana is assumed to serve as a gateway to use of more pernicious drugs (Willis, 1996).

How vast is the gambling epidemic? The best estimate of problem gambling among adolescents during a recent year was about 15%, and pathological gambling was about 6% (Ladouceur, 1996; Ladoceur et al., 1994). Among adults, problem gambling increases about 3% each year, and pathological gambling grows about 1% (Louisiana Compulsive Gambling Study Committee, 1996; Volberg, 1996).

For adults involved in the criminal justice system, the lifetime rates are: 15% for problem gambling and about 14% for pathological gambling. Almost one in three jailed prisoners has a gambling problem, but the numbers are closer to two in three for incarcerated juveniles in Louisiana (McCown & Keiser, 2000).

It is not known whether increased gambling behavior among adolescents is a function of additional opportunities or a normal developmental phase. [In Louisiana, where some of the best data are now available, the prevalence of pathological gambling behavior is 6% in persons in grades 6 to 12; 3% in persons aged 18 to 21 years; and 1% in persons older than 21 years. When problem and pathological gambling are measured together, the numbers rise to 16%, 14%, and 4%, respectively, for these age groups (Volberg, 1995).] Some very preliminary data suggest that gambling experimentation is increasing in young people. Lifetime prevalence is now 86%, compared with 78% in earlier studies.

The average age of onset of gambling—approximately 13 years—is the same as for alcohol and illicit drugs. Tobacco typically is used a year or so earlier (Fisher & Harrison, 1997). One of the most replicable findings is that early use maximizes the probability of subsequent abuse (Gaboury & Ladouceur, 1993). Several scenarios are possible for a relationship between early drug/alcohol use and subsequent abuse: (1) a general factor of addictive personality or social deviancy causes early drug use and leads to later drug abuse; (2) early use itself may cause deviancy; or (3) a combination of environmental and host characteristics best explains the development of the disease. Strategies designed to change either the individual or the environment can be applied to prevent the eventual manifestation of the full-blown disease syndrome.

Epidemiology overlaps *medical sociology*, which concentrates on the conditions or behaviors of groups and society's treatment and allocation of disease, and *behavioral medicine/medical psychology*, which highlights risk factors associated with the onset of disease or with disease prevention. From the medical sociology standpoint, the earlier use begins the greater the possibility of the disease. In other words, the worst outcomes are associated with early use. Unfortunately, this has not been studied longitudinally. However, as we have presented earlier, there is some evidence that gambling is increasing in young people. McCown and Keiser (2000) administered the College Student Gambling Inventory to 367 students. They found a correlation of age and total score. Younger students gambled more than university students, perhaps because the older students had responsibilities, such as families or outside employment, that precluded their gambling.

When working with children, it is one author's habit to ask them what they would wish for if they had three wishes. In the past five years, the most common response from all age groups (beginning with age 3) is "I want to win the lotto." Historically, children have often wished for "lots of money" or "a million dollars." Now, however, their fantasy of wealth and success is more specifically tied to winning at gambling. Many parents have also shared with us that lottery tickets are popular presents for their children at birthdays or holidays. It seems clear that children are becoming more conscious of gambling activities at younger ages. More research is needed before we can ascertain how significant the gambling problem is for young people.

PARADIGMS AND SOCIAL POLICY

Our paradigms undoubtedly influence our views toward social policies and the spread of gambling. Moralists on the far right or far left condemn both present and future expansions of gambling, yet they fail to grasp the subtleties of the fact that individuals' vulnerabilities to gambling disorders are different. Adherents of a disease model usually remain agnostic, at least in theory, regarding the spread of gambling. After all, if it is a disease, then not everyone who is exposed will become a compulsive gambler!

Evolutionary and sociological theorists often believe that gambling is ubiquitous. To them, gambling is a necessary "evil" of modern civilization and should probably be decriminalized. To paraphrase a social commentary by the late comedian Lenny Bruce, nothing would be stupider than to put gamblers in jail; prisoners constantly gamble on anything! Many evolutionary behaviorists also advocate a strong libertarian social policy.

Persons who advocate a personality-oriented paradigm are wary of the spread of gambling until more is known about identifying and modifying risk factors. This position is probably echoed by epidemiologists, who want to assess how a change in the environment can influence the host. Again, however, political considerations add to the confusion of what should be essentially a scientific discussion (Meier, 1994).

Regardless of the paradigms advocated, gambling is spreading at very rapid rates, and it is doubtful that its spread can be completely contained. Its most rapid spread is among those least able to afford it: the poor, the young, and the elderly. It is too early to assess any related increase in problem gambling behaviors, but many gambling laws seem to have been passed to provide a "quick fix" for revenue problems. Perhaps equally absurd, a new prohibition on gambling may be stirring, based on religious values that are not shared by all persons in our pluralistic society.

In Louisiana, people were apparently shocked to learn, from a statewide study, that the average gambler actually loses money. Unfortunately, gambling is being promoted to people who believe gambling participation will almost inevitably enhance their own personal wealth. As long as this view is promoted—by the casino industry, the video industry, or state lottery agencies—the results will be drastic for at least a subset of persons who gamble.

On the other hand, many semiprofessionals in the "therapy business" collect large consulting fees for assisting with blocking gambling's expansion, primarily by exaggerating its deleterious impact on individuals and society. Finally, some subgroups of mental health professionals seem to be involved in a shakedown of the gambling industry. In essence, they will tacitly accept gambling as long as dedicated funds are provided for treatment *and the funds are earmarked for them.* In principle, treatment funds are a lofty goal, but many of these therapists hope to receive lucrative paychecks that are beyond the purview of managed health care reimbursement.

When they exaggerate or underplay the dangers of problem gambling, clinicians and policymakers add to both the political confusion and personal misery (Simurda, 1994). We advocate that clinicians must suspend any reactionary moral statements and concentrate instead on what they are trained and paid to do: help clients change. Advocacy of social policy under the guise of science is simply dishonest. It will ultimately hurt those whom we are entrusted to help.

Many decisions are needed, under risky conditions and without complete information. A whole area of cognitive psychology and an even broader area of behavioral science are now studying the process of making risky decisions under conditions of uncertainty. Tversky and Kahneman (1993), for example, examined these situations in great detail and found that humans routinely take mental shortcuts, called heuristics, in making decisions under uncertainty. Often, these heuristics are not optimal for present-day decision making. However, at one time, they may have been more useful, especially for humans were limited experience.

CHAPTER 3

The Phenomenology
of Gambling

I meet a lot of gamblers who are extremely smart and hardworking.
Some of them are quite good at predicting the outcome of games or
sports. But I've never met one who has the sense to predict what [his or
her] own future will be.
                          —John W., a recovering pathological gambler
                                           (21 years of abstinence)

THE *DSM-IV* distinguishes between alcohol abuse and alcohol dependence. Compulsive gambling is not given a similar distinction. Yet, as
we noted in Chapter 2, gambling disorders can exist on a continuum,
whether they are habitual or episodic. A critical distinction is missed in
the *DSM-IV*. Problem gambling, presumably less severe than compulsive
gambling, may simply make life difficult or tedious—or, contrarily, exciting. Addictive gambling (our synonym for compulsive gambling) usually
makes life all but intolerable. We prefer the term *addictive* because the
word *compulsive* is used in multiple and often confusing contexts in the
psychiatric community.

Problem and addictive gamblers are almost always identified by a
changed or heightened physiological state while they are gambling
(Griffiths, 1996b). They also show a faster return to baseline, a common
trait in almost all forms of acquired compulsions (Solomon, 1980). The
danger with gambling is that whether a person has a low or a high state
of basal arousal, the gambling is attractive.

For people in a pathological state of low arousal, increased physiological states associated with gambling are almost always identified as excitement. The prospect of winning money is extraordinarily exciting; even

the most puritanical observers can understand that reaction. The heightened negative physiological states may be misinterpreted as positive. The Schachter/Singer theory of emotions states that undifferentiated emotions are interpreted within a social context. The image generated by folklore and by the gambling industry is that the activity is highly pleasurable, whether one wins or loses. The arousal it offers, from winning or from losing, can be interpreted pleasurably, due to social facilitation. A similar phenomenon has been identified with alcohol consumption (Marlatt, 1998). The "demand characteristics" or response set of a situation (e.g., Earn & Kroger, 1976) can persuade even a losing player that he or she is happy. At any casino or racetrack, this phenomenon can be observed directly by watching people while they are losing. Losers—even big losers—never mourn their losses for more than a second or two. Their facial expressions tend to be more neutral than sad or angry. Only winners evidence much emotion. Facial expressions tend to be ecstatic, though some winners remain quite stoic. The proverbial "poker face" is frequently in evidence, particularly with addicted gamblers.

Because responses to gambling winnings and losses tend to be so idiosyncratic, it may be useful to speak of the *phenomenological spectrum* of gambling. Problem gambling and addictive gambling involve several processes, but their complete sequence may not be necessary. Each process, however, boosts the likelihood of future problems and can be referred to as a "gateway" to an ultimate end point of addictive gambling. This is tantamount to the concept that certain drugs are being "gateways" to more seriously addictive substances (Walters, 1994).

THE GATEWAY CONCEPT OF GAMBLING DISORDERS

We identify five processes that constitute gateways to addictive gambling. In the majority of cases where people develop problem or addictive gambling, the first, and probably the most necessary process is that the physiological changes involved in the excitement of gambling must *initially* be interpreted positively. For example, because gambling can provide distraction from life's difficulties, gambling acts as a negative reinforcer, primarily by reducing depression and anxiety (Griffiths, 1995). It may also act as a positive reinforcer if it is perceived as being exciting and offering the possibility of extraordinary profit. People who do not respond to gambling with physiological changes and enjoyment are not likely to become gambling abusers.

In the second process, the person comes under the influence of a variable ratio of reinforcement (Domjan, 1998). This ratio occurs when organisms cannot predict how many responses are required before reinforcement occurs. Responses are usually present at a high and steady rate and are hard to extinguish. Slot machines, as well as table games, are extremely addictive because they provide precisely this type of reinforcement. (In many undergraduate psychology textbooks, casino gambling is used to illustrate variable-ratio reinforcement.) It is important to realize that the reinforcement in gambling and other addictions may be vicarious (Cattell, 1982). People with exotic fantasy lives may be likely to imagine winnings, or may spend their time planning, in the words of one of our clients, "how I'm going to spend that money I know I'll win . . . if I play enough."

The likelihood of problem gambling is increased in the third process if the person experiences a potent operant rewarding experience—a "big win"—early in the gambling experience. Studies of operant conditioning also show that habits are formed faster as the magnitude of the reward increases.[1] Knowing someone who has had a big win may also be helpful. The immediacy of the reward—being able to handle the cash or chips within a matter of seconds—adds to the potency of the reinforcement experience. One race track manager told us, "Say a group of fifty people show up from a social club or work. One or two of them will hit it big. They'll be back, for sure. And those that were with them when they hit it big—who saw how easy it looks—they'll be back, too."

In the fourth process, the likelihood of problem gambling is increased if the participant believes he or she has substantial control over the outcome of the game (Friedland, Keinan, & Regev, 1992). For stocks, futures, and horse racing, where some skill is possible, this belief can be reasonably, if largely incorrectly, held over the long run (Lee, 1971). However, for most casino games, which are essentially games of chance, there is a cognitive distortion involving control of chance. The role of personality certainly interacts with the need for the illusion of control (McClelland & Watson, 1973). People with more need for power, for example, are likely to experience gambling as reinforcing only if they feel some skill is involved. People with a high degree of "learned helplessness," or externality regarding a locus of control, are probably more likely to play games of chance in which subjective control is deemed less important.

The fifth process is ironic. The possibility that a problem will develop is enhanced if the person believes in luck or magic. Persons who believe they have the capacity to know when they are lucky—for example,

---

[1] The reward in a casino does not have to be monetary. We are aware of one young man who had a series of positive sexual experiences at a number of casinos. This generalized to an apparent gambling addiction. Later, he stopped looking for sexual partners at casinos and began an insidious pathway of downward chasing, similar to that described below. He never experienced a "big win" in the monetary sense, yet he developed a severe gambling problem.

schizotypal personalities—are at much higher risk to search out video machines or dice tables where they "feel" they can win. This behavior can be seen in any number of studies. Most recently, McCown and Keiser (2000) found that bizarre thinking correlated .56 with severity of gambling problems in a population in treatment. People who believe in too much control *or* too little control over gambling events are predisposed to develop gambling problems.

CUSTER'S SUBTYPES OF GAMBLERS

A useful heuristic for understanding gamblers is based on subtypes that exhibit particular behavioral patterns (Cattell, 1990). The late Dr. Robert Custer (Custer & Milt, 1985), a pioneer in the field of gambling treatment, delineated six different types of gamblers. Not all are problematic gamblers, and not all meet the traditional criteria of "disease model" patients. The variations are:

1. Professional gamblers
2. Antisocial gamblers
3. Casual social gamblers
4. Serious social gamblers
5. Neurotic gamblers
6. Compulsive gamblers

Professional gamblers are relatively rare today. They were much better known in the old West and in turn-of-the-century gambling parlors. They tend to be very skilled in the games they choose to play. They are almost always able to control the time spent gambling and the amount of money they spend. In essence, they know when to quit. Usually, they are not addicted to gambling.

Many colorful figures in North American history were professional gamblers. They included "Cincinnati Red," "Pittsburgh Phil," the contemporary author/handicapper Andy Beyer, a famous trial lawyer who used the pseudonym "Robert Scott," and the mythical African American named Joshua, who in the 1950s, apparently on his own, constructed a method of multiple regression (which he performed in his head!) to predict the final time of harness racing horses. Most, however, are obscure persons who made minimal wages in a life that only *seemed* exotic.

It is estimated that fewer than 3,000 people in the United States and Canada make a living as professional gamblers (Eric Rosenmeyer, personal communications, February 1999). Most earn an amount that approximates the United States minimum wage, and it is believed that fewer than 50 make over $100,000 annually. (We contacted the Internal Revenue

Service about this statistic, but were told that the information was confidential.) Oddly, many people who claim to have a winning "system" inflate their IRS filings as "proof" that they win more than they lose. Professional touts, for example, claim more income than they earn with their "private methods," to encourage others to buy their advice.

Professional gamblers these days are largely confined to blackjack, a sport or game that can be beaten (although with much effort), and poker, a game that requires the development of a great deal of skill. Only one study, as far as we know, has ever been conducted on professional gamblers' personality. McCown and Keiser (2000) used Cattell's 16 Personality Factors Test (16PF; Cattell, 1972) to compare successful career horseplayers ($N = 21$) with casual ($N = 40$) and addicted ($N = 40$) players. Only 21 career horse players, who could verify that they made their living gambling, could be identified over the entire country.

The profile of professional horse gamblers was not particularly flattering. They tended to be intelligent but cold, emotionally stable but somewhat boring, socially insensitive, extremely unsentimental, hypervigilant, and very tense. Casual gamblers were gregarious, self-confident, and much more relaxed. Chronic gamblers were less conscientious, much more calculating, and very tense. They were also higher on narcissism, but equally as gregarious as casual gamblers.

A career as a professional gambler is not particularly enjoyable. Some people used to think it was impossible to have an advantage at table games. However, in 1961, a brilliant MIT mathematician demonstrated that blackjack is the only table game in which a player has a theoretical advantage. This claim has been expanded further; inexpensive computer programs will assist a player in learning the necessary but extraordinarily difficult skills. Despite the fact that casinos go to great length to identify professional "card counters," they probably make much more money from persons who attempt to card count unsuccessfully and then try to recoup their losses through progressive betting. Casinos, like the gamblers who frequent them, are often obsessed with the illusions of control.

Sandra

An example of a professional gambler is Sandra. Sandra is a 35-year-old woman who has earned a living as a professional gambler for nearly 15 years. She is an attractive, well-dressed woman, who has never been married, and lives on her own in a small apartment. Sandra did not seek therapy for gambling problems, she was depressed, due in large part to her lifestyle. Her primary complaint was depression. Specifically, she was lonely and felt isolated from her contemporaries. Sandra made a living as a professional gambler by working cruise ships. She was invited by the cruise lines to work in the onboard casinos and entice other passengers to play poker.

She used her own money and generally made a reasonable, middle class income. Most of her life was spent traveling and playing poker with strangers. Sandra managed her stake very carefully and ran her gambling as a business. Although she experienced occasional loses, she never "chased" loses (tried to recover the loss by gambling more) and could easily leave a game when she was being out-played (which was rare). Because she was associated with the cruises and they wanted passengers to have a good time, she also rarely won large amounts and played conservatively.

At first, the travel and lifestyle appealed to her. She met many interesting people, but had very limited opportunities for socializing with them since she was "working." The hours were long and she found that, despite her skill at the game, playing poker for 8 to 10 hours a day 6 days a week became arduous and boring. Being gone for such long periods on the cruises made it difficult for her to build friendships or pursue other interests. "I started to hate the job. I couldn't really play poker because the 'customers' would get upset with losing. I couldn't stop playing because I needed the money. It's a career that ultimately goes nowhere. I'm essentially a factory worker."

Knowing the fetid conditions that professional gamblers actually face, we have used this fact and incorporated professional gamblers as an adjunct to treatment. In the early 1980s, when one of the authors was conducting sessions for gambling addicts, he brought into the group a professional horseplayer. He spent several hours disabusing members about the lifestyle he led. He described in great detail the horrendous hours, tremendous work demands, and endless streaks of poverty, bad food, and rotten motels. He concluded by telling the gamblers in the treatment group that had he spent as much time reading "something constructive" as he had scouring the Daily Racing Form™, he would probably have a doctorate and a happy life. "Hell, if I used half the brainpower I waste on picking races on *being somebody*, I'd be sitting in some corporate office with a view out the window, instead of a view of the gutter. . . ."

Custer identifies a second type: antisocial gamblers. These are not necessarily people with the antisocial tendencies noted in Chapter 2. Instead, they are people who are involved in fixing races or playing with marked cards. Bergler (1957) described them in detail. Often, they proliferate in large urban areas. Shell games are very popular with them. On the East Coast, three card monte is also used to scam tourists. Frequently, they have a confederate to assist them in "ripping off" the "suckers." More sophisticated examples include persons who try to fix slot machines. Las Vegas wages an elaborate war against these "rip-off" artists, often responding a step behind them.

Such "artists," as they prefer to call themselves, often develop gambling problems themselves, despite their propensity to "fix" numerous games of chance. They may even seek treatment, though unless they are being actively pursued (by law officers, organized crime, family, and so on), they steadfastly avoid inpatient services. Their prognosis is probably poor, as it is for anyone with an antisocial personality disorder. Gambling is a means to an end for these people, who often have multiple addictions. Meyer and Deitsch (1996) describe this type of person as an "ineffective criminal personality." An example follows.

Jennifer

Jennifer is a 32-year-old woman who used to make a living in prostitution and drug deals for rock stars. When her looks "faded," as was inevitable with her personally abusive lifestyle, she thought of a novel method of making money. She became a "gambling groupie" for a number of rock bands with disposable incomes. Rock groups—or, in one case, a classical music performer—who wanted to gamble in a town where it was illegal would learn of her services and then call her up. For a large overhead, she would participate in rigged dice games and marked card sessions. She even brought along a portable computer for slot playing and sports betting. All of the odds were grossly stacked in her favor. She allowed her patrons to win occasionally, especially when they were new to her services. Thereafter, she would engage in cheating, extracting as much as a 50% take from her customers.

She made contact with one of the authors on a "Sports Chat Line," one of the ubiquitous services that charges gamblers high telephone fees to talk with one another anonymously, in conference calls. (Usually, they use such lines as sources of additional information relevant to specific wagers.) She had no desire to change her behavior, but was very open to the anonymous voice of the author, perhaps thousands of miles away. After several hours of conversation, she revealed data that confirmed that her story was truthful. She began to unfold a story that evoked ambivalent emotions. She realized that while she was too old to provide sexual services to "high rollers in the rock field," she could provide them with "an addiction as powerful as any drug. . . . They know me all over America. And the thing is, they are all suckers."

"Do you realize how—what it feels like—to hear a record by [a famous rock band] and know I have taken them for $8,000 the night before? God, what a rush! I swear, it's better than crack . . . better than gambling yourself . . . 'ripping off suckers' is what they used to call it.

"On the other hand, you know, I don't see me doing this when I'm 40, much less 50. I'm putting my money away for the day my credibility fades."

This type of antisocial person is also described by Lykken (1995) and Walters (1999). In general, the literature suggests that the best prognoses occur when there are depressive or anxious symptoms, which can be tied to behaviors through arduous therapy.

Custer defines the third type of gambler as a casual social gambler, a person who gambles primarily for recreation and entertainment. For this type, gambling is a harmless form of relaxation that is tantamount to the usually innocuous behaviors of temperate drinkers (Margolis & Zweben, 1998). Gambling never interferes with social or vocational obligations or with family ties (Kandel, 1984).

Because the distinction is rather fuzzy between a casual social gambler and a serious social gambler (the fourth type identified by Custer), the concept of a spectrum disorder is very useful here. On one end, we have a casual gambler who "goes to the boats" or buys a lottery ticket simply for amusement. This continuum continues toward the serious social gambler, who invests more of his or her time in gambling than the casual gambler. Gambling behaviors are this person's major source of relaxation and entertainment, but without substantially interfering with family (or other) obligations. Serious social gamblers may lack leisure or other social skills, but they manage to function on a daily basis (Hill & O'Brien, 1999).

Serious social gamblers are often found at racetracks and other places where they believe their sense of skill may provide them an advantage. The serious social gambler, for example, may spend hundreds of hours a year on a computer, trying to predict horse winners or beat a point spread. As one serious gambler told one of the authors, "The pleasure is in the method, not necessarily the winning or luck." Another noted that she spent more money on gambling-related books than on gambling. Another reported that he spent more on the Daily Racing Form and sports handicapping "tout sheets" than on actual wagering.

Serious social gamblers may be experiencing behaviors that are normal and are part of an ongoing developmental phase. Dating couples (heterosexual or homosexual) often engage in heavy gambling until they reproduce or have their mutual attention shifted toward greater career successes. This is reflected in the fact that most chronic serious gamblers tend to be underachievers, even if their gambling does not reach the level of an addiction. An example is a person with a doctorate in chemistry, who works in a commercial laboratory at night, essentially so that she can study different blackjack simulations. Another example is a doctoral candidate in mathematics, who has delayed his career for years so that he may perform computer simulations of atmospheric differences and their effects on roulette.

Heavy social gambling can facilitate successful dating. Couples who cannot talk to one another have something to do in common. They can share emotions that otherwise would escape discussion, or engage in a "pseudomutuality" of following teams, wins and losses, and handicap lines. As one recovering gambler told us recently, "Hell, yes, gambling kept my marriage together. How could I yell at my wife over all the noise in the casino?" It provides a way to be together while avoiding intimacy.

Custer's fifth type is described here as the neurotic gambler, although Custer did not use the term himself. These gamblers tend to have numerous life and psychological problems, including anxiety, loneliness, and depression. [A detailed case study is presented in McCown and Johnson (1993).] They gamble primarily to distract themselves from the miserable aspects of their empty lives or dysfunctional emotional states. A good example is the lonely spouse at a video poker machine. Very frequently, they are poor or disenfranchised. To use one gambler's phrase, they "didn't get the poker hand God gave everyone else." For these people, gambling is both a drug that dulls their senses and a purchase of a dream (Westphal & Rush, 1996). Central to their sense of failure in life is their low self-concept, which may have existed across their life span (Byrne, 1996).

Susan

Susan, age 26, is an example of a neurotic gambler. She lives with her mother and three of her five children in an old mobile home on an old boyfriend's land. The part of town she lives in is notorious for its violent bars, blaring country and western music, and the ever-present sound of video poker. Susan has been married three times. All of her husbands abused her. With an eleventh-grade education from a notoriously poor school system, Susan finds it difficult to imagine obtaining a well-paying job. Instead, Susan works three part-time jobs, none of which offers benefits. In a typical six- or seven-day workweek, she works 12 to 14 hours per day.

"I play video [poker] all of the time," she says. "Once or twice I won big. Not that big, but big enough. Mostly, though, I just play to distract myself. I just sit there and forget about the kids, my mom's health, the fact I won't get no more from life than I got already."

"I'm not like a lot of those people who play. I don't really think I'm going to win. I don't drink either, because it just doesn't agree with me. I just like to sit on the stool in front of the machine and see what happens. I could do it for hours. It's peaceful, like fishing or something."

Unfortunately for Susan, her gambling habit is much more expensive than fishing. When we helped her realize that over half of her minimum-wage pay goes to feed her gambling habit, she shrugged.

"There's nothing else to look forward to in life. Some people have Jesus and some of them have liquor. It's a mean town here. Gambling and cigarettes are all I have. I won't let anyone take them from me."

Custer (Custer & Milt, 1985) believes that, for these people, gambling is an analgesic rather than an actual euphoria or a high. He denies that these people are *compulsive* gamblers. He believes they are more similar to people who drink to escape anxiety or depression (Wiesenhutter, 1974). They are "problem" gamblers, analogous to alcohol abusers in the *DSM-IV* (APA, 1994). Women are more likely to fall in this category of gamblers; those who gamble to escape.

The sixth type of gambler labeled by Custer is the "classic" compulsive gambler—the type who receives the most attention in the mental health literature (Rachlin, 1990). Clinical observation seems to suggest that these persons have truly lost control over their gambling lives (Blume, 1994). Gambling and gambling-related activities are the most important things in their life. The majority engage in the process of "chasing," described below. In Gamblers Anonymous, these people are often considered to have hit a "low bottom."

Tanya

Tanya is an example of a chronic compulsive gambler. She works in a restaurant. She has difficulty resisting any bet, whether it is on how many games the New Orleans Saints will lose or how long it will take a busboy to clear a table. She says, "You know, I've done a lot of drugs in my life. But for me, the thrill of picking winners is better than cocaine. Better than sex. Better than money, even. . . . I like the money and I couldn't get motivated about betting without it. But the big thing is, it's such fun picking winners."

Tanya owes several thousand dollars to friends and to credit card companies. She is nonplussed by all of this. "One day I will hit big. At a boat or at the Super Bowl. Fuck it, until then I will stay in debt. When I hit it big, I will quit."

Surprisingly, Tanya is also very religious. "God will give me the winning ticket when it is time. Then, I'll pay off my debts, spend more time studying, and go to occupational therapy school. Really. I know you don't believe me, but that's what is going to happen. Then I will quit. I'll quit when I catch up."

Custer (Custer & Milt, 1985) notes that the hallmark of these types of gamblers is that they become more and more in debt. They tend to believe in a variety of odd cognitive mechanisms to justify their increasing debts. Always, they believe that they will eventually catch up if they just "chase" longer (Lesieur, 1986).

The probability that these people will commit crime to pay for their gambling losses is extremely high (Rosenthal & Lesieur, 1996). They may, for example, embezzle from their employers or family or lose a job for the opportunity to gamble. Or they will borrow money from organized crime, even though the payback involves selling drugs or engaging in other illegal activities (Wexler & Wexler, 1993). Women in this group of gamblers may turn to prostitution. Unfortunately, when these people come to treatment, they may have multiple addictions, extreme debts, an exhausted social support system, and a variety of psychological problems. Ironically, as is so typical in contemporary mental health data, persons with the most need of treatment have the least access to it (Herron & Welt, 1992; Richards & Bergin, 1997).

Custer believes that this sixth type of gambler behaves in a manner that we could label as genuinely compulsive. An anticipatory tension buildup is followed by commission of the action, relief or euphoria, and, ultimately, guilt. Affect regulation and appropriate development of the self may often be lacking (Schore, 1994). This type of compulsive behavior is frequently associated with serotonergic deficits (Zuckerman, 1999). The latter apparently may be inherited or may follow a history of trauma or early emotional deprivation (Foy, 1992).

Bob

Bob is an industrial consultant with an academic background. He admits, "I would be lying if I said I didn't like all of this. Just going to play the videos, thinking about it, it is so damn exciting. I dream about it. I can't get my mind off of it. The horses, cards, it doesn't matter! It's like tension, like the need for food or something. I have to have it. I can't . . . can't really tell you . . . I wouldn't expect you to understand . . . it's a need, like when I used to smoke, but worse. Have you ever known an alcoholic . . . someone in love? It's worse. Much worse.

"It gets like an obsession. I can't think of anything else. And then I go play—whatever—and usually lose all my money. Even if I am ahead, forget it . . . I just can't stop 'til I have blown it all. I mean, Jesus, last week I was $3,000 ahead and left broke.

"I feel guilty; of course I do. I feel like a loser; wouldn't you? But then, the tension is gone. On the other hand, there is the guilt. God, the guilt! I've thought about hurting myself—I mean offing myself, you know. I don't know what serious gambler who's lost doesn't. Can you imagine telling your high school kids, 'Jerry, Mike, I spent your college funds on the damn poker games. . . .

"But the tension starts to build again. I don't know why. It's like the tension gets in the way of the guilt. And then when the tension rises, you can't help it.

"The whole cycle takes a couple of weeks . . . sometimes as long as a month, sometimes a day. You psychological types should study why we have to have this cycle. It's interesting. Too bad it happens to be me that has it.

"I went to psychiatrists. They told me I was manic-depressive, because of the cycle shit. None of the medications did anything. Then they put me on Prozac or some shit. It didn't do anything either. Xanax, Atavan—Christ, nothing much helped. I still craved the action, betting on anything.

". . . I know it's going to be offensive to say—sorry—but it's like when you are in early adolescence and you have the urge to masturbate. I mean men do; I don't know about women. It just dominates your mind and you do it and then you feel awful, especially if you are Catholic like I am. The guilt, you'd think would be—I mean, it would stop you; but it doesn't work that way. I had a counselor one time—he told me gambling was like mental masturbation. Something about that stuck. I don't know why. I just have that image when I gamble now.

"I know I need help, but you know, there's a lot of fun with the whole thing. Fun and guilt and suicide. It's really fucked, isn't it? Every time I go to

GA, it's like . . . I can't identify with these people. Their 'stories' are all the same. 'I hit skid row and tried to kill myself while the mob was trying to kill me,' or something like that. 'Now I own the county's largest mobile home dealership. I'm rolling in the money and cheating on my wife, neglecting my kids. . . .

"I hate the lifestyle, but, you know, I hate the recovery. What I hate most is the urge, the relief, and then the guilt. That's all life is for me. A struggle, a surrender, and then regret."

Formal treatment is probably necessary for both the fifth and sixth types of gamblers. When we discuss treatment strategies in later chapters, we will highlight differential methods of treatment planning and implementation.

SUBJECTIVE CRAVING

It is impossible for a nonaddicted gambler to genuinely understand the overwhelming desire that many serious compulsive gamblers have for performing their addictions. For this reason, it is important for anyone contemplating working with gambling addicts to attend open meetings of Gamblers Anonymous and listen to the various stories (J.R. Wilson, 1992). Many are horrifying. Some evoke an odd sense of crypto-voyeurism. Almost all reveal a dimension of despair that is beyond sympathy, beyond moral condemnation. Perhaps the best antidote to the simplistic conclusions of the moral model is attendance at a few GA meetings.

Recently, one of the authors was at a 12-step group and heard one of the speakers state that addiction to gambling was harder to control than addiction to cocaine. This prompted a study (in progress) to determine the dimensions of craving associated with various addictions. Earlier works on gambling (Herman, 1969) emphasized the aspect of impulsive craving. This has been reiterated in recent research (Steel & Blaszczynski, 1996).

Our own research (McCown & Keiser, 2000) has shown that words related to craving or lack of impulse control that are generated in response to the Thematic Apperception Test do not differ significantly in frequency for cocaine, gambling, or alcohol. Tobacco generated significantly more craving-related words. This may be congruent with research suggesting that nicotine exerts its addicting influence through multiple pathways, and therefore has a generally higher addiction potential than other abused substances (Brick & Erickson, 1998).

As part of an additional study in progress, in a content analysis of people's "stories" from GA and CA, we found no difference in the words related to relapse or craving. This suggests, as does other evidence, that gambling is as severe an addiction as cocaine. Furthermore, from the evolutionary perspective, we all must gamble daily. Relapse from gambling may be more common because people have to wager all their lives. They have to make choices, often without optimal information, but no one *has* to use cocaine. In this manner, gambling may be more difficult to treat than any other addictive disorder. Specific subtypes of gambling may also be more addicting, although data addressing this remain sparse.

CHASING: THE HEART OF THE PROBLEM GAMBLING HABIT

At the heart of most chronic gambling is the paradoxical phenomenon of the chase (McGurrin, 1992). Chasing, the process of accelerating the amount and frequency of wagering, is pivotal to the observations of Custer (Custer & Milt, 1985) and of Lesieur (1986). Chasing occurs in at least two major phasic variations. Initially, it is the playful thrill of the big win, an ephemeral feeling that is never really duplicated. In the nongambler, this can be simulated (but not duplicated) by calling a "chat line," where people flirt wildly with one another, leaving outrageous messages that promise future rewards. In some Internet chat rooms where people are engaged in imaginary foreplay and teasing, similar chasing can be seen. We have seen people addicted to these so-called "love lines" (not to be confused with phone sex services), but the intensity does not come close to the chasing associated with gambling.

Later, this thrill, perhaps through a process of backward conditioning, generalizes to all gambling play. The invidiousness of gambling is that factors associated with it—the smell of the horses, the photos of the sports team—may serve as powerful cues for relapse. The gambler begins to fantasize about winning, or even about betting and losing. Gambling becomes a genuine obsession (Kaufman, 1994), an addiction that is profoundly difficult to treat (Wexler & Wexler, 1993).

To an outsider, the thrill is simply impossible to describe. It has been likened by clients to mania, cocaine, amphetamines, "that first cigarette," sex, and childbirth—an astounding combination of descriptors. No wonder there is an amazing addiction potential!

John, a 27-year-old welder who plays over $400 in lottery tickets weekly, is a client who recently joined Gamblers Anonymous. During his first few weeks of playing the lottery, he "hit" three times for $11,000. Since then, he admits to being "hooked."

"To me, buying that ticket and anticipating the announcement of the number—it's better than food, better than sex, better than anything you can imagine. I can only describe it as like a roller coaster that goes on for a few hours before they do the daily lottery. . . . Frankly, it would be hard to imagine living life without this kind of thrill."

This thrill cannot be described by anyone who has not had a gambling problem. John's defense is that he has no other pleasures in life, and he should be free to do whatever he wants with his money. To the liberal minded clinician, this is fair enough.

Unfortunately, for John and those like him, despite the pleasures involved, gambling, like any other potentially problematic pattern of action, becomes a pathological behavior when its thrill or reinforcement value interferes with the gambler's social, personal, familial, or vocational functioning (Hill & O'Brien, 1999). This is not a binary (yes or no) process; usually, as with other addictions, it is one of accretion through several years (Margolis & Zweben, 1998). Despite the fact that gamblers may remember a "big win," their gambling slowly and in the course of time exceeds behavioral control (Minnesota Counsel on Compulsive Gambling, 1995).

It is extraordinarily rare for a person to suddenly begin a dysfunctional gambling habit in earnest. With the exception of certain people who demonstrate gambling dysfunction only when there is a powerful new host (Westphal & Rush, 1996; also see Chapter 2), problem gambling, like problem drinking (Sobell & Sobell, 1993), develops fairly slowly. Months, even years, even decades, are required before the habit grows out of control (Wiesenhutter, 1974). This pattern is typical of substance abuse (Welt & Herron, 1990; Willis, 1996).

Later, chasing becomes more insidious, as is illustrated in an excellent exposition by Lesieur (1986), who argues that the second phase of chasing becomes necessary to make up for the money lost from wagering. Initially, a gambler chases the high; later, he or she is chasing to recoup the inevitable losses (Wexler & Wexler, 1993).

This later type of chasing is likely to occur quickly when games are less "zero sum"—that is, the state, a casino, or organized crime extracts a high percentage of the money in the winning pool. When the wagering remains a zero-sum game, there is very little evidence that chasing is problematic. However, when large amounts are taken out for taxes or overhead, the possibility for addiction is increased dramatically, simply because people accumulate more debt, at a much quicker rate (Kusyszyn, 1984). Because they have a lower rate of return, they try to compensate by gambling higher amounts, to cover their losses. They chase more, to try to recover their faster mounting debts. Heavy taxing of gambling may then result in more addiction than where games of chance are not as heavily taxed.

This is expertly reported by "Mary," a GA member whose account is both enlightening and tragic.

Mary

"Okay . . . I'm a social worker. Everyone gives me the grief about how I should have known better. All I can say is, people who don't realize that gambling is as powerful as any drug out there—at least for people like me—

who are they fooling? One of the problems is, you get into debt and you keep wanting to make the big score. So I maxed out on my credit cards. Mortgaged my house, eventually—yeah—statistics were on my side, I guess, but I managed to almost break even. It was *almost*. Never could I just say, 'Hey, you are down a couple thousand for the year, call it quits for good.' So, I mean, I sold some coke [cocaine], even turned a couple of tricks. I don't even want to go there. . . .

"What's that expression—'Been there, done that'—the whole time I am working in an alcohol unit and telling people to go to GA.

"For me, the bottom was when I had to put up with some sexual abuse on my job to get a promotion. I mean, my boss, he knew I had a problem and he knew I needed four thousand extra a year. All to put back into the casino so I could get even. Well, I mean, for me, that was the end of the line.

"But still, I am driven. A driven woman. . . . I keep feeling, just one more time, just one more big hit, and it would cure me. . . . I have to be honest. There were times when I was ahead. I bought my house with—well, the down payment was with the payoff from slots. I could have quit right there. I had some religious kind of delusion going. God is going to bless my gambling or something. But still, the thing is chasing. When you get down, you get desperate. You bet more and more, progressive betting. This just means you double up. You lose a dollar, you bet two. Get lucky, you do okay . . . get unlucky and you lose hundreds.

"Me? I lost thousands. . . . I kind of feel if they had warned people about betting to get even, then maybe things wouldn't have been so bad. I don't know . . . I mean, I have an illness. But for God's sake, it got like a cancer when I got in the hole."

EXPERIMENTAL ANALYSES OF "THE TAKE" AND "THE CHASE"

Recently, researchers from our group (McCown & Keiser, 2000) tested whether experimental slot machine "taxes" increased chasing. The design was simple. Subjects were asked to gamble as much as they wished. Each was given 1,000 imaginary quarters. They were told that if they "ran out of money," they could simply ask for more. There was no expectation that they would be rewarded from these imaginary coins or that they would win. In one group, the "tax" from the machine was set to 17%. In other words, on average, 83% was returned for each unit bet. In the other group, the tax was set at 5%.

The group with the higher tax tended to "tap out" (lose all of their money) quicker. Remarkably, however, once they tapped out, they tended to play with more vigor and at a more furious pace. They placed more multiple bets, as if to attempt to compensate. Again, they went "broke" and repeated the process.

These results need replication, but they may illustrate a general principle: The higher the "take," the more people may wager. This may be the essence of the chase. Higher takes mean more frequent tapping out, which accelerates the rate of the gambling. This sequence should raise some serious questions regarding the desirability of increasing gambling taxes to pay for needed government services. Slot machines, at least, appear to function under a law of reverse elasticity. The higher the house "take," the faster people bet to recoup inevitable losses. Future research needs to match computer and laboratory models of gambling, house and government "take," and empirical data available from casinos and sports books. It is very likely that an optimal function can be found that discourages pathological gambling but maximizes revenues that can be safely obtained.

NEWER VARIETIES OF THE CHASE

Modern times have developed new methods applicable to fostering the chase (Volberg, 1995; Walker, 1988). A gambling disorder is rapidly forming among people who wager on the Internet, a still poorly understood phenomenon. McCown and Keiser (2000) estimates that 2% of Internet users will engage in gambling sometime in the next five years. Of these, perhaps 10% may develop periodic problem behaviors. Despite recent congressional action to limit Internet wagering, it will not go away. Pirated software has not disappeared with legislation.

In addition to team sports, horse racing, roulette, slots, video, blackjack, keno, and almost any other game imaginable, there is an interesting phenomenon of rapid Internet auctions. As is well known by people who spend a great deal of time on the Internet, innumerable auctions are available. Rather than describe what they are in technical terms, we offer this account from Charles, an I-Auction Addict whom we met on an on-line support group.

Charles

"I like to go to the auctions on line. I get my credit card and bid for all kinds of things I may need or maybe don't need. It's as much a thrill as gambling was when I was a horseplayer. What I usually do is, I place a quote for a lot just slightly above the minimum. Little chances that I will get it. But if I do, it is a thrill. I mean, getting a computer for a third of the price of list, even though I don't need one . . . it's a high, checking all the other bids, trying to outmaneuver anyone else playing. It's like the races, I guess.

"I realized that I had a problem when I had $19,000 of credit card debts in one month. I mean, I bought two computers, a copy machine, and a sports car . . . all kinds of stuff I didn't need but that was a good deal. I could see doing this if I was some sort of dealer, but I'm a chef. Well, not a chef, actually. I'm in charge of concessions at _____. I do a lot of bulk buying in my job. Maybe that's why I can't resist a deal. But what good is a $5,000 computer that I get for a quarter of the price going to do me, especially if I already have four of them?

"No, I don't hoard things. I sell them . . . generally—well, it's true I guess—at a big loss. Hang out with me long enough and I'll get you some great computer bargains. My expense.

"But you know, last night, I almost bought some property on line. Very scary. That's why I need help. Property . . . why? I don't have any—I don't have the slightest need for anything like that.

"But God, is it a thrill! It's a different kind of gambling than tables, machines, anything. The excitement is incredible. I'm sure you hear this all the time. But it's better than sex, better than anything I can think of."

Internet wagering will become a growing gambling problem during the next few years. With Internet auctions being used as entertainment by college students and people with insomnia—among others—the opportunities for addiction to an agent not even invented merely two years ago are phenomenal. We have previously mentioned how behavior in chat rooms resembles chasing. We are also aware that people speculate in autographs, pop memorabilia, rare books, and other collectibles. One previously heavy gambler whom we treated speculated heavily in memorabilia involving Frank Sinatra. When Sinatra died, our client sold his collection for about three times the amount he paid for it. However, this dealer has also been unlucky regarding similar purchases. He got "stuck" with a large amount of sports memorabilia, which prompted him to mortgage his house and "speculate," based on Sinatra's age, health, and eventual demise. As this person states, "Yeah, I know, I am chasing. But I pretend I am doing it for business reasons."

There is very little difference between this behavior and betting on horses or the outcome of a specific ballgame. Many chasers have no histories of excessive gambling. They enjoy speculation, and they believe that their success is a sign of their superior cognitive abilities. When they fail, they blame their loss on bad luck and start the chase cycle. Here is one of the most fascinating cases we have ever seen in a nongambler.

Charles

Charles is a 46-year-old antique dealer who lives in an upscale area of Boston. His specialty is stained glass acquisition and repair. When he thought the market was soft, he would spend thousands or even tens of thousands of dollars on "the easy antiques. I call them that because people don't know quality from quantity . . . they just like color."

However, when he sensed the market was approaching its height, he would unload his stained glass merchandise—ideally, at a huge profit. When he failed to make a profit, he would invest enough to cover his losses the second time around. Although his purchases usually involved stained glass, they also included more speculative works of art, on some of which "I took a bad beating. . . . It can be a rough market."

Charles had the inevitable cycles of winning and losing, profits and losses, that initially do not appear to be distinctive from the normal business patterns of most small business owners. However, each of Charles's losses was followed by a heavier, slightly riskier investment, usually financed by exhausted family or friends. In other words, he chased. Very soon, his behavior became similar to that of heavy sports bettors. He was soundly in debt and needed to win in order to get out of a crushing financial burden. Charles eventually went bankrupt. He also realized that his problem with speculative purchases was very similar to gambling. He is now participating in GA, although he believes that it is "irrelevant, really, to the problems of business types."

Charles raises a valid issue: "What I do in my gambling—I mean, my profession—that's socially okay. I make people happy with good deals, and I hire people and provide jobs. Society says that's great. But you know, if I succeed in all of this, I will have to be lucky on what I buy. I have to take a chance, based on what I know. The hard thing is how to walk the line—you know, make a living taking a chance, but not too big a one. I think anyone who works for himself is a bit of a gambler."

Chasing is also common in persons who work in the real estate and investment professions. Deals can be made quickly. Fortunes can be won and lost in a matter of hours or days, depending on the activity level that a specific area generates. There is strong temptation to cover losing opportunities with additional money. The dynamics of this type of behavior match almost exactly those of any other type of chronic gambling.

CHASING AND SKILL: EMPIRICAL RESEARCH

Our initial hypothesis suggested that chasing is most likely to be related to three factors: (1) the amount of winning that is possible, (2) the amount taken "by the house," and (3) the feeling that the wager is not a factor of luck—it involves skill. These hypotheses were based on various literature sources and theoretical orientations (Hermans & Hermans-Jansen, 1995; Hollander & Wong, 1995; Langer, 1975; Letarte, Ladouceur, & Mayrand, 1986).

The wagering option with one of the highest possibilities for chasing is keno, a common game where little effort is expended and multiple bets are possible. Keno is popular because it has a variety of wagering strategies and can offer huge payoffs. It is particularly pernicious because it has one of the highest house advantages of any game (50%) and is essentially effortless for the player. Keno can be played at a casino buffet or bar with no thought whatsoever. In Las Vegas, it is known as a "lazy sucker's game" because of the advantage of the house and the fact that playing it for hours requires no skill or effort.

We thought that keno, more than any other game, would produce the most chasing. Some clinical observations also seemed to suggest that this might be true. However, a more rigorous study proved otherwise. To study chasing in greater depth, we developed a "Chasing Inventory," which has undergone a number of revisions. Our current data indicate that chasing is primarily a function of the perceived control of gambling activity that a person can exhibit (Lightfoot, 1997). At present, among college students, chasing appears to be less likely for games of pure chance, moderately likely for horse racing, and extremely likely for sports team betting (McCown & Keiser, 2000).

Using a slightly different set of data, we attempted to determine whether chasing was a function of both the amount of the "take" and a bettor's belief that he or she has controllability. A structural equation model showed only a slight decrease in the overall "unfitness" when the variable of the house take was included. In other words, the amount of the take, while important, is secondary to a person's subjective feeling that he or she has control over the outcome of a wagering strategy.

These findings were derived from college samples and may not necessarily apply to every type of gambler. The subgroup of gamblers who do not believe that intelligence or skill is important may represent a growing sizable minority. These are people who frequently play video games and believe that certain machines are "hot." There is a natural limit to chasing with such machines. Most machines will accept no more than 10 gambling units, whether they are silver dollars or ten-dollar chips. Horse race chasing, known as "progressive betting" (Quinn, 1987), is usually not practiced seriously by any track denizen for any length of time. Every serious student of the racetrack has denounced it as economic folly. Even the best all-time handicappers have had tremendous losing streaks. Parimutuel wagering is so complex and so subject to random error that the winning streaks necessary for progressive betting cannot be guaranteed.

CHASING AND
INTERMITTENT REINFORCEMENT

Nongamblers regard chasing as such a bizarre behavior that we feel immediately compelled to attempt an explanation. One of the reasons people chase is that the behavior is intermittently reinforcing, If enough money is wagered, then *some* will probably be won back. The amount and timing of the win are unpredictable. However, because the laws of probability state that something will be won eventually, the chasing lifestyle is constantly being reinforced by wagers that become frequent.

A compendium of motivational research (McClelland, 1987) has consistently demonstrated that rewards are more positively interpreted when they have previously been deprived. Losing money makes winning more reinforcing, either through a basic psychological contrast effect or through any one of several mechanisms that may involve cognitive comparisons. Pathological gamblers frequently say that they experience more pleasure after being "down financially." The excitement of winning becomes more intense.

Chris Anderson, with the Illinois Council on Problem Gambling, relates a story one compulsive gambler told him. The gambler went into a casino to play his game: blackjack. The dealer gave an ace and jack to the gambler on his first hand. The gambler indicated to the dealer to "hit me" again. When the dealer pointed out that he had a 21, the gambler insisted on getting another card. His rationale was that "it's no fun to hit right away, that takes the pleasure out of it." Some treatment professionals feel that the excitement of the chase, of coming from behind, might be more stimulating for pathological gamblers than actually winning.

In an unpublished study, we attempted to demonstrate this tendency in the laboratory. Using a simulated casino game, we manipulated the wins and losses of students by changing the ratios of reinforcements. We then asked students to rate satisfaction with their performances. Students rated smaller wins as more reinforcing when they had been "on a losing streak." Larger wins were less reinforcing when students had been "on a winning run." This finding is congruent with a variety of experiments in learning theory, as well as contemporary neuroscience.

Lesieur's (1979) brilliant exposition of the phenomenology of the chase also highlights the fact that a gambler cannot quit while ahead. This is likely a factor of the variable reinforcement qualities associated with gambling. There is an increasing pattern of gambling as long as there is money available for wagering. A history of early success, synonymous with a higher risk of addiction following early drug use (Robins, 1985), may help increase this aspect of the chase.

If the closing of a casino or an aberrant action of friends interrupts gambling, the gambler is even more likely to return if he or she wins. In laboratory experiments, interrupted gambling was rated as more pleasurable, whether winning or losing. Ultimately, smaller wins become less reinforcing and the gambler cannot win enough. The size of bets is increased, and the chase produces tolerance.

This results in gambling for longer periods and wagering higher amounts than were initially planned. Often, this is a first step in the progressive loss of control that accompanies problem and addictive gambling. The process of less gambling is simply seen by the chaser as less exciting, just as a smaller dose of narcotics is less exciting to the heroin abuser.

THERAPY FOR CHASERS

This chapter has not been primarily aimed at treatment, but it may be useful to introduce specific methodology relevant to interrupting the vicious cycle of chasing. The first step involves the clinician's identifying the existence of a pattern of chasing in a particular client. Having the client keep a detailed log (discussed in later chapters) may be helpful, but clients who gamble heavily are not able to perform this task. However, even in failure, they may recognize an upwardly cycling pattern of losses.

The second step addresses cognitive misunderstandings as mistakes that are inherent in the chase and its mathematical pseudo-philosophy. The cognitive underpinnings of chasers are different. Some, according to gambling experts, simply do not understand basic mathematics (Quinn, 1987). Others are more complex and may involve subtler cognitive distortions (McMurran, 1994).

When persons believe in luck, it may be possible to extinguish this belief through simulated gambling experiments conducted in a controlled environment. Limits on this type of strategy will be discussed in later chapters.

What may be harder to extinguish is some chasers' belief that they possess special skills. Examples are "gambling intelligence" or "gambling wisdom."[2] These "skills" make them more liable to believe that they can succeed in wagering. Compulsive gamblers often describe elaborate "systems" for betting or playing their games, even if the game is a purely "luck" based game like keno. The role of cognitive distortions in fostering these beliefs will be discussed in later chapters.

Some of the most difficult cases we have seen involve people who have temporarily succeeded—on the basis of luck—in very high-stakes games or wagers. The framework laid down by these experiences seems to prime people to chase when they encounter an inevitable cycle of losing. This is especially true of people who are involved with large financial dealings, such as stock or currency futures. They may be very likely to attribute success from random luck to their own abilities (Greenson, 1978), in part because of their narcissistic need to be special (Guidano, 1987).

For a more narcissistic person it may be helpful to find another avenue that allows feeling important: work that involves the Twelve Steps, or other social, spiritual, or intellectual activity. We once worked with an addicted gambler who put his expertise to use by working for a state

---

[2]During a recent visit to a casino gift shop, we saw for sale a "Gambling Luck Test," a questionnaire that claimed to be able to predict whether a person is intrinsically lucky. Thinking this was a joke, we investigated further. The sellers were attempting to pass this "instrument" off as a real scientific device. Needless to say, from a psychometric view, the test was skewed toward the "false positive" end of error.

gambling commission in another state. He was able to persuade himself that he was "too smart" to be suckered into wagering again, and that his past had been a valuable lesson. (Indeed, it had! He had learned all about corruption in gambling.)

CHASING AND THE OBSTREPEROUS PERSONALITY: A SPECIAL PROBLEM

As mentioned previously, in a game such as blackjack it may be possible to use highly honed skills to gain a small personal advantage over the house (Harvey, 1999). This is known as card counting, and it requires hundreds of hours of memorization and dry-run practice sessions. We have never known a gambling addict—recovering or otherwise—who has made more than the minimum U.S. hourly wage by mastering this immensely complex skill. The intellectual acumen involved is better spent in other efforts, but, for some people, the thrill comes from beating the system, at least until the ever-present casino security personnel permanently bar the card counter from the wagering premises.

Many very bright people "waste" extensive time at pari-mutuel racing and related sports. The degree of intellectual discussion on particular portions of the Internet is highly mathematical. Lest the stereotype of the chronic, down-and-out gambler be applied to this group, consider the following statement by a psychologist handicapper, James Quinn (1987): "In the 1970s and 1980s, a new wave of writers, several with advanced academic credentials, concentrated on one or a combination of handicapping factors in far greater depth, promoting their ideas and practices as 'methodologies' that combined systematic techniques and an ultimate reliance on interpretation and judgment" (p. 18).

For these writers, Quinn notes, the obsession was not in making money or in the thrill of gambling. Instead, it was in the intellectual pursuit of beating the masses, which is necessary for pari-mutuel success. Not much progress has been made toward this goal. As Quinn notes, any "gambling system" applied to pari-mutuel wagering is eventually self-defeating. Others will find out and use it, thus reducing any advantage it may have previously afforded.

These people are chasers, but they are chasing something more elusive than money. Their thrill is in winning percentages. Most would be happier with a two-dollar bet that produced a 300% profit than a $50 bet that increased their money again by half. Their obsession is to outsmart their fellow players. They want to beat other gamblers "in theory." Usually, they can be persuaded to try out any new "system" on paper for several hundred simulations before they actually lose money with it. Like absent-minded inventors, part genius and part deluded, they eventually realize their folly and set out again to build the perfect handicapping machine.

Often, they are addicted to information or statistics. They like numbers. They enjoy the process of "data crunching." The more information they have, the more interesting the "angle" or the more desirable the wager. They have little interest in games that are entirely chance-based. Usually, they are more interested in the mathematics of the wager than the actual process of winning (Hausch, Ziemba, & Lo, 1994).

Do these people need treatment? If they do, it is usually for more global issues than their gambling problems (Meth & Pasick, 1990). Brief psychodynamic therapies (Messer & Warren, 1995) may be helpful in refocusing their lives toward more productive goals. It is unlikely that persons with such profoundly bleak internal worlds will respond to gambling treatment alone. More "core" problems are frequently the sources of such emptiness (Luborsky & Crits-Christoph, 1998; Magnavita, 1997).

CONCLUSION

Addictions are multifaceted (Rozin & Stoess, 1993). Gambling represents an option for addiction that is as old as civilization (Wexler & Wexler, 1992). As Griffiths (1996b) exquisitely notes, the exact causes and reasons for continued problem or addictive gambling are dependent on the individual. However, among the pathways to this pattern are some commonalities. Too often, the career of the gambler follows a specific pattern, eventually involving criminality and financial ruin (Bergler, 1957; Blaszczynski & Silove, 1995). This pattern appears to be occurring more frequently, as gambling opportunities expand (Wadle & Owens, 1996). Because of the financial factors associated with chronic gambling, the pattern is much more common than the diverse routes that addiction to substances often foster in a client (Kaufman, 1994).

To be successful, clinicians need a phenomenological understanding of gambling (Lesieur, 1990). A similar understanding is probably needed for treating most addictions (McAuliffe & Alber, 1992), but empathy with gambling may be difficult for a nongambler (Meyer & Deitsch, 1996), especially if he or she is a busy generalist clinician. However, if we are to successfully treat gambling disorders, we must develop some nonjudgmental understanding of them. Among the many "common factors" in successful counseling or therapy, this seems to be one of the most important (Rockland, 1992; Roth & Fonagy, 1996; Rutan & Stone, 1993). An understanding of the process of the chase is a necessary first step toward becoming a successful therapist of problem and addictive gamblers.

CHAPTER 4

Etiologies and Maintenance of Gambling Disorders: A Brief Review

Honestly, I don't know why I do gamble. It doesn't feel good and has ruined my marriage, killed my family, and cost me a job. I have no idea why I gamble, but I'd be willing to bet all of last year's winnings that you can't figure it out either.

—A gambler in group therapy, 1998

WHY DO some people gamble only casually and apparently have no problems maintaining this behavior for life? Conversely, why do some people almost immediately develop problem gambling behaviors, seemingly from their first gambling experiences? Why are these problems so difficult to treat? What is the mystery that makes gambling so attractive? For years, clinicians have been asking these questions. Nelson's (1998) recent novel about the exciting and perilous world of gamblers provides an excellent literary account, as did Dostoyevsky's classic, *The Gambler*, in the nineteenth century. These questions remain sources for future novelists; they still have not been answered satisfactorily (R.I.F. Brown, 1987; Griffiths, 1996a).

As a society, we have additional concerns. Is there any understandable reason why problem gambling is apparently on the increase? Data since the early 1990s have indicated that teen gambling is becoming more widespread (Haubrich-Casperson & Van Niespen, 1993). Yet, parents seem to be in mass denial regarding this problem (George & Schroeder, n.d.). The pattern seems to follow that of substance abuse; moderate but important trends are seen in increased experimentation and possible habitual abuse (Willis, 1996).

To counselors or therapists who have had no experience with clients who have problems with gambling, it seems inconceivable that these self-defeating behaviors can be so attractive and addictive. Yet there is incontrovertible evidence that gambling disorders represent some of the most serious addictive processes that a person may have. As we stated in Chapter 1, problem gambling behavior is a substanceless addiction, a phenomenon with the exact dynamics of other addictions, but without the obvious ingestion of a chemical (McGurrin, 1992). This adds to the mystery of an adequate explanation of this entrenched behavior. Much of our knowledge regarding the etiology and maintenance of addictions involves hypothesized relationships between ingested substances and neurotransmitters (Smith & Darlington, 1996). With gambling, it is not clear which neurochemicals are released and why they combine to produce addictive behaviors.

Also puzzling is the mysterious situation of a previously casual recreational gambler who suddenly develops compulsive gambling problems. This may occur after years of enjoying social gambling as an innocent, nonaddictive pasttime. Under what circumstances do casual gamblers become problem gamblers? Is there an event or a developmental period that makes them more susceptible to the addiction? If so, can it be identified or foreseen? Can we identify anyone who might be at high risk?

Horvath (1998) argues that pathological gamblers are individuals with multiple handicaps. Deficits may involve a biological vulnerability as well as a learned dysfunction that causes gaps in identity and ego constructs and renders cognitive and emotional frameworks inadequate. These problems make it difficult for these individuals to manage many aspects of life, particularly negative emotions, interpersonal relationships, intimacy, and behavioral impulsivity. But then shouldn't we find similarities in the psychological and behavioral patterns of problem and addictive gamblers? These questions have puzzled clinicians and researchers for many years (e.g., Kusyszyn, 1973).

Unfortunately, with our present knowledge, many of these questions are unanswerable. In this chapter, we attempt a sporadic and clinically relevant review of a large amount of data (much of it not specific to gambling) in order to discuss the etiologies and maintenance of gambling problems. None of the theories presented in this chapter is universally applicable to every problem or addicted gambler. The theories are neither "right" nor "wrong." They should be thought of as heuristics that are generally useful in helping us to understand the history and treatment needs of our clients.

This chapter does not attempt a complete or even a systematic overview of the research regarding gambling. Instead, its selective coverage is directed toward busy practicing clinicians who are interested in learning how to manage gambling behaviors. Among the important gaps in this brief overview is the psychoanalytic tradition (e.g., Freud, 1929/1950), which is clinically rich and often useful. Similarly, we ignore the etiology and maintenance of family-based problem gambling (McCown & Johnson, 1993). These areas deserve their own dedicated works and will be discussed further in later sections that highlight treatment methods.

This chapter can be conceptualized as a clinical overview to which we have added new, occasionally summarized research from our group. Excellent and much more thorough reviews of research on possible etiological factors influencing pathological gambling are available elsewhere (Griffiths, 1996b; Spunt, Dupont, Lesieur, Liberty, & Hunt, 1998; Walker, 1992) and are certainly worth clinicians' research efforts. The edited collection and clinical guide by Shaffer, Stein, Gambino, and Cumming (1989) remains invaluable and points to a general failure to address these and similar critical issues, despite the massive increase in available opportunities to wager.

Very current topical reviews are available via the Internet from the Harvard Medical School, in cooperation with the Massachusetts Council on Compulsive Gambling. The WAGER (Weekly Addiction Gambling Educational Report) is devoted entirely to increasing the accessibility of gambling-related research and news to clinicians and to the public. Although it is supported by a variety of funding sources that have contradictory agendas, the WAGER has established itself as an unbiased source of distilled commentary. It is currently free of charge and is available via the Internet or in traditional printed format. In an area where objectivity is easily compromised by overwhelming emotions and subtle biases, the WAGER has remained objective, clear, and overwhelmingly relevant to clinical research and practice.

Most states now have councils that can offer a variety of information specific to local concerns. The councils often sponsor local or regional conferences and coordinate prevention and treatment efforts in many areas. Many publish newsletters, provide resources for mental health professionals, and have speakers available for educational presentations. In addition, the National Council on Problem Gambling and the Institute for the Study of Gambling and Commercial Gaming cosponsor the quarterly publication of the *Journal of Gambling Studies*. The journal is available through membership in the National Council or can be ordered through the National Council on Problem Gambling, Inc., 445 West 59th Street, New York, NY 10019.

REINFORCEMENT THEORIES:
THE MOST COMMON EXPLANATIONS FOR
THE COMPLEX BEHAVIORS OF GAMBLERS

The simplest and perhaps the most parsimonious way to account for the acquisition of gambling is with the variety of reinforcement theories that are present in contemporary behavioral sciences. The application of operant reinforcement theory to the understanding of gambling is so common that, typically, in undergraduate psychology textbooks, the example of gambling behavior is used to *teach* some of the major concepts of operant conditioning (Franken, 1998).

A brief overview is helpful for people who do not recall the occasionally confusing but important introductory theories of learning. Gambling behavior is rewarded or reinforced (i.e., the gambler wins) on what is known as a variable ratio (VR) of reinforcement (Skinner, 1953). Variable ratios of reinforcement provide for definite or certain behavioral reinforcement for response, but with an interesting twist. These schedules vary the amount of responses necessary for reward, and the reward intervals are generated randomly around a specific mean. For example, on a variable ratio schedule 20 (VR 20), an organism is reinforced every 20 times *on average.* However, in some cases, the reinforcement may occur two or three times in a row, after only a single response. Similarly, it may occur only at tremendously long intervals, perhaps after hundreds of responses. The organism has no way of predicting exactly when the reinforcement will occur; it only knows that it *will* occur. Reinforcement is simultaneously certain (in its inevitability) and uncertain (in its timing) (Domjan, 1998).

Such schedules of reinforcement are the hardest of any to extinguish, or to eliminate. Extinction of VR is extraordinarily slow, and there are frequent spontaneous returns to previously reinforced behavior, a phenomenon known to psychologists as an *extinction burst.* Extinction of VR reinforced behavior may take many thousands of nonreinforced trials. Domjan (1998) discussed situations in which pigeons placed on VR reinforcements pecked 150,000 times before extinction occurred. One of the best ways to make sure that any behavior is maintained for long periods without reinforcement is to reinforce it on a high variable ratio.

The reason for the hardiness of behavior that is reinforced on a variable ratio can probably best be understood from an informational perspective. The organism that is responding—in our case, the gambler—knows that eventually he or she will obtain a reward. However, each previous trial is essentially unpredictive regarding the possibility of reinforcement on the next trial. Consequently, long trials of nonreinforcement are not perceived as punishing or predictive of future rewards. The organism will respond and respond, despite long absences of rewards between trials. This may be one reason why gambling is so difficult to eliminate.

Problems with Reinforcement Theory as an Explanation of Gambling

A simple VR explanation of the acquisition and maintenance of gambling behavior omits an important fact. Variable ratios are very hard for organisms to learn and to maintain. Very often, organisms will not engage in behavior for a length of time that is sufficient for a variable ratio to sustain their subsequent behaviors. Rewards usually do not come quickly enough, and behavior usually ceases before it is reinforced at all.

As is taught in almost any Introduction to Psychology class, the best way to acquire a behavior is by a fixed ratio of reinforcement. Behavior is more apt to be acquired if it is reinforced every time it is performed. Besides being the hardest to extinguish, VR schedules of reinforcement are also the hardest to initially acquire, and in some cases are impossible to acquire. At this point in our discussion, learning theory seems to be able to explain the maintenance of chronic gambling behavior, but not necessarily its acquisition.

Contrast the development of problem gambling behavior with that of problems with alcohol or other drug (AOD) abuse. The results of AOD abuse tend to be less variable (Castellani & Rugle, 1995). Although the intensity of the AOD experience is frequently a function of mood and setting, it is also on a relatively low VR of reinforcement. If an alcoholic drank heavily seven times but got drunk only once, these results were unpredictable and it seems unlikely that he or she would continue drinking. The physiological negative aspects of drinking demand that the behavior be maintained by a more constantly reinforcing ratio.

Gambling, however, may and does occur with more difficult reinforcement schedules. A payoff may occur every twentieth or fiftieth time; similarly, there is little "dose dependence" in rewards because the amount expended to play correlates poorly with the amount of reward. In contrast, the AOD abuser knows that he or she will probably achieve results within a specific range if a certain amount of a particular substance is ingested. Usually, five drinks, tokes, hits, or whatever units of doses are popular, will have more impact than one or two. Although psychological factors play a major role in AOD abuse, biological factors also assist the user with some degree of hedonic predictability.

The gambler, on the other hand, has no guarantee of such consistency of reward. A dollar fed into a slot machine may bring back a dollar or, depending on the machine, perhaps $100,000 or maybe even $1,000,000. Usually, however, the dollar will bring back nothing at all. Ultimately, this frustrating process of nonreward is punishing to the gambler, as elucidated on a psychobiological level by Gray (1988).

Because most gambling experiences are punishing, we should note that the real issue is not how some people are able to make the transition to intermittent schedules of reinforcement, but whether any people do so at all. One explanation might be that the initial stimulus response is reinforced by other behaviors besides the gambling payoff. This phenomenon is seen in behaviors that offer more consistent dose-response rewards. Many drugs or experiences that are addicting are initially unrewarding and are indulged in for reasons that are not merely hedonic (A.T. Beck, Wright, Newman, & Liese, 1993). Most smokers, for example, had to learn to enjoy cigarettes, and most heroin users do not report positive feelings during their first usage (Fisher & Harrison, 1997). Usually, social pressure or other cultural or psychological factors encourage use and continued reuse until schedules of reinforcement can become causally operative (Halpern, 1995; McKeever, 1998).

Besides an initial schedule of reinforcement, other factors might be needed for the acquisition of problem gambling behaviors. The initial successful reinforcers might be social factors, cognitive expectations, the ambiance of the gambling venue, or numerous other contingencies that are not usually recognized by the future client. Perhaps after a person gambles for a longer period and eventually obtains a series of wins on a variable ratio, the gambling behavior itself is reinforced and maintained. At that point, it becomes progressively difficult—and in some cases, almost impossible—to extinguish this behavior. Further research in this area could help elucidate the role of these nonmonetary reinforcers in providing the impetus to gamble, despite a pattern of initial early losses.

THE ACCIDENTAL WIN, EXPECTATION, AND REINFORCEMENT

People who accidentally win big—and are therefore inadvertently conditioned (from their own perspective, not the casino's) early in their gambling career—tend to have a very high likelihood of developing gambling problems. Numerous studies have shown that a "big winner" is much more likely to develop subsequent gambling dysfunctions (Snyder, 1978). Popular books on gambling exhort novice gamblers to be careful if they experience an early windfall (Binkel, 1999). "The experience of an early win," said one casino manager to us, "that's the thing that keeps so many of them returning day in and day out."

In our own research, we have added a covariant to the phenomenon of the development of gambling problems following a big win. We have interviewed people prior to their first attendance at a casino, and measured their expectations of winning. We then interviewed them after they came out of the casino ($N = 45$). For persons with high expectations, a *big win* was associated with a desire to return to the casino. A loss was highly aversive and correlated negatively with the desire to return. For persons with low or moderate expectations, a loss was unassociated with a desire to stay away from the casino. A win of any amount was associated with a desire to return, regardless of expectations.

Small and moderate losses were not associated with a desire to avoid the casino, unless the losers had large expectations. Gamblers with small and moderate expectations are at highest risk for having expectations that are lower than their accidental "big win" and then developing the beginnings of a compulsive gambling habit. *The most vulnerable patrons seem to be those who expect to win big and do so, and those who don't expect to win at all and lose only a small amount.* Perhaps prevention strategies should be aimed at these vulnerable groups. However, from this research, our recommendation might be to increase the expectations of winning. This strategy might decrease the desire to return, since it presents a situation that is likely to be highly at odds with the reality of the casino. On the other hand, such an approach might backfire by supercharging the addictive potential of people who expect to win big and actually succeed at this irrational expectation.

VARIABLE REWARDS AS BEHAVIORAL INCENTIVES

Little is known about winning varying amounts and whether it enhances gambling patrons' exaggerated behavioral responses (Skinner, 1953). Variable winnings are extremely common in video poker and video slot machines. Because the variation in reward intensity and frequency also acts as a variable ratio, it provides two very potent ratios of reward acting in tandem. This may help explain why gambling behaviors are so difficult to extinguish: They have actually been rewarded on two different VR schedules.

Cognitive expectations, however, also must play a part in this addictive process. With extremely high jackpots now possible with typical slot machines, this formerly self-limiting modality is especially dangerous. A payoff may occur on every play or on every fiftieth play (on average). When there is a payoff, it may be one coin or a life-changing jackpot. This dual ratio of reinforcement, where both the frequency and the amount of reward are uncertain and variable, may combine to make gambling via slots and video poker, among other outlets, so uniquely attractive. Again, more research is needed in these areas to determine whether changes in the reinforcement ratios of these machines will make them potentially less addictive.

MOTIVATION AND AROUSAL THEORIES AND PROBLEM GAMBLING

As the preceding discussion suggests, monetary rewards may play a key role in determining who develops a compulsive gambling habit. One set of theories states that people gamble because they have specific needs— often unconscious—that are met by gambling. For example, Chantal, Vallerand, and Vallieres (1995) argued that motivation is a key determinant of gambling involvement. They hypothesized that participants who exhibit a high self-determined motivational profile (i.e., engage in gambling for fun and have a sense of choice) would have a higher degree of involvement. These results were supported in their study.

In other words, people who find gambling more fun and feel they have chosen it themselves as a recreational activity are more apt to become gambling addicts. This may seem commonsensible; however, combined with the previous findings regarding VRs, it has some important implications. First, problem gambling is likely to occur among people who enjoy it. Eventually, someone who enjoys it will experience a big win, which places the person on a variable ratio that will make extinction difficult. Gambling will then accelerate, and problem gambling behavior will be the result.

The role of *autonomic* arousal has also been cited in the genesis and maintenance of gambling disorders. Sharpe et al. (1995) investigated the role of arousal in the process of the development of problem gambling. The three groups of subjects recruited into the study corresponded to problem gamblers and high-frequency and low-frequency social gamblers. Five different conditions were employed to determine under which conditions gambling-related cues were linked to increased autonomic arousal, as measured by skin conductance level (SCL), heart rate (HR), and frontalis electromyography (EMG). The five conditions were: (1) a neutral task, (2 and 3) a videotaped poker machine gambling scenario presented with and without distraction, (4) a personally relevant "win" situation, and (5) a videotaped horse race. Comparisons of the responses for the videotaped poker machine gambling stimuli and those for a horseracing video task demonstrated differences only for the problem gambling group and only for SCL. No differences between these tasks emerged on the HR and EMG indexes, and no differences were evident for either of the social gambling groups. No changes were observed in any group when subjects' cognitions were prevented by asking the subjects to count the number of wins made during the video play period while watching the same poker machine video.

However, when personally relevant situations were presented and compared to a neutral task, differences were observed in all three groups. The nature of these differences varied between the groups, and there were different indexes of arousal. For problem gamblers, increases were evident in all three measures (SCL, HR, and EMG). Increases were also observed for the control groups in comparison to the neutral task, but only in HR and SCL and not for EMG. For HR, the increases were equivalent across all three gambling groups.

The SCL for the problem gambling group became significantly more aroused than for the control groups, but no differences were observed between the high- and low-frequency gamblers. Only the problem gambling group evidenced significant EMG increases in the personally relevant task (compared to the neutral task).

From this study, it appears that problem gamblers, whether engaged in high or low risk, show a different physiological arousal pattern. In a similar study with equal relevance, we have examined the relationship between levels of arousal, as measured by heart rate, and the number of erroneous cognitive perceptions about winning, among regular, problem, and occasional video poker players. Significant correlations were found between physiological arousal and the number of erroneous verbalizations about the results. In other words, the process of physiological arousal, which problem gamblers appear to be primed to experience, encourages cognitive distortion about the probabilities of winning and encourages the tendency to see patterns where there are none.

More recently, our research group replicated this study with college students. An aggregate measure of change from baseline in SCL and HR correlated .46 with the amount of verbalized cognitive distortions about the likelihood that a random series of numbers had an underlying pattern. Physiological arousal apparently is associated with beliefs in erroneous patterns that do not exist. From an evolutionary perspective, this may make some sense for species survival. Under conditions of arousal, we may be primed to scan the environment and grasp any inklings of patterns for external phenomena. Although this may give us a survival edge when faced with otherwise unpredictable stressors, it also may make us evolutionarily prone to excessive gambling.

Does a person have to be a problem gambler to experience this cognitively biasing physiological arousal? Evidence would suggest not. Griffiths (1995) assessed the mood of regular and pathological gamblers and found that each experienced a more depressed mood before playing and, compared to nonregular gamblers, each exhibited significantly more excitement during gambling. Apparently, *any* history of gambling is associated with increased excitement, which, in turn, is associated with cognitive distortions. Additional research is needed to clarify whether this tendency toward excessive excitement is a function of previous winning while gambling.

Additional factors might be relevant to a motivational maintenance of gambling behaviors. In a series of classic research studies with a broad range of applicability, Atkinson (1958) showed that people tend to work the hardest when there is only a moderate likelihood that they will succeed. By itself, this finding would make it unlikely that *anyone* would develop problem gambling behavior. However, the major exception seems to be where the great secondary reinforcer, money, is involved. The possibility of a higher monetary reward encourages harder work, despite the odds of reward and across a variety of situations.

Money seems to work best as a reinforcer when other incentives are not operating or are not salient. In an ingenious experiment, Atkinson (1958) showed that the contribution of achievement incentive, a well-recognized motivational force, becomes prevalent only when the money incentive is low. In other words, a large amount of money seems to block out many motivational factors, including important and far-reaching motives such as the need to achieve, to experience affiliation, and to gain power and intimacy (McClelland, 1987).

Specific motives, such as the need to achieve, can be important determinants regarding styles of gambling behavior. Consistent data indicate that people who have a high need for achievement:

- Prefer being personally responsible for their performance results (Franken, 1998). In this way, they are likely to feel satisfaction in doing something well.
- Prefer moderate risks to very short or very long odds.
- Prefer gambling that involves some degree of skill (e.g., poker or sports handicapping).
- May be especially liable to experience problems in sports betting.
- Prefer frequent feedback regarding their performance successes.
- Will often bet just to show that they are right or that they can do a "good job."
- Often scan their environments for opportunities for gambling and for testing new "theories" about successful wagering.
- Tend to disagree with the concept of "gambler's magic," with common ideas of luck, and with trusting in superstition (A.W. Wilson, 1972). At the racetrack, for example, they are much more likely to buy and study a racing form.

Although we believe that extraversion correlates negatively with slot machine playing, alcohol, which causes a state similar to enhanced extraversion, may increase gambling incentives and motives. It has been found that men (but not women—that experiment is yet to be performed) who are forced by a laboratory situation to feel inadequate about life's responsibilities drink more, apparently to feel more powerful. Drinking also gives men increased feelings of power and decreases their inhibitory thinking.

There is also a phasic response to power and alcohol. As subjects initially drink, they tend to feel more powerful, more sociable, and more benevolent toward others. After several drinks, however, the sociability turns into agitation, and the benevolence turns more toward blatant self-serving fantasies. This occurs while the feelings of power are increasing. Consequently, as one of our clients stated, "With one or two drinks, people are healing the world. With seven or eight, they are splitting heads."

We recently attempted an extension of this type of research to the relationship of alcohol and gambling, and we found several similarities. Problem gambling is often associated with higher needs for power that are apparently not met in a person's environment. As subjects drink, they tend to go through a biphasic response regarding their desire to spend their winnings. With moderate alcohol consumption, gambling is associated with fantasies about the "social good" that could be accomplished with winnings. Heavy drinking, however, introduces fantasies that are more significantly concerned with implementing personal power over others.

When moderate drinkers lose, they may recognize their losses and quit. However, with the "investment" of motivation associated with heavy drinking, the pattern is different. In the heavy drinker, losses are seen as deep rivals of personal power. This causes a strong motivation to continue to play, or to chase. In other words, a person who is drinking while losing at gambling is more likely to "take it personally" and become a danger both to his or her personal finances and to the security of the gambling establishment.

More research is clearly needed in the area of motivation and gambling. Behavioral science has only the slightest theoretical underpinning regarding how motives develop. For example, the origins of the power motives probably have a biological component. There is evidence that loss of status relates to a need for power. This might explain why the poor, disenfranchised, and socially nonrewarded segments of our society are apt to gamble. Gambling, even when one is losing, provides the illusion of power, at least temporarily. Very likely, biological propensities, superimposed on long-term situational variables, may be factors in causing or perpetuating aberrant gambling behaviors.

BIOLOGICAL ETIOLOGIES

Relatively little attention has focused on psychobiological causes or correlates of gambling (Spunt et al., 1998). Although there are several studies on the roles of the central noradrenergic system (Roy, deJong, Ferraro, et al., 1989; Roy & Linnoila, 1989) and hypoactivity of the serotonergic system in pathological gambling, relatively little attention has been directed toward gross cerebral function and frontal lobe involvement.

Despite the fact that pathological gambling has been characterized as an impulse control disorder, it has also been associated with compulsivity (Kusyzyn, 1977). Preliminary neurobiological studies implicate serotonergic dysfunction in pathological gamblers. Treatment with serotonin reuptake inhibitors (SSRIs), such as clomipramine and fluvoxamine, may be effective in treating this disorder. Well-defined and controlled clinical trials in large samples of pathological gamblers are needed (Griffiths, 1998).

Specker et al. (1995) provide further evidence of the relation of serotonergic deficits to gambling. They hypothesize that if serotonergic deficits are related to gambling, then there should be a spectrum of persons who have a number of comorbid features associated with impulse control disorders. They describe the occurrence of attention deficit disorder and impulse control disorders in 40 pathological gamblers in treatment for gambling problems, and 64 controls. Impulse control disorders other than pathological gambling were noted in 35% of the pathological gamblers, compared to 3% of the controls. In the gambling group, these included such diverse disorders as compulsive buying and compulsive sexual behavior. A strong association was found among pathological gambling, attention deficit, and other impulse control disorders. Attention deficit disorder was seen in at least 20% of the pathological gamblers. Finally, and often not addressed by many studies, the rates of impulse control disorders did not differ by gender. This strongly suggests that a central serotonergic mechanism or dysfunction contributes to this spectrum of disorders, which may culminate in suicidal behavior and has also been linked to low levels of serotonin (Roy, 1994).

On the other hand, Black, Goldstein, Noyes, and Blum (1994) examined the lifetime prevalence of eating disorders and pathologic gambling in first-degree relatives of subjects with obsessive-compulsive disorder (OCD) and in controls. There were no significant differences between the groups. The authors conclude that eating disorder and pathologic gambling have no familial relationship to OCD. This argues against the notion that gambling is related to a spectrum disorder of obsessive-compulsive behaviors. At this time, although the data support some role of serotonergic dysfunctioning, the exact relation to causality is uncertain.

If gambling is related to serotonin deficits, it should also be related to a tendency toward depression. Some studies, not all, have demonstrated this to be true. Some of the possible disparities have been raised in a review article by Hollander and Wong (1995), who focused on body dysmorphic disorder (BDD), pathological gambling, and sexual compulsions within the realm of obsessive-compulsive spectrum disorders. These three disorders affect sizable numbers of the population, have early-age onset and chronic courses, and seem to have preferential response to SSRIs (Roy, 1994). They also have a high comorbidity with obsessive-compulsive disorder, depression, and other impulse control disorders.

According to Hollander and Wong (1994), BDD patients are more toward the compulsive/risk-aversive end of the dimensional model of obsessive-compulsive spectrum disorder, and they often have poor insight. Pathological gambling clients hypothetically are closer toward the impulsivity/novelty-seeking end of the OCD spectrum. They often have features of inattention. Sexual obsessions and/or compulsions encompass a heterogeneous group of disorders, as exhibited by differential response to SSRIs within this group.

If serotonin activity is related to gambling, then gamblers should demonstrate low platelet monoamine oxidase activity. Carrasco, Saiz-Ruiz, Hollander, Cesar, and Lopez-Ibor (1994) found this in a small but methodologically thorough study. Surprisingly, this methodology, which is much easier to perform than research regarding serotonin, has not received the attention it deserves.

In conclusion, deficits in serotonin regulation seem to be important as factors in the pathological gambling process. To date, however, no prospective studies have demonstrated that serotonergic deficits predate the onset of gambling behaviors. On the other hand, gambling losses are depressing, especially if they are severe. It would not be surprising if these depressive series of behaviors associated with gambling losses reduced the bioavailability of serotonin. In other words, we should assume nothing regarding the direction of causality. Meanwhile, there is some evidence that SSRIs may be helpful, but are not a panacea, for persons with gambling problems.

THE BIOLOGY OF THE REWARD SYSTEM AND GAMBLING BEHAVIORS: GAMBLERS AS PLEASURE-SENSITIVE PEOPLE

In very recent years, it has become known that specific pathways or circuits in the brain are dedicated to the neural mediation of reward and pleasure. The activation of this system of reward mechanisms seems to be a common feature shared by most if not all abusable substances, and perhaps even by pleasurable experiences (Brick & Erickson, 1998). Drugs that are abused act on these brain mechanisms to produce a subjective reward, known as a "high" or "rush." Data indicate that "abusable" drugs almost always have a final common mechanism of action, despite vast differences in their pharmacological properties. These drugs ultimately stimulate the nucleus accumbens, an area with large numbers of dopamine receptor cells (Kalat, 1998).[1]

Drugs that apparently have a negative hedonic effect and are not pleasurable, such as haloparidol, seem to inhibit the activity of this system. By blocking dopamine, especially at the nucleus accumbens, they temporarily block the capacity for pleasurable drugs to be reinforcing. Hence, they lose their abuse potential almost completely. It is likely that nonpharmacological addictions are also mediated through these specific neural pathways and areas.

Current research shows that there are actually two major dopamine systems in the midbrain. A primary or first-stage system comprises descending or caudally projecting fibers of dopaminergic neurons. The ventral tegmental areas of the midbrain contain dopamine neurons, and their cell axons project to the mesolimbic brain areas, including the medial prefrontal cortex and the nucleus accumbens. Projections also extend to the amygdala and the hippocampus. The activity of neurotransmitters on the presynaptic nerve terminals of the dopamine-releasing axons in these latter projection sites is proposed as the key reinforcing property of a variety of abusable drugs.

In the second dopamine area are the axons of the ventral tegmental area cells as they ascend in the medial forebrain bundle and project into neurons of the forebrain—largely, the nucleus accumbens, frontal cortex, amygdala, and septal areas. In essence, this two-process system is a complex dopaminergic loop between the forebrain and the ventral tegmental area. Its cell bodies are located in the nucleus accumbens (the "pleasure center") and in several structures of the limbic system. A secondary pathway runs approximately within the medial forebrain bundle; cell bodies are located in the ventral tegmental area of the midbrain. The second-stage fibers are the axons of the ventral tegmental area's cells. They ascend into the medial forebrain bundle and ultimately project into neurons of the forebrain (Smith & Darlington, 1996).

Amphetamines—and probably cocaine—act on the first- and second-stage neuronal terminals (Hester & Miller, 1995). These drugs apparently

---

[1] An exception may be hallucinogens, which appear to work through serotonergic activity. Not surprisingly, many people do not find these drugs initially pleasing (Zuckerman, 1979, 1983).

mimic the effect of direct electrical stimulation and may also be the biological underpinnings for the relationship between sexuality and aggression, noted by the classic psychoanalysts (Zillman, 1998). Other
behavioral reinforcing drugs act primarily (or only) on the second-stage
dopamine neurons, probably through action of the endogenous opioid
system. This occurs because cell bodies, axons, and synaptic terminals
of the enkephalinergic and endorphinergic neurons are found in extraordinary abundance in this hypothesized reward area. Endogenous opioid peptides neurons synapse directly onto the mesotelencephalic
dopamine axon terminals, forming an elaborate system that is now only
beginning to be understood. Opiate-mediated activity, however, is now
known to directly affect the dopaminergic reward areas (Smith & Darlington, 1996).

This is a simplified word sketch of a very complex picture. The second-
stage component of the reward circuitry is under the modulation of a wide
variety of other neural systems. These include GABA and serotonergic,
noradrenergic, and diverse neuropeptide systems, many of which are
only poorly understood. Others probably have not even been identified.
Dopamine appears to form a critical link for all reward media, including
opiates and sedatives. Ten years ago, this statement would have been
merely speculative. Now, the general consensus is that addiction is related to a dopamine dysfunction.

Blum, Sheridan, and their associates (1997) have postulated a specific
deficit in the dopamine reward system. Hypothesized dopamine D2 receptor gene variants are involved. Other neurotransmitters have also
been implicated, but, to date, the only molecular genetic defect that has
been found to associate with alcoholism, drug dependency, obesity,
smoking, pathological gambling, attention deficit–hyperactivity disorder
(ADHD), Tourette's syndrome, as well as other related compulsive behaviors, is a variant of the dopamine D2 receptor gene (DRD2). In their review of the available data on the subject, Blum et al. reported a number of
independent meta-analyses that confirm an association of DRD2 poly-
morphism and impulsive-additive-compulsive behavior (IACB), which
they have termed "reward deficiency syndrome."

The dopamine D2 receptor gene in pathological gambling was studied
directly by Rule, Muhleman, Chiu, Dietz, and Gade (1996). These authors
note that the Taq A1 variant of the human DRD2 gene is associated with
drug addiction, some forms of severe alcoholism, and other impulsive and
addictive behaviors. They sought to determine whether there is a similar
association of this gene with pathological gambling. Of the 171 pathological gamblers studied, about 51% carried the D2A1 allele versus about
26% of the control subjects. This allele was also associated with higher,

more reckless patterns of gambling in persons who had pathological gambling behaviors.

This discussion does not uncover the existence of a magic bullet explaining the disease of gambling, but it does suggest that inherited or acquired genetic variants may make some people less, or differentially, sensitive to rewards. How these people behave psychologically will only be answered by a combination of behavioral and genetic scientists, working in tandem.

A BRIEF THEORY OF REWARD SENSITIVITY, AVOIDANCE, AND IMPULSIVITY

So far, we have largely discussed reward sensitivity and dopamine, especially as it is regulated through beta endorphins and other endogenous opioids. However, as any introductory psychology textbook now states, the serotonergic system plays an important role in responding to rewards and novelty (Zuckerman, 1999). Deficits in the serotonergic system would also be expected to be related to gambling.

Oddly, the selective serotonergic reuptake inhibitors (SSRIs), the newer generation of antidepressants, work with two classes of gamblers, even though they would seem to require different medications: (1) those who are overaroused and (2) those who are underaroused. (We discuss these subtypes later in the chapter.)

Elsewhere (McCown & Keiser, 2000), in discussing the neural basis of conscientiousness and procrastination, we have postulated that not only reward system conclusion points, but also the actual reward processes of afferent signals help determine approach and avoidance behaviors. Denial, which is encountered in a variety of addictions (Wakefield, Williams, Yost, & Patterson, 1996), is common among persons who do not appreciate signals of punishment but have a hypersensitivity to rewards. Excessive response to punishment anticipation with lower capacity for reward produces anxiety, with little possibility for abuse potential. Excessive response to reward sensitivity, but not to reward, produces perfectionistic behaviors. When such people do gamble they tend to become bogged down not so much in actual play but in the secondary aspects of gambling, such as elaborate handicapping schemes.

This model recognizes the role of excitement or general arousal in facilitating reward sensitivity and fostering impulsivity. It should also be realized that if gambling disorders are due, in part, to general arousal when rewards are present, it might be possible to dampen this response with substances such as carbamzapine, which does not lower overall inhibition, but does dampen hyperresponsiveness to reward situations.

Haller and Hinterhuber (1994) report such a finding, which is in need of replication.

COMORBID PSYCHIATRIC DISEASES AS THE CAUSE OF PROBLEM GAMBLING

Anxiety and depression are the most common comorbid conditions in chronic gamblers. They are followed closely by addictions to other pharmacological and nonpharmacological agents. Anxiety syndromes include obsessive-compulsive disorder, panic attacks, and phobias.

There is a predictable relationship between nonpharmacological addictions and anxiety and depression. All nonpharmacological addictions clearly affect the brain and produce changes in mood and behavior. These alterations occur in a variety of conditions. For example, gambling—which, as we have seen, may be analogous to cocaine or amphetamine use—can produce signs of anxiety and anxious moods, rapid heart rate, and, at higher doses, panic attacks (Griffiths, 1993).

With drugs and alcohol, there is usually an improvement in mood following cessation. Instead, the recovering gambler will frequently experience long-term dysphoria. If alcohol, benzodiazepines, and barbiturates are used, the dysphoria is worse. Prolonged gambling appears to produce serious states of depression. Our clinical impression is that the depression is more prolonged than with detoxification from ingested substances and may be more likely to produce a mood-induced relapse. People attempting to quit gambling may resume simply because they feel better, even when they lose.

Other data suggest that people who are anxious and depressed may be more likely to gamble to relieve this dysphoria (Griffiths, 1996b). People gamble because it is distracting. Even though over the long run it may make them more depressed, in the immediate situation, it is reinforcing because it provides relief from internal or external cognitive stressors. In other words, it is negatively reinforcing, in addition to positively reinforcing whatever winning history the subject has. Part of the addictive attraction of gambling might be its capacity to provide relief from negative psychological states.

This relief is fairly easy to control in its duration. It is not as disrupting as alcohol or drug use, because it does not require several hours or days to "sober up." People can gamble, feel relief from life's stresses, and then return to a stressful situation without any noticeable impairment. This does not usually happen with alcohol or drugs, except in the end stages of the disease. Despite the fact that winnings or positive reinforcements in gambling are not dose-dependent, negative reinforcers are much more so than with AODs. A sustaining mechanism in the process of acquiring problem gambling behavior may be that gambling produces relief without evidence of intoxication or obvious impairment. Because of this, people with a variety of emotional difficulties, including anxiety and depression, may be predisposed to gamble as a form of self-medication.

Occasionally, chronic gambling can produce an apparent psychotic symptomatology that resembles the psychotic behavior seen in cocaine abuse. This probably follows one of three patterns: (1) a brief but aggressive paranoid psychosis, (2) an emergent bipolar disorder or neglect of an ongoing psychotropic disorder, or (3) emergence of a preexisting psychotic symptom. This suggests that gambling may be a form of poor self-medication, where an anxious or depressed person gambles to induce dysphoria, which works only temporarily, but ultimately increases psychotic proneness, probably through release of excessive dopamine in the mechanisms described in the previous section.

DISSOCIATIVE EXPERIENCES AS A CAUSAL STATE

One hypothesis strongly suggested by clinical experience is that persons who gamble, especially video gamblers, may be experiencing a dissociative experience. This hypothesis is easily generated by anyone attending any activity where gambling is occurring. All one has to do is look at the faces and levels of interest and distractibility in people actively gambling. In one study, our group found that, given a task to determine which of several facial expressions occurred during the context of wagering, college students could successfully classify over 90% of such faces. Moreover, comments from neutral, nongambling patrons reflected the fact that facial expressions vacillate from intense interest to utter boredom in a matter of a second or two. Even when gamblers win, their joy is short-lived. To paraphrase the paraphrase of a recovering gambler quoting Gertrude Stein, "I had no there, there, when I was gambling . . . not unless I was winning."

If gambling produces dissociation in some people, then it is easy to understand how these gamblers might be blind to the punishing aspects of losing money and might be primed only to experience rewards. They might be more likely to avoid the responses of others, who are telling them to stop their gambling. In other words, they would be relatively insensitive to social cues.

Although the evidence is anecdotal, many of us who work with gamblers find their descriptions of long periods of fruit and video poker machine gambling echo the descriptions of trance phenomena in hypnotic states. Many compulsive machine players relate sitting in front of their machine for as much as eight to ten hours without feeling any hunger or other physical discomfort. They describe the sensation of time stopping and the rest of the environment fading from their awareness. If interrupted from play, they may be somewhat disoriented or irritated. Particularly for those gamblers who seek escape or relaxation through gambling, this experience may be exactly what they desire.

The evidence for gambling's actually being associated with dissociative experiences is contradictory. Kofoed, Morgan, Buchkowski, and Carr (1997) investigated the relation between dissociative states and addictions in 58 pathological gamblers and 25 control subjects, who, in this case, were alcoholics. The authors hypothesized that greater dissociative experiences might reflect increased vulnerability to pathological gambling and particularly to video lottery gambling. The subjects were classified into one of three gambling types: (1) video lottery only (VLO); (2) video lottery mixed with other forms of gambling (VLM); and (3) non-video mediated gamblers (NVL). The control subjects were alcoholics. The subjects completed both the Dissociative Experiences Scale (DES) and the Minnesota Multiphasic Personality Inventory-2 (MMPI-2). Of 58 gamblers, 88% were pathologically involved in video lottery gambling. Higher DES scores were seen in VLM subjects, who were involved in many gambling forms. High levels of prior dissociative experience were not associated with VLO pathological gambling.

Unfortunately, there are problems with this study, such as the very small sample size and the concurrent lack of statistical power. Using alcoholics as a control group may not be wise, inasmuch as any memory problems that they may have because of the neurotoxicity of alcohol may be interpreted as dissociative states, especially during initial phases of treatment, when cognition is very clouded.

Finally, and most important, dissociative experiences may not be common while a person is not gambling, but may be unique to the act of gambling. In other words, to use psychological terminology, these experiences are state-dependent. Because they may be encountered only during gambling, and by definition involve dissociation, there is little likelihood that they would be recalled at all or that questionnaire data would be able to help assess such conditions.

A more ecologically valid experiment might have significant others rate the behaviors of their partners who have gambling disorders. Our research involves having 14 spouses or longtime significant others rate the behaviors of their partners, all of whom scored past the cutoff on a gambling inventory. Prior to this research, a special inventory was developed for administration directly after the gambling experience, and was modified to include ratings of others. The internal consistency of both the self (.81) and the other (.72) was adequate for research purposes.

Chronic problem video gamblers were rated by their significant others for dissociative behaviors experienced while gambling, as compared to while watching television or eating dinner. The data are preliminary and reflect only a very small sample—which certainly was not blind and was probably very biased—but there are substantial and extremely significant differences between gambling and either watching television or eating. This suggests that dissociation may be especially severe in video gambling, a concern raised by other authors (e.g., Griffiths, 1993). Again, additional research in this area is warranted.

COGNITIVE BIASES AS CAUSAL PROCESSES IN GAMBLING DISORDERS

Bujold, Ladouceur, Sylvain, and Boisvert (1994) have argued that, in treating gambling, it is useful to have gamblers predict the likelihood of winning and then compare these predictions to the true odds. The ability to predict is usually greatly overestimated. Such cognitive bias likely plays a role in maintaining gambling behaviors (Dusenbury & Fennema, 1996; Ladouceur, Paquet, & Dube, 1996).

One of the goals in our treatment philosophy is to determine the extent to which a person believes skill, blind luck, or a winning streak is responsible for gambling success. These are relatively independent constructs (Kusyszyn, 1980). A sports bettor may believe that skill is important. A more superstitious gambler may "feel" lucky. An optimist may report a "lucky streak" that promises a win.

Sharpe and Tarrier (1992) described a treatment approach that emphasizes the importance of clients' cognitions and beliefs in maintaining gambling behavior. Walker (1992) found that any slot players voiced more irrational thinking than nonplayers. Recently, we have studied the self-narratives of gamblers, where autobiographies were used as part of treatment and became available as archival data. The self-narratives (Hermans & Hermans-Jansen, 1995) showed great variability regarding lucky periods of time or "streaks." Whereas non-problem-gamblers or nongamblers tended to divide blocks of time into larger portions ("1998 was a good year for me"), gamblers were more specific about supposed variations in luck over individual months or weeks. For example, one gambler in treatment stated: "The third week of February has always been good to me, much better than anything in the first couple of weeks of March. . . . Always."

At the heart of this pattern may be a cognitive bias regarding encoding and understanding of streaks of luck. There may also be differences in perceptions of time between abusive gamblers and others. Presently, research suggests that nongamblers tend to encode their lives in a series of meta-emotions: love, periods of sadness, loneliness, and the like (L.S. Greenberg & Safran, 1987). Clinicians are especially prone to this self-analytical meta-thinking about emotions (Garb, 1998). Problem and addicted gamblers, on the other hand, are much more likely to segment their lives according to much smaller units that represent periods or perceptions of subjective luck ("What year—yeah, 1997, August, second week I believe. Goddamn, was I on a streak . . . I couldn't lose for trying") and periods defined by gaming opportunities ("Arizona was great—eight days of straight poker, with no house limits"). Consequently, their lives seem to lack coherence, or any theme at all, aside from wagering. The complexity that is part of the human experience is replaced by a nomothetic identity. One of the real tragedies of excessive gambling may be that it robs the human spirit of the diversity of living.

COGNITIVE BIAS AND THE ZEIGARNIK EFFECT

One important question concerns gamblers' apparent bias toward believing that they are winners. Some of the cognitive psychology of 40 years ago may supply answers to this question. In a sequence of experiments, subjects were required to complete a series of tasks. Some of the subjects were interrupted while the tasks were being completed. It was found that subjects remembered the incomplete tasks better than the completed ones. In addition, if given the opportunity, subjects returned to resume work on the interrupted tasks. This is called the Zeigarnik effect, after its discoverer.

What appears to be responsible for the Zeigarnik effect is the expectation by most adults, that people should finish any job they have started (McClelland, 1987). Shifting the demand characteristics alters the encoding of relevant memories. People with a high demand characteristic to see themselves as winners will be more likely to remember wins. In our society, most people see themselves in a positive light. Therefore, there is a strong cognitive bias toward believing that one is winning and a stronger bias toward revising one's memories to reflect this conceptualization of the self.

The Zeigarnik effect may also explain why people who are losing continue to gamble, even in the face of mounting losses. If subjects identify their gambling behavior as "I'm here to win money," any losses represent uncompleted tasks. The task is only completed if consistent winning is involved. If subjects are interrupted during a winning streak, they tend to remember the interruption and this reinforces the processes involved in generating their self-image as winning gamblers. On the other hand, if they are interrupted while losing, they usually tend to have a higher drive to continue to gamble later. They want to complete their task of making money. If asked to tell how well they did, subjects tend to recall more tasks completed, which, from their perspective, describes the process of winning money.

ILLUSORY CONTROL AND UNCONTROLLABLE STRESS

Researchers have recently focused on the role of uncontrollable stressors in fostering a variety of behavioral problems (J. Johnson & McCown, 1997). Compared to controllable stressors, uncontrollable stress generates a different biobehavioral set of responses. What is most interesting is that it does not matter whether the stress is actually controllable, or there is only an illusion of control. Even the false belief that environmental events are controllable has a profound effect on both psychological and physiological responses to stress.

The illusion of control is largely related to cognitive development. Faulty perceptions regarding control are more likely among regular video poker players (Coulombe, Ladouceur, Desharnais, & Jobin, 1992). Their biased evaluation is related to persistence in gambling, despite losses (Gilovich, 1983), and their thoughts are often associated with childish cognitive development—specifically, preoperational thinking. This phase of development may explain why misattribution regarding probability is a developmentally related process in gambling (Derevensky et al., 1996).

A fascinating study comes from a group of clever researchers in Israel (Friedland et al., 1992). It was hypothesized that individual failure to exercise actual control over an event might be compensated for by trying to bolster a personal and subjective sense of control. This led to the hypothesis that stress would engender a tendency toward illusory perceptions of increased controllability. Results supported the hypothesis and may be interpreted as meaning that uncontrollable stress is associated with the tendency to find patterns in gambling activity that is random. Controllable stress, on the other hand, does not seem related to this tendency.

This may help to explain why "near misses" in gambling are so reinforcing (Langer & Roth, 1975; Reid, 1986). Near misses subjectively maintain a sense of control. The gambler says, "If only I had done it slightly differently. . . ." Near misses are so subjectively reinforcing that slot machines are designed to produce them and to foster the illusion of control. Much of the effectiveness of these machines in inducing gambling behavior may also be rooted in the evolutionary psychology of the near miss. It causes us to work even harder for a goal we think is obtainable.

Findings such as these might explain why people who are depressed, anxious, or interpersonally stressed are more likely to develop gambling problems. Such persons are probably psychologically primed to find patterns where none exists. Again, from an evolutionary perspective, it is doubtlessly advantageous to manifest this cognitive bias. When there is no control in the environment, humans tend to find any possible explanation. This explanation might help us survive when we have uncertain information about natural conditions. However, it also fosters a tendency toward gambling as an addictive process.

In related studies, other researchers have shown that windfall gains are spent more readily than other types of assets (Arkes, Joyner, Pezzo, & Nash, 1994). This may relate to predictability of the reward. Unpredictable rewards are apparently spent more quickly, which may explain why gamblers who win often bet more heavily, rather than quitting while they are ahead (Quinn, 1987). The gambling industry relies on this response to boost profitability (King, 1969). Gamblers, on the other hand, persuade themselves that the variable that is causing their winning is the transient friend known as "luck." The gambling industry would be far less lucrative if people resisted the tendency to spend their gambling winnings on additional gambling.

The vicious paradox regarding luck often becomes quickly apparent to the outsider but is impossible for the gambler to see. The existence of personal periods of enhanced gambling luck is impossible to falsify, to use the important phrase and scientific orientation of Karl Popper (1934). Gamblers who are winning will continue to play and often will say that luck is "on my side today." Gamblers who are losing often feel they need to continue to play to determine whether "luck has left me." Despite any past massive losses, they need to continue gambling to "bring luck back." Winning is evidence of the existence of luck and its favor toward the gambler. Losing is not a falsification of the idea of luck; it is evidence that luck has temporarily "left me." Luck appears to have an agency all its own—in part, because of the biases that gamblers may be primed to develop.

A similar phenomenon may be the "bad bet" experienced by problem gamblers (R.J. Rosenthal, 1995). This occurs when a wager that is subjectively assessed as a "sure thing" does not yield winnings or "come in." Bad bets are often followed by larger and more irrational bets, especially by problem gamblers, but nonproblem gamblers usually take the losing experience as a cue to quit. Apparently, when a sure bet goes bad, the illusion of control is shattered and a chronic gambler has to compensate by attempting to overcontrol the next sequence of wagers. Ultimately, this pattern leads to quick financial ruin, as Quinn (1987) has noted.

THE ABSENCE OF COGNITIVE RESPONSES AS A HEURISTIC BIAS

Kahneman and Tversky (1982) describe heuristic biases as shortcuts in thinking that may have had some previous evolutionary advantage. One of the more curious aspects of problem gambling is that it often may be characterized by grossly simplified or even by absent higher cognitions during the losing gambling process (Kusyszyn, 1977). Writers of popular advice books for gamblers note that people begin to develop gambling problems when they are placed in situations where they gamble "too fast, too much." In other words, they play "at the level where they don't think" (Singleton, 1999).

One popular book summed up the role of cognitive factors in gambling quite succinctly:

> Avoid games where you are encouraged not to think. The more decisions you have to make, the more likely you are not to slip up. Even worse, playing games that require no decision lull you into a mindlessness that encourages errors on your part. The best way to go broke very quickly is to gamble a lot (sic) in a game that keeps you from thinking. You can kiss your money goodbye. (Binkel, 1999)

This may conflict with the implication that the illusion of control is important in developing gambling disorders. Yet these statements are not necessarily exclusive. Faulty cognitions regarding probabilities *or* no cognitions regarding probabilities may encourage aberrant gambling behaviors. If gamblers do not think about the odds, or believe that their chance of winning over the long run is illusory, they have no quick and natural feedback regarding the reasonableness of their behavior. Instead, they are operating on reinforcements associated with excitement or other aspects of immediate stimulus control.

To date, little research has been conducted on the lack of cognitions in gambling. One exception has been our ongoing research on the newest type of gambling to become problematic: rapid play video mediated gambling (RVMG). Generally offered as electronic slot or video poker, RVMG is among the fastest growing gambling available and it is becoming a common pastime for millions of Americans. Comparatively inexpensive microtechnology, novel marketing strategies, and high profit potential have encouraged state governments to promote these devices in casinos, taverns, restaurants, and many other accessible locations. Data suggest that these machines have an enormous "addiction potential." One study indicates an 8.7% classification rate of adolescents as problem gamblers, largely related to RVMG (Winters, Stinchfield, & Fulkerson, 1993). Accounts also suggest that marketing of RVMG is most directed toward those who can least afford this activity: the poor, disenfranchised minorities, women, and the elderly.

Traditional theories of addictive sports, table gambling, or fruit machine gambling using older mechanized slot machines may be largely inappropriate in explaining the repetitive behavior of persons engaged in

RVMG. First, the rate of play (amount of gambling actions) in RVMG may be several hundred times more than that of horse racing or sports betting. It likely also exceeds the rate of play associated with manual fruit machines (with traditional lever pulling). Most video and fruit machines presently manufactured are now button-activated, reducing player effort and allowing much more rapid play.

Second, the cognitive decisions and perceived skills necessary for winning are minimized with RVMG. Video poker and blackjack games now include displays showing the player's best options for winning a particular hand, reducing the need for any deliberate choice mediated by perceived skill.

Third, behavioral inhibitors that slowed the rate of play with traditional fruit machines are substantially reduced Credit cards, casino play cards, or paper money "loaders" make it unnecessary to continually "feed" quarters or dollars into the machines or even to wait for personnel to provide change. The stereotype of a gambler feeding change into a "one-armed bandit" is now replaced by someone rapidly and repeatedly pressing a single play button, in the absence of behavioral constraints of money insertion or the need to pull a relatively slow, spring-activated lever.

Fourth, other factors limit the relevance of traditional pathological gambling explanations to RVMG. Theories emphasizing arousal have proven inadequate and may be especially irrelevant to the systematic repetitiveness associated with this modality (Wildman, 1992). Perceived skill, which has been strongly associated with the addiction potential of sports gambling or of "playing the numbers," does not apply to RVMG because, essentially, no knowledge, skill, or expertise is necessary. For example, as we indicated in Chapter 3, traditional forms of chronic problem gambling are often characterized by "chasing" (Lesieur, 1984)—losing bets are followed by an increased wager to recoup losses. Video machines, with their limit on wagers per play, do not allow this strategy. Similarly, cognitive models based on presumed erroneous reward expectancies (e.g., Taber & McCormick, 1987) do not account for the fact that most people who engage in RVMG may readily acknowledge their anticipation of losing. Behavioral explanations involving variable reinforcement ratios do not account for the fact that RVMG usually has extraordinarily punishing effects: players consistently lose large amounts of money with little or no expectation of gaining it back. Consistent behavioral literature has indicated that frustrative nonreward is typically a highly potent extinguisher of behavior, but this does not appear to be a factor dissuading losers from chronic RVMG.

Fifth, personality variables such as sensation seeking or low self-esteem do not appear to be promising explanations for RVMG, inasmuch as great personality variation characterizes chronic video gamblers as well as other types of problem gamblers.

We directly examined the relationship between video play pace and cognitions. In one study, we had persons verbalize their cognitive expressions while playing laboratory-simulated RPVM games. There was a correlation of −.34 (p < .001) between the amount of cognitions voiced and the aggregate amount of play. Interestingly, it did not matter whether cognitions were positive or negative. The more a person thought about gambling while performing, the less likely he or she would wager extravagant sums. This suggests that video gambling may be related to a state that fosters a lack of cognitive processes. If this is the case, then programs that promote cognitive responses during gambling may be helpful in reducing gambling problems and subsequent addictive behaviors.

PERSONALITY THEORY

The most common "lay" causes of gambling disorder are related to aspects of personality. Yet the role of personality in contributing to addiction has been given a rough road during the past 25 years of the cognitive revolution in psychology and the behavioral sciences. This contrasts with the experience of people in Twelve Step programs, where frequent reference is made to "addictive personalities."

The word *personality* itself remains controversial (Comer, 1992). It includes social internalized variables, motivation aspects, cognitive factors, temperamental factors, genetic differences, and individual differences. All of these overlap, and any discussion attempting to arbitrarily divide these areas is rather fuzzy. With this in mind, we will restrict our discussion of personality to variables that have been more traditionally associated with temperamental aspects of human behavior (Eysenck & Eysenck, 1985). In other words, these are relatively stable, enduring traits that appear to have physiological correlates (Eysenck, 1983).

THE ADDICTION-PRONE PERSONALITY

One explanation for why people develop problem gambling behavior is that they are "addiction prone" (Rozin & Stoess, 1993). This explanation is circuitous and answers little. It argues that people who become addicted are people who are predisposed to become addicted, but the predisposition that fosters this addictive process is not clarified.

Other researchers are moving beyond the concept of addiction proneness and attempting to hypothesize what factors might relate to this constant tendency. For example, this is a belief that there is a general tendency to become addicted, and that several dimensions are involved. They include: capacity for addiction craving, ability to develop stimulus or substance tolerance, significance of withdrawal symptoms, and lack of personal control. Persons who are on the upper ends of any or all of these facets might be considered addiction-prone.

Other authors who suggest that alcohol and gambling are independent diseases take a more negative position. Addiction in one area, they argue, does not necessarily mean that addiction in another area is likely. Dickerson (1993) takes the more radical view that different psychological processes contribute to the development of impaired control, even in different types of gambling. To Dickerson, there is no evidence of a general propensity to gamble, much less a general propensity toward addictive proneness. This is congruent with the cognitive explanations of gambling favored by many others (e.g., J.S. Beck, 1995; Benjamin, 1996; Bohart & Tallman, 1999; Cullari, 1996). The only common pattern for developing problem gambling is stated to be negative emotions (see below), followed by a pattern of crushing personal indebtedness, similar to the pattern found in chasing.

We have reviewed the literature regarding personality and addictions from the perspective of our bias toward the conception of personality as relatively stable temperament variables (Janda, 1998). We believe that three temperament variables, two of which are included in the popular so-called "Big Five" of personality (Retzlaff, 1995) are extremely important for determining patterns of addiction and risk of addiction proneness (Wachtel, 1997).

IMPULSIVITY

Perhaps the most important variable for predicting gambling disorders is impulsiveness—acting without thinking (McCown et al., 1993). Based on the above discussion regarding the lack of cognitions in gamblers who develop problems, it may be likely that impulsivity is a risk factor. Impulsivity has been divided between the so-called "functional" impulsivity, which relates to verve, moxie, and spontaneity, and dysfunctional impulsivity, which relates to disinhibitory behavior that is usually regretted later (Dickman, 1993). For clinicians, dysfunctional impulsivity is of most importance.

From a biocognitive perspective, there are several theories regarding impulsive behaviors. Some others have begun an information processing theory regarding dysfunctional impulsivity. McCown, Palmer, and Roden (1997) present evidence that impulsivity is related to an inability to divide attention and perform cognitive set shifting. Consequently, there are no cognitive feedbacks on potentially negative behaviors. Biological explanations stress the role of monoamine oxidase, deficits in serotonin, and perhaps also dopaminergic dysfunctions. These are simply flip sides of the same behavioral syndrome.

Impulsivity has been highly correlated with a variety of addictions. For example, Castanelli (1995) found that persons who were gamblers scored higher on impulsivity and inability to resist craving than cocaine abusers or alcoholics. McCown (1989) found that people who were multiply addicted tended to be more impulsive. More recently, Steel and Blaszczynski (1996) used principal components analysis to investigate the relationship between psychological constructs measured by their impulsivity and addiction. Four primary factors emerged, of which three are relevant to the present discussion. One related to psychological stress. One related to sensation seeking. Another factor related to antisocial behaviors.

This suggests that impulsivity may have several facets that relate to the high probability of developing gambling behaviors. First, impulsive people may have higher stress levels, in part because of unmet obligations (Ferrari, Johnson, & McCown, 1996). This may act to fuel the urge for gambling as a distraction.

Second, impulsive people may be at higher risk to try aberrant lifestyles because of their general exaggerated tendencies to sample a wider variety of experiences. They are much more likely to be "experience hungry" and therefore may try gambling at a higher rate than people who are low on impulsivity (Zuckerman, 1991). In other words, using the epidemiological model, these people may be subjecting themselves to more exposure to risk factors.

Third, and perhaps most important, once they do gamble, impulsive people may be less likely to restrain themselves. They are not in the habit of dividing their attention enough to restrain their behaviors. They are caught up in the moment, without the ability to step outside of themselves and limit their behaviors.

NEUROTICISM

Neuroticism is a broad personality factor that relates to autonomic arousal or negative emotionality (Comer, 1992; Eysenck & Eysenck, 1985). It has been found in virtually every major factor-analytic study of personality and is so well established as a broad construct that it is included on every factor theorist's list of major dimensions of personality (Digman, 1989). About one-quarter of the variance of neuroticism is inherited. The rest appears to be due to incidental and unpredictable experiences during childhood, suggesting the role of chaos, which we explore in later chapters, in the development of personality.

Persons who score high on tests for neuroticism are likely to experience problems with anxiety, depression, phobias, obsessive-compulsive behaviors, low self-esteem, and psychosomatic disorders (Digman, 1990; Eysenck, 1993). On the positive side, neuroticism seems to be positively related to the capacity to feel experiences intensely (Costa & McCrae, 1989). This can be valuable for poets, artists, and, certainly, lovers (Eysenck, 1993).

One of the problems with relating neuroticism to gambling behavior is the direction of causality. We have discussed this in regard to depression and anxiety, but it deserves reiterating. Losing money makes people depressed, especially when they begin to be deeply indebted. Therefore, gambling losses may increase neuroticism. On the other hand, there is ample evidence that people who are depressed, anxious, or otherwise unhappy may gamble to distract themselves. This has made it difficult to ascertain the direction of causality in gambling disorders.

We are aware of only one study, still unpublished, that has examined this correlation through time. Our research group has looked at the relationship between neurotic symptoms of anxiety, depression, traumatic stress, and somatic complaints, and ongoing gambling behaviors. In a time series study using structural equation modeling, the best fit for the data was the cocausality of neurotic symptoms and frequency of gambling. Frequent gambling causes neurotic feelings, and neurotic feelings cause frequent gambling. Thus, the direction of causation is mutual and complex. A further limitation on this study is that it was conducted with college students and not with seriously indebted gamblers. Future research will need to ascertain whether negative affect is a cause or a result, or both, of gambling.

EXTROVERSION

Most current theory regards the personality variable of extroversion as a behavioral manifestation of a broader trait that relates to reward sensitivity and conditioning (Zuckerman, 1994). (This is true despite the fact that there is no evidence linking extroversion to dopamine, which suggests that a different reward system is in operation.) Although disagreement continues in this area, the available data seem to indicate that extroverts are more sensitive to rewards and are somewhat slower to be classically conditioned, especially to punishment (Gray, 1991). Extroverts need a broader variety of stimuli. They tire of routine more quickly than introverted people, and they seem to need to experience more things more intensely (Eysenck & Eysenck, 1985).

In an interesting study that used Gray's model as a theoretical anchor, it was hypothesized that introverts would be more susceptible to gambling-related stimuli of punishment than to monetary rewards (Bartussek,

Diedrich, Naumann, & Collet, 1993). Dependent measures included event-related potential stimuli for signaling winnings and losses. This hypothesis was supported and was recently verified in our laboratory.

Subsequent research has shown that extroverts and introverts often engage in different types of gambling. Extroverts prefer table gambling in casinos. Introverts prefer the slots, the racetrack, and sports betting via bookies. When they do gamble on the slots, extroverts gamble more irregularly, playing less but overestimating their winnings.

Our research team has recently postulated a new theory relating personality to addictions (McCown & Keiser, 2000). This view is in line with contemporary accounts that suggest that reward and punishment are both important for addictions (Geary, 1998; Zuckerman, 1999). The reinforcing properties of addictive experiences are powerful motivational forces that are preferred by certain subjects—perhaps those with biological and personality mechanisms that are overtly sensitive.

Extremes of extroversion, neuroticism, or impulsivity are apt to produce tendencies toward both biological and psychological factors that promote addictions. This holds true for substance abuse or for nonpharmacological behavioral addictions. Note the complex and complementary interplay among personality factors, psychological diagnoses, and biological states. The line between traits and psychobiology may be blurred, but the illustration represents a reasonable portrait of the complexities of human behavior.

This is not the all-inclusive model that we promised, earlier in the chapter, to reveal. Gambling is too complex to be reduced to a single variable (Kusyszyn, 1980). Predictions of human behavior must always regard the vast pathways available in volitional action (Howard & Conway, 1986). Causes of human behavior are even more complex and are impossible to fully describe (Howard & Myers, 1990). As Horowitz (1998) has noted, there are as many causes of aberrant behavior as there are life stories.

EPILOGUE: GAMBLING, ADDICTIONS, AND THE NEED FOR SCIENTIFICALLY BASED TOLERANCE

Persons with addictions have behavioral disorders that are often heuristically conceptualized as diseases. Few people now argue that the "disease model" is useful in most situations. A number of factors serve to trigger this disease process and none is mutually exclusive. Learning, biology, psychological disorders, and personality, as well as cognitions, all might play important roles in the acquisition and maintenance of addictive behavior.

Although we are very far from understanding addictive behavior, we can state one clear conclusion: There is no place for a moral perspective in the comprehensive understanding of addictive processes. Addicts, whether gamblers, alcoholics, or cocaine users, need treatment, not moral condemnation. We reiterate this because of the disturbing punitive trends in the treatment of persons who, a generation ago, would have been labeled as "sick" (Hill & O'Brien, 1999). Today, people seeking voluntary substance abuse or gambling treatment may be criminalized, stigmatized, denied treatment, and further alienated from whatever connections they have with mainstream social institutions.

Punishment will not change the tendencies of people to gamble to excess. Basic behaviorism (Skinner, 1953)—as well as alternative models (Hull, 1943)—illustrates that this is true in animals. In a human democratic society, we hope that no one is willing to require the draconian measures that would eliminate gamblers from ongoing interaction with society. Efforts at prohibition of gambling opportunities may limit some exposure to gambling but they will not change the host's susceptibility, which is based on complex psychological, biological, and social factors. Additional stigmatization of people with the complex psychobehavioral problems of addictions will only serve to make the problem worse, as we have seen from social ineffectiveness in coping with the HIV epidemic (Kalichman, 1998).

As an aside, and perhaps as an appropriate way to end this chapter, we disagree with some of the anecdotal trends in addicts' treatment, especially those that maintain a puritanical stance about the depression, anxiety, sleep and eating disturbances, and panic disorder that accompany gambling cessation (R.J. Rosenthal & Lesieur, 1996) or attempts to abstain from drugs of abuse (Smith & Darlington, 1996). We believe that strong psychotherapeutic and pharmacotherapeutic efforts are indicated in the treatment of comorbid psychiatric disorders (Pinsker, 1997; Price, 1996).

A history of addiction does not disqualify a person from the therapeutic regimen available through psychiatry. For example, some psychiatrists refuse to treat alcoholics or gambling addicts with antidepressants because they believe their depression will cause them to "work the program more seriously." This is nonsense bordering on malpractice. High-risk patients—for example, those who might be likely to both benefit from and abuse drugs such as benzodiazepines—may require the additional monitoring that our health care system seems reticent to provide. However, a belief that people with psychiatric symptoms inherently must suffer in order to make gains is morally repugnant.

At the heart of this attitude is a return to naïve Puritan values. Gambling is enjoyable for many people (Spanier, 1995). For those who cannot gamble safely, just as for those who cannot drink safely, therapy is more humane and practical than punishment (Vannicelli, 1992). The social and legal responses to addictive behaviors have been characterized as illogical, inconsistent, inhuman, unscientific, and simply counterproductive (J. Johnson & McCown, 1996). Equally unproductive are simple unidimensional approaches to addictions.

Additional research is urgently warranted to help ameliorate present and future gambling problems. We need to foster our understanding of risk factors, demographics, biology, comorbidity, and, most important, *prevention* of problem gambling behaviors. This was true a generation ago (Gossop, 1989). Regrettably, little progress has been made, as can be seen in any comparison of what we once knew (Gambino & Cummings, 1989) and what we now know. Gambling may be an inherent human activity, but problem gambling does not have to be. Only a unified effort of scientists and practitioners can help reduce its potentially devastating impact.

CHAPTER 5

Treatment for Pathological Gambling: Inpatient Programs and Gamblers Anonymous

Percentage of Managed Mental Health Care Groups That Will Pay for Inpatient Treatment for Gambling: 0%

Percentage of Managed Mental Health Care Groups That Suggest Referral to GA for People with Gambling Problems: 100%

Percentage of Members of Gamblers Anonymous Who Believe That Hospitalization Is "Often or More" Necessary for the Treatment of Gambling Related Disorders: 100%

Percentage of Gamblers Treated as Inpatients Who Initially Resisted Treatment in This Modality (N = 254): 93%

Percentage of Gamblers Treated as Inpatients Who Two Years Later Credit This Treatment as "Largely Responsible or More" for Continued Gambling Abstinence (N = 132): 97%

—From McCown and Keiser (2000)

Looking at these numbers, I guess our referral sources might feel we are letting them down. So do our treatment providers. That's too bad. Clinical wisdom shows they don't get much better, regardless of what you do.

—Anonymous Managed Care Administrator, on the Internet

THIS CHAPTER highlights the traditional and well recognized treatments of inpatient hospitalization and membership in Gamblers Anonymous. It assumes that the reader has a background in contemporary psychiatric and psychological diagnoses and treatments, including those for substance abuse. Knowledge of specific gambling treatments is not presumed.

In this chapter, we attempt to highlight the scientific literature regarding these treatment modalities. Unfortunately, there are almost no empirically rigorous studies that examine the effectiveness of these common therapeutic methods and none is expected in the foreseeable future, so we are forced to rely on informed clinical experience.

There are both limitations and advantages to the knowledge that can be gained from clinical experience alone. The advantages are offered in working on a day-to-day basis with dysfunctional gamblers. This chapter highlights the care that clinicians must exercise before they can claim to possess appropriate knowledge regarding treatment. Our hope is that some of the mistakes made by addiction care providers in other domains will not be repeated.

As we argue later in the chapter, unbridled use of clinical experience as the final arbitrator of decision making has had an adverse impact on addiction treatment (J. Johnson & McCown, 1997). Prior to clarifying this argument further, however, we must ask the clinician to accompany us on a brief excursion into the role of knowledge and clinical experience in therapeutic choices.

KNOWLEDGE VERSUS CLINICAL EXPERIENCE: AS CLINICIANS, WHAT DO WE DO UNTIL WE KNOW WHAT WE ARE DOING?

In this chapter, we draw primarily on our own clinical experiences, those of coworkers, and those presented by other practitioners in the literature on gambling. In other words, we are relying on clinical expertise. There are two schools of thought regarding expertise derived from clinical experiences. One extreme discounts clinical experiences almost completely, believing that they represent pseudo-knowledge. Experience, it is argued, is a poor substitute for the rigorousness that scientific knowledge should produce.

Proponents of this view draw support from the fact that clinical knowledge regarding twentieth-century mental health practices has, in large part, been only mildly effective. At times, such "knowledge" has been highly harmful. Electroshock, psychosurgery, insulin therapy, psychoanalysis, and aversion therapy were all widely employed before they were rigorously tested (Kendall, 1997). All of these treatments were also hailed by the popular press as being highly effective. Today, they are restricted to unusual conditions because the initial enthusiasm they generated did not meet the reality of their impact or their capacity to change behavior in a positive direction. This was true despite the clinically derived "knowledge" that assured practitioners that these treatments were highly effectual.

This faulty clinical "knowledge" came from an aggregate of clinical experiences—individual cases of success that were amplified throughout the professional community (Ogles, Lambert, & Masters, 1996). Questions about long-term effects of psychiatric treatments—and side effects, in particular—were often ignored. Unfortunately, the mental health community, which often acts as a positive feedback loop (Bütz et al., 1997), proved very slow to express concern with these and other procedures that were "validated" by common clinical practices.

Lest we believe that these were fallacies of a less sophisticated time, we should consider the use of psychoactive medications to control symptoms. For example, common clinical practice in psychiatry encouraged the massive use of antipsychotic drugs. The prescribed dosages were often grossly higher than the amounts supported by scientific findings (Meyer & Deitsch, 1996). However, "clinical knowledge" convinced practitioners that these exaggerated doses of medication were warranted. This was wrong. High dosages did nothing to help patients, and they fostered untoward side effects that could have been avoided.

Another example concerns clinical knowledge and the use and abuse of addictive prescription medications. Since the 1950s, antianxiety drugs have been routinely used for conditions where there was no evidence that they had an effect (Kendall, 1998). Most of these drugs have enormous addictive potential. For example, in a study of patients taking benzodiazepines for anxiety, only 43% were able to tolerate discontinuing the medication for even one week (Rickels, Schweizer, Case, & Greenblatt, 1991). Tolerance and dependence were major reasons for return to the medications. Common clinical practice still encourages the irresponsible use of these drugs, despite clear indications to the contrary (Brick & Erickson, 1998). Clinical knowledge may sometimes lead to ineffective and dangerous treatments.

HANS EYSENCK AND THE DEMAND FOR SCIENTIFIC EVIDENCE

Systematic application of the belief that clinical knowledge is of little value owes much to the initial and continuing critiques of psychotherapy (and other mental health therapies) by Hans Eysenck (Eysenck, 1993; see Comer, 1992, for a review). Eysenck argued that only empirically evaluated treatments that had demonstrated an effectiveness should be administered. Eysenck was never a clinician, but he was an extraordinary scientist who strove to simplify clinical problems by relating them to both traditional and novel psychological theory (e.g., Eysenck, 1985; Eysenck & Eysenck, 1985). In the absence of scientific knowledge, Eysenck believed that psychology and other mental health disciplines should remain agnostic. In other words, unless a specific intervention—say, Gamblers

Anonymous—has demonstrated itself to be effective, the scientifically minded clinician cannot take sides on its efficacy. This limits what and whom the practitioner can treat, because few psychological or psychiatric problems have well-defined, scientifically derived treatment protocols.

From our view as scientists and practitioners, Eysenck's rigorous attempts to empirically anchor psychotherapy are scientifically admirable (Garb, 1998). However, from the standpoint of busy practicing clinicians, we realize that much of what we do in counseling and therapy remains poorly understood (Cormier & Hackney, 1999). Society has entrusted us to be the change agents for people with very complex problems of living (McCown & Johnson, 1993). Empirical research in mental health sometimes produces rapid changes in potential methodologies. What was yesterday's "state-of-the-art knowledge" becomes outmoded or is subsequently demonstrated to be simply not true (Cooper, 1983). If we waited for a completely scientific body of knowledge to solidify and legitimize interventions, we would almost never be able to meet our social obligations as change agents (Foy, 1992).

One of the best examples of our reliance on clinical knowledge is the current treatment of dysfunctional gamblers. Because society has only recently become interested in problem and addictive gambling, there is almost no systematic research. This places conscientious clinicians in a dilemma. We can do nothing and refuse to treat problem gambling, because we do not have a knowledge basis that is truly "scientific." A strong ethical argument can be made for this position: Our interventions may make the problems we are trying to treat much worse. Yet this conservative path seems inhumane. It also conflicts with the clinical experiences of practitioners who have helped people recover from disordered gambling.

Bütz et al. (1997) discussed the ethics of attempting to help change behavior when therapists cannot be reasonably assured of a specific clinical outcome or prognosis. These authors deferred to the concept of clinical "wisdom" to help make ethical interventions in the absence of data. Nowhere is this wisdom needed more than in the treatment of problem and addicted gamblers, whose needs are often intense and life-threatening. The ultimate goal of mental health practitioners should be a scientific set of interventions. In the meantime, we must remain "informed helpers" (Egan, 1975), aware that we must do the best we can, with what we know and have experienced.

KNOWLEDGE AND CLINICAL WISDOM

The polar opposite of Eysenck's position is the belief that clinical experience is superior to empirically derived knowledge—even knowledge obtained from well-designed and relevant mental health studies. The basis of this belief is the notion that clinical experience is somehow more "real," accurate, or truthful than the cold and often abstract findings of artificially controlled research (R. Anderson, 1994). Often, an appropriate argument is raised: Research laboratory conditions are too contrived to simulate the broad range of mental health problems clinicians encounter on a daily basis. Clinical knowledge, these proponents claim, involves a superior type of knowledge derived from socially shared "wisdom." Complicating matters further is the fact that wisdom as a psychological phenomenon is a concept that is exceedingly important, yet still poorly understood (Sternberg, 1998).

Wisdom, as we now understand it, is a process rather than an end point. Wisdom emphasizes acquisition and discovery of "tacit knowledge"—aspects of practical situations that are hard to quantify (Sternberg, 1998). Wisdom, according to this view, is the capacity to solve problems that have many inherent ambiguities. Wisdom is flexible and increases with relevant experience, as long as the practitioner is open to it. Wisdom thrives where there are no perfect answers and where ambiguities are possible.

Knowledge, on the other hand, is an awareness of factors that act to reduce ambiguities. Knowledge allows the clinician to avoid fuzzy decisions by discarding complexities. According to Sternberg (1998), knowledge is an independent concept that is statistically unrelated to wisdom. In many circumstances, knowledge may interfere with wisdom. If, for example, we take Eysenck's position that intervention without knowledge is inappropriate, we will have no way to exercise clinical wisdom.

Both knowledge and wisdom may be necessary for the practicing clinician. Clinical wisdom thrives in situations where there are ambiguities. In many situations, human behavior is highly ambiguous and we don't have definite answers. Empirical knowledge, on the other hand, is able to look beyond the haze of superfluous facts and to focus on identifiable relations that are likely to maximize a specific goal.

Our position, not unlike Sternberg's (1998), is that a balance of knowledge and wisdom is most helpful. We believe that clinical experience alone is never an ideal substitute for valid scientific findings. Unfortunately, scientific knowledge regarding psychobehavioral problems is obtained very, very slowly. Because of the complex nature of human behavior, scores of studies may be needed to demonstrate the clinical effectiveness of a specific procedure. In the absence of such an abundance of studies, clinical experience is a useful start, as it is in medicine, which relies much more on clinical judgment and lore than most of us realize.

Clinical experience also represents hypotheses about behavioral changes. Presently, such experience may be all the practitioner can rely on when the scientific literature is sparse or systematically lacking. The more lofty goal of attempting to match optimal treatment of varieties of psychotherapy to particular clients in specific situations has almost never been met.

CLINICAL EXPERIENCE AND "PSEUDO-WISDOM"

Sternberg (1998) emphasizes that wisdom is most useful where the knowledge base is either poorly developed or irrelevant. As practitioners and researchers who deal with addictions, and gambling in particular, Sternberg's distinctions help us identify a major clinical problem that we consistently encounter. Much of what passes as "wisdom" is simply heuristic bias. It is, in essence, a type of antiwisdom. Clinical wisdom optimizes decisions under conditions of ambiguity. Genuine knowledge optimizes such decisions by reducing the ambiguity. Much of what people identify as "clinical knowledge" is simply tradition or lore that no one has bothered to test—or, sometimes, to even challenge.

Sometimes, the outcomes for clients or patients are egregious. During the 1960s, "clinical knowledge" said that lithium would not help bipolar disordered patients. Clinical lore suggested that, usually, these patients eventually stabilized. Traditional analytic theory (which, we believe, was wrongly applied and misunderstood concerning these patients) postulated that manic patients needed to have their unconscious "bubble out" until they reached a point of equilibrium. In the 1970s, for those who can recall the oral history of substance abuse treatment, "clinical wisdom" in some Narcotics Anonymous groups encouraged heroin addicts to get drunk together instead of using narcotics. In some AA groups we have recently seen, compulsive gambling is advocated as a "safer" recreational alternative to drinking. Much of what we pass off to our colleagues, to patients, and to other professionals as clinical knowledge is, at best, our informed opinions. It certainly is not wisdom.

CLINICAL OPINIONS AS A LEGITIMATE COMPROMISE

Opinions are necessary when there is an absence of confirming data that produce universal agreement. In this chapter, we describe traditional treatment approaches. We share our own and our colleagues' experiences. However, where we lack data, we quite honestly volunteer our opinions and discuss how those opinions were formed. We attempt to remain eclectic and pragmatic while presenting our opinions. This task is more difficult than it seems, as we indicated in Chapter 2. We have made one observation regarding the behavior of clinicians: All of us have a tendency to pay attention only to discussions that are congruent with our personal theoretical paradigms. Typically, biologically oriented physicians are less interested in Gamblers Anonymous and other 12-step programs than they are in the effects of psychotropic medications. People from a 12-step disease tradition may be less interested in relapse prevention and cognitive therapies. Behaviorists are not interested in psychodynamic approaches, even if they work! This unfortunate situation produces collective ignorance.

In our quest to adhere to specific models, we often fail to remember that helping the client is more important than theoretical purity. One modest goal of this chapter is to encourage flexible and eclectic treatment approaches, with the eventual hope of determining what works best and for whom. Admittedly, we are distanced from a scientific psychotherapy advanced by Eysenck and his legacy. However, if we prematurely close the door to potentially effective treatments, especially those validated by informed experience, an empirical set of treatment methods will never be found. This situation is only complicated further when we refuse to realize that no single orientation—whether 12-step, biological, behavioral, systemic, cognitive, or psychodynamic—has all of the answers that we will some day know.

THE GOALS OF TREATMENT: ABSTINENCE OR CONTROLLED GAMBLING?

In Chapter 2, we discussed paradigms of gambling and the need for practitioners to admit to cognitive biases regarding paradigms and directly related therapeutic issues. *Our own belief is that abstinence is the preferable goal of treatment for any gambling disorders.* Our personal clinical orientations have become increasingly removed from advocating the goal of controlled gambling, simply because it does not seem worth the risk of prompting a potential relapse.

Gambling may be enjoyable, but it is not necessary for life. Optimally, the client needs to learn new ways of coping, of spending leisure time, and, most of all, of sharing intimacies (L'Abate, 1999). He or she will then be less likely to experience a relapse (Wildman, 1989). One reason is that sharing of intimacies involves discussing vulnerabilities, which is often a powerful inoculation to prevent relapse (L'Abate, 1994). Other reasons involve the help in problem solving, stress reduction, and social support that the nongambling lifestyle tends to foster.

Put simply, our informed clinical opinions at this time are that controlled gambling should not be the treatment goal. Gambling abstinence is safer. (More will be said later about this controversial issue.)

HOW SHOULD WE MEASURE
TREATMENT SUCCESS?

Even a cursory examination of addictions literature indicates that success can be measured in a number of ways. They include: rates of relapse, days of abstinence, vocational performance, increase in life satisfaction, decrease in family dysfunctioning, and many other variables. In gambling, more than in any other addiction, success is limited to continued abstinence. Anything else is a therapeutic failure.

Unfortunately, relapse is endemic in all addictions. Often, a reduction in the rate of gambling is the best that can be expected as a viable treatment outcome. This is also true for other addictions (A.T. Beck et al., 1993; Benjamin, 1996; Cormier & Hackney, 1999; Garb, 1998). Treatment is much more effectively measured when it is conceptualized as "Days abstinent" instead of "Percentage of people totally abstinent at the end of five years." If this seems like a distortion of data (i.e., cheating), it certainly is not. In the treatment of any serious disease with a high relapse or mortality rate, success is measured in days, weeks, or months, rather than in percentage cured. As they say in Gamblers Anonymous, "One day at a time." As much as we may wish for total "cures," this goal is part of the illusion of control referred to previously (Greenson, 1978).

Problem gambling implies unplanned behavior that usually results in undesirable consequences. Gambling problems have both biological and social/cognitive components that likely represent the complex interaction between genetic and environmental factors. We choose to speak of "managing gambling disorders" rather than successfully "curing" them. This is an important concept for therapists to grasp. Often, it is antithetical to the medical-model training of many practitioners. Yet, with the exception of a small group of people whom we are not able to identify in advance, such an outcome may be impossible.

OTHER TREATMENT GOALS

Among its other goals, treatment should be as humane and noninvasive as possible. Unlike schizophrenia or depression, pathological gambling in any individual would be relatively easy to completely control and even eliminate. All we would have to do is incarcerate the person in solitary confinement, perhaps in restraints, to prevent any markings on the hospital or cell walls. (A colleague who peer-reviewed this chapter noted that this statement was wrong. Chronic gamblers often have bets with themselves in their own minds!)

Thankfully, few of us would be willing to support incarceration as a viable treatment option. However, this rather far-fetched scenario illustrates that although a treatment might be effective, it may also be un-ethical or distinctly immoral. We could probably reduce gambling prob-lems by increasing heroin or crack cocaine use, but only drug dealers would argue that this is an acceptable trade-off. Important ethical ques-tions may recur, regarding behavioral therapies and gambling.

The worst examples of clinical lore passed off as wisdom involve treat-ment options and restrictions. For many years—until insurance com-panies and scientific data suggested other alternatives—inpatient therapy for substance abuse was the only treatment considered viable. "Clinical wisdom" was simply a faulty heuristic for reducing ambiguity (J. Johnson, 1994). A retired physician recently summarized his 45 years of experience with substance abuse: "Everyone went inpatient and everyone went to AA. Junkies were considered too hopeless to treat. Besides, clinical wisdom said that they contaminated the treatment of alcoholics."

The reality of addiction treatment is that most people can be treated at least as successfully on an outpatient basis as they can in an inpatient program (Fisher & Harrison, 1997; Hester & Miller, 1995; Marlatt, 1985). There are many exceptions, and research is just beginning to identify what type of patient needs more restrictive and expensive inpatient treatments. Furthermore, and more controversial to traditional "disease model" pro-ponents, there are alternatives to AA that may work as well for alcoholics (Kaufman, 1994; Marlatt et al., 1988; McBrady, 1985; McCown & Johnson, 1992; Mello & Mendelson, 1978; Pargament, 1986; Sobell & Sobell, 1993). Again, we are just starting to examine what works for whom.

However, our blindness and arrogance enabled critics to successfully pursue their own agendas. Presently, in most areas in America, it is vir-tually impossible to hospitalize a privately insured patient for long-term addiction treatment. This is true even if, for clinical reasons, it would be in the patient's best interest. The reason for this situation is that the addictions community closed itself off to any treatment options other than the ones that were "known" to be successful, although nei-ther knowledge nor wisdom was employed. The collective lie was that the *only* way to get sober was to go through a 28-day treatment program and then go to AA meetings daily and forever. For many people, this is a valid approach; for others, it is not. Because evidence and mounting clinical experience were ignored a less than altruistic agenda emerged. In this chapter, we attempt to qualify carefully what is merely our opin-ion, or the opinions of our colleagues, as compared with what is sup-ported by the scientific literature.

Another treatment consideration involves balancing the costs of treat-ment with outcome benefits. All factors being equal, the least expensive and restrictive treatment is obviously the most preferable. However, any physical or mental health intervention requires a cost benefit analysis. If

50% of patients improve with a particular treatment, how much extra should a 1% improvement cost? Suppose each percentage of increase in treatment effectiveness is obtained only after a geometric increase in costs? A logarithmic increase? An exponential increase?

One client whom we know stated that, to keep from gambling, he found it necessary to hire 24-hour guards who muscled him into abstinence. (This person had the resources to do this, and a strong economic incentive not to gamble.) For him, this appeared to be the least restrictive treatment environment possible. Nothing else worked for him; Gamblers Anonymous was particularly ineffective. Using his own radical treatment, he stopped gambling. Several years later, this supervision continues.

Most of us would consider this treatment intervention too restrictive and not likely to be cost-effective. This individual had a profound problem that was incredibly treatment-resistant, and he had the resources to pay for what essentially was physical restraint. The circumstances of his financial livelihood gave him a reason to comply with what most of us would consider a nightmarish existence. However, for most of society, increased treatment effectiveness must be weighed, at some point, against the possibilities of increasing costs. This is a moral decision, not a psychomedical one, but the costs of programs should be clearly understood.

IS ABSTINENCE REALLY NECESSARY FOR THE RECOVERING GAMBLER?

We can't be comfortable in answering this question simply. We hear it asked too often. Still, we will answer it simply and say that, in our informed opinion, the answer is "Yes." Perhaps, though, our explanation is as important as our conclusion.

There is scant, but growing and methodologically sound, scientific evidence that controlled gambling may work. Data seem to indicate that controlled gambling is an option for some people. (Most of the research has come from laboratories in Australia, and may reflect different cultural factors not fully explored.) But the subset of persons who succeed with controlled gambling cannot be specified in advance, and the risk of ruining a life by experimenting unsuccessfully with controlled gambling is too devastating to ponder. In our experience in treating gamblers, abstinence *is* necessary.

If anyone who has a potential behavioral syndrome that points toward the devastating end stage of gambling disorders fails to take advantage of all of the treatment options, we would consider that person deluded, or at best, grossly uninformed. GA attendance may be unpleasant, but it is far less personally traumatic than chemotherapy, open heart surgery, or other life-saving medical treatments that many people endure. Abstinence may result in missed opportunities for a favorite enjoyment, but it makes possible many other rewards in life.

While abstinence is the goal for most gamblers in remission or recovery, it is important for treatment professionals to understand the dilemmas faced by compulsive gamblers given the persuasiveness of opportunities to gamble in our society. For example, one GA member told of his almost comic attempt to avoid gambling while ordering a hamburger at a fast food restaurant. He placed his order and was handed a "scratch ticket" which gave him the opportunity to win anything from a free beverage to several hundred thousand dollars. When he tried to refuse the ticket, the server actually argued with him saying that "it was dumb to pass up a chance to win something." The GA member actually found it necessary to disclose that he was a compulsive gambler in order to get the server to take the ticket back. He described feeling tremendously uncomfortable, almost "irresponsible," not taking the ticket. He knew, however, that even a few moments indulgence in the fantasy of getting something for nothing could undermine the reality he had worked so hard to create in his abstinence.

Given how ubiquitous the "you may already be a winner" mentality is in our culture, it is an incredible challenge for compulsive gamblers to constantly monitor the environment to avoid gambling opportunities. The authors have noticed that even conferences devoted to recovery from addictions often feature prize drawings or other games of chance through sponsors booths or as incentives for attendance. We hope that as information becomes more available and awareness is improved, promoters and sponsors of these conferences will find other ways to entice attendees and customers.

Once a person develops a gambling-free lifestyle, the desire to return to social gambling usually ceases. If it does not, that person is at high risk for relapse, following even brief bouts of social gambling. Abstinence is a goal of choice, just as cigarette cessation is the goal of choice for people with asthma or a history of impaired pulmonary functioning. Some people apparently cannot quit smoking, despite related health problems. Only then is "controlled smoking" an option. Controlled gambling, in our opinion, is never the first option, nor should it be considered until numerous treatment failures have occurred.

When clients ask whether they can ever return to gambling, we are able to answer fairly straightforwardly: "A few people have tried and succeeded. Many hundreds more have tried and failed. At this time, there is practically no way for us to know whether you are at risk, although a desire to return to gambling would indicate that you are. Total abstinence is the best, most reasonable, and safest goal. In the long run, it is also the least expensive."

We have found that clients accept this honesty. Many will still harbor a desire to return to gambling. Gambling dreaming, gaming memorabilia, and talk about gambling may still be prominent aspects of their lives. Yet, slowly, we believe that abstinence is possible.

GAMBLERS ANONYMOUS: THE HEART OF ABSTINENCE-BASED PROGRAMS

Our principal method of treatment is gambling abstinence, reinforced through affiliation with 12-step groups such as Gamblers Anonymous (GA). This is hardly a revolutionary therapy (Griffiths, 1996a), despite the fact that GA groups are too few and far between. The 12-step forms of disease management have been largely excluded from the reviews on gambling treatment, either because of small numbers of studies in the literature or because the studies of the abstinence-based methods did not possess sufficient scientifically accepted controls. In other words, they lacked random assignment and appropriate double-blind controls, as well as appropriate dependent measures.

The abstinence-based method for gambling was derived from the principles of Alcoholics Anonymous (AA), the world's most famous volunteer group-therapy modality (Benard & MacKenzie, 1994). Founded in 1935 by two alcoholics, a stockbroker and a physician (Hester & Miller, 1995), this program is based on the fundamental belief that alcoholism is a disease that is incurable and chronic. AA has "Twelve Traditions," which preclude an official association with specific treatment facilities. No professional treatment providers are employed during any meetings. For many, one of the "miracles" of AA and related groups is that people with diverse psychopathologies can gather together and focus on a common, mutual good.

As is well known, the process of recovery in GA is similar to that in AA (Gowen & Speyerer, 1995). The Twelve Steps and Twelve Traditions of these two organizations are almost identical. A person recovers through "working the program"—that is, completing personal, financial, and moral reforms associated with each of GA's steps (Taber & McCormick, 1987).

However, despite the similarities, there are a number of differences between AA and GA that the clinician needs to understand, lest she or he make embarrassing and potentially therapeutically important mistakes. First, because of the rapid expansion of GA, many meetings do not have enough people to use the "sponsor" model of AA, where a person working the program confides intensely in another person who has a lengthier recovery history and with whom he or she can identify. To some extent, this may affect the rates of recovery, though we do not know this yet. The absence of a sponsor is often disconcerting for someone who has achieved substance abstinence through a 12-step program.

Also, because of the rapid expansion of GA, there often tend to be fewer closed meetings—that is, meetings only opened to self-admitted compulsive gamblers and not to outsiders. Open meetings may be more didactic—similar to the step meetings of AA. There are also more substantial regional differences in meetings; GA groups tend to be less uniform than AA groups. Hence, if you are fortunate enough to have several groups in your area, and the client does not like one, he or she can try another. The dimension of personal fit is even more pronounced than with AA.

GA also tends to be more pragmatic and less spiritual. B.R. Brown (1994) argues sardonically that while it maintains the image of spirituality common in 12-step organizations, GA is actually a highly secular group. This bothers many people who have found help in the spiritual aspects of AA (Cullari, 1996). Explanations for this lack of spirituality include the abiding influence of a founding member who is an atheist. Many people who have used their religious faith as a crutch to continue gambling ("Dear God, just let me hit this jackpot so I can pay my rent") may come to regard it as negative reinforcement.

Many people who attend both AA and GA feel that the tone of GA groups is often more tough-minded. One senses that there is less "hand holding" in GA, probably because of the participants' deeper level of desperation. Closed meetings may be particularly brutal and confrontational. Another thesis in progress indicates that more confrontational language is used in GA meetings than in AA or NA groups.

Not surprisingly, given the direct and often confrontational tone more common in GA, the attrition rates from GA generally tend to be somewhat higher than from AA or NA. Anecdotal accounts suggest that the dropout rate from GA is well over 70%. Persons who drop out appear to be dissatisfied with the format and methods of GA, including the tone of meetings (R.I.F. Brown, 1987).

However, despite the tension and even the confrontation that may be encountered in GA, it may have a number of advantages that AA and other 12-step groups do not have. For example, GA seems to be much more open to new experiences and treatments than AA. There is also a clinical impression that GA is willing to go outside of the "official" literature and explore contributions of behavioral sciences that may help in maintaining abstinence. At one recent GA meeting, one of the authors saw on display well-known books by psychologists on topics such as anxiety (D.H. Barlow, 1988) and self-regulation (Baumeister et al., 1994). Typically, at AA meetings, most of the available literature reflects the imprimatur of The AA Services Board or the Hazeldon Foundation, a publisher of 12-step-related books.

As a result of this openness to new experiences and treatments, the antimedication bias that some 12-step groups may have is all but absent in most GA meetings. Our impression in conducting on-line research is that GA members strongly favor any type of pharmacotherapy possible, as long as it will help reduce their capacities for relapse. In fact, in recent days, we have learned more about the development of potential investigatory drugs from GA members than from many pharmaceutical companies!

Another major difference in AA and GA is the availability through GA of the "pressure relief" group. Once a GA member has a certain amount of time abstinent from gambling and attendance at GA, they can request a pressure relief group meeting. The meeting includes the gambler, his or her spouse or partner, and several individuals and couples from GA and Gamanon (the organization for family members and friends). In the meeting, a detailed budget which includes plans for repayment of all debts is negotiated. The older members and their partners assist by providing guidelines and support for the newer member. Payments to all creditors are arranged, even "loan sharks," bookies, and other illegal creditors. GA members will sometimes even help the gambler in contacting these sources and establishing payment plans. Unlike the partner of an alcoholic who is usually told by Alanon to take less responsibility for his or her partner, in the GA pressure relief plan, the nongambling partner is often told to take control of the household finances. Recommendations often include removing the gambler from bank and credit accounts and establishing a minimal cash allowance every week. Given that very few mental health professionals have experience in dealing with financial matters with clients, GA serves a particularly important purpose. It provides a real, manageable plan for financial recovery for the gambler and his or her family.

GA has also been much more open to allowing social science access to its members for research purposes (Blaszczynski & McConaghy, 1994; Fabian, 1995; Lester, 1994). In AA, the desire for anonymity usually precludes any cooperation regarding research.

Although the "personalities" of groups reflect different geographical regions and the attitudes within each group, GA offers much greater emphasis on pragmatism and daily functioning, rather than spirituality. New members can get amazingly practical information from people who have "been there, done that, and have the T-shirt," to quote a GA participant.

For a person who does not "click" with GA, it is often helpful to find another 12-step program. We sometimes refer people to both GA and AA, and let them decide what works best for them. Many people continue in both programs before eventually settling on one modality.

Despite our continued use of GA, we realize that initial scientific investigations of it have not been necessarily favorable (R.I.F. Brown, 1987). All existent studies have serious methodological flaws. We conclude that although GA does not eventually prove to be right for everyone, it warrants a serious trial by every problem or addicted gambler.

INTERNET SELF-HELP GAMBLERS ANONYMOUS GROUPS

An interesting development in the past four years has been the extensive use of 12-step-related Internet or other computer network groups. Finn (1996), in a prescient article, commented on the web-based self-help groups. They include 12-step groups for compulsive sexuality, spending, and smoking, and more commonly encountered groups such as AA and GA. Finn notes a number of potential benefits of on-line groups. They include greater and more immediate access to support; specialized group meetings for people with esoteric or specific needs; reduction in the social status barriers that sometimes accompany self-help groups; and a special advantage to those who are very shy or socially inhibited.

However, web-based methods also have potential disadvantages. They include (1) an increase in isolation, which is associated with Internet usage, and (2) possible Internet addiction, a still humorous but real (and some say genuine) phenomenon. Persons whose addictions to gambling are primarily through the Internet would be at highest risk to slip with such therapeutic techniques. Yet, Internet-based 12-step groups may have some important uses. They are a more accessible source of basic information and, as such, many serve as a "gateway" to more direct GA involvement.

In our experience, three classes of people may successfully use computers for self-help. In the first class are the simply curious—those who are not convinced that they have a problem or are concerned that they may be ostracized by family, employers, or friends. In essence, computers offer them a way to "try the waters" regarding their treatment. Often—and here we admit to having no data—they are confronted with the severity of their problems and seek additional avenues of help.

In the second group are problem or addicted gamblers who use computers when they cannot attend 12-step meetings, or when there are geographic impediments. For example, a person with agoraphobia might do well with a computerized self-help group, as would a new mother or father who is relatively housebound caring for an infant. "Home groups" can be contacted via the Internet even when the gambler is traveling. Also, persons whose drivers' licenses have been suspended for alcohol infractions may make excellent use of on-line 12-step interventions. This latter subgroup might prefer "real" as compared to "virtual" 12-step groups. However, because of problems with multiple addictions, they may not have any other viable options for treating their major disorders.

A third group of recovering people relies exclusively on 12-step computer programs, by personal preference. An obvious disadvantage is isolation, which may contribute to difficulties in recovery. Yet, anecdotal accounts suggest that these programs may be helpful, especially for people with multiple addictions or diverse lifestyles. Here is an example:

Jane

Jane was a 44-year-old transvestite who did not feel at ease at Gamblers Anonymous meetings. She always dressed in drag when she was gambling, and therefore figured that she should appear in drag during recovery efforts. Although no one at GA was particularly cruel or inappropriate to her, she thought that her flashy presence distracted from both her problems and the difficulties of others. She further thought—perhaps erroneously, we do not know—that her appearance frightened off new members.

Using the Internet, she was able to locate a group for transvestites who had compulsive gambling problems. She was able to "dress" in the solitariness of her home. Eventually, she obtained a camera for her Internet connection so she could "compliment the other ladies on line."

An irony to this situation was that Jane was married and his wife did not know that he was a cross-dresser. She simply thought that "Jamie" (his male name) was "off being a computer nerd somewhere in the basement." As a side advantage, in addition to gambling problems, Jane was able to address the conflict she felt in her life and the lack of intimacy that had evolved in her marriage by keeping her cross-dressing a secret. Although the marriage eventually ended in divorce, both Jane and her partner were happier and remained good friends. Jane's pathological gambling remained in remission for as long as she was followed—a period of three years.

Other users of computers for self-help are persons who are in socially sensitive positions. For example, our preliminary data show that persons can gain access to on-line 12-step groups, especially when they want to remain totally anonymous. Police officers, for example, are in an awkward position if they attempt to attend 12-step gambling groups. Frequently, they may see people whom they have arrested, which destroys their anonymity and creates an unpleasant situation under some circumstances.

Does Gamblers Anonymous Actually Work?

The question we are asked more than any other is: "Does GA work?" Clients ask because they want help and because they see themselves burdened by a life of continuous meetings. Families ask because they are desperate. Mental health professionals ask because they want to provide effective treatment. Scientists ask because it is their nature to analyze and criticize.

Mindful of the data that do exist, we answer this question as follows: "GA works as long as a person works GA." This means that as long as a person stays involved with GA, there is less likelihood that he or she will gamble. Treatment, like rehabilitation, needs to be considered a lifelong process. In our opinion, the prognosis of any recovering gambling abuser is logarithmically enhanced by GA attendance. We have no hard data to present. We do, however, have numerous anecdotal accounts of persons who stopped GA attendance and began gambling again. We also have accounts, as do alcohol therapists, of persons who began lying about their recovery and then experienced a slip. This is tantamount to individuals who lie to their dietician about what they are eating and experience a cardiac deterioration. Because of the severe problems that family members also face when living with a compulsive gambler, we also emphasize the importance of GAMANON attendance for spouses and partners. Given the impact on family finances, trust, and intimacy in relationships with problem gamblers, their partners inevitably need support and information to manage their own distress. Also, as noted in the information on pressure relief groups, partners are often called on to take an active role in monitoring family finances and limiting the amount of money available to the gambler. Certainly, the degree of betrayal and rage that partners often experience needs a safe environment for expression; GAMANON can offer that place.

To date, we have never seen anyone who has honestly and conscientiously "worked a program" relapse for more than a few months. This contrasts to periods of 20 to 40 years of heavy gambling that did not spontaneously disappear when untreated. GA is not magic, but it seems to foster "Fewer relapses, milder relapses. . . ." If people attend AA and gamble, their gambling is reduced. If they slip, their relapses are shorter; they may have single occurrences rather than protracted lifestyle changes.

Again, this is a clinical opinion. However, we believe that it is as eclectic and unbiased as an opinion by any practitioners in the field. We agree with the conclusions of Meyer and Deitsch (1996) regarding Alcoholics Anonymous. GA helps establish a gambling-free lifestyle, which, along with an ongoing commitment to GA, perpetuates a cycle of continued abstinence. Any objections to GA attendance, especially very early in treatment, are best interpreted as an aspect of the client's refusal to acknowledge the severity and chronicity of his or her gambling problem.

HOSPITALIZATION AS A CORNERSTONE OF TREATMENT

Often, a key decision a clinician faces, when seeing a patient who is a pathological gambler, is whether hospitalization is appropriate. Given a diagnosis of pathological gambling, treatment of the accessory psychopathology and the somatic condition is important and may indeed involve hospitalization. During hospitalization, a variety of intense therapies can be offered on a frequent basis, and evaluation can benefit from the input of multiple clinicians.

Unfortunately, even in extreme circumstances, inpatient hospitalization is often impossible. Insurance companies are adamant about refusing to pay for such services. Gamblers differ from other substance abusers in that their problems may be more hidden. They cannot directly overdose, and there is usually no known biological point in their abuse when they develop a medical emergency. Often, they encounter hospitals only when they attempt suicide.

Yet, because of their tremendous financial and psychological difficulties, problem gamblers may require removal from their present environment to a safe, supportive, and medically oriented facility. Few resources, such as inpatient treatment programs, are available for gamblers and their families. A decade ago, there were only 16 inpatient programs for gamblers in the United States. Despite the tripling of gambling during this period, there are under 50 today. There are more inpatient facilities for substance abusers in the New York City area than there are for pathological gamblers in the entire country. The first dedicated unit for gambling disorders was established as recently as 1972, in a Veterans' Hospital in Cleveland (Taber & McCormick, 1987). The available facilities report positive success with inpatient programs, and, in our opinion, they are a favorable choice. However, it almost seems superfluous to discuss their desirability or the criteria associated with inpatient services. Few people can afford to pay for them.

If inpatient services are available and their cost can be managed, they may be medically necessary for a client who has experienced a major life disruption—a vocational, financial, or marital disaster associated with either excessive gambling or suicidal attempts. Inpatient treatment probably is also indicated if the patient is experiencing insomnia, anxiety attacks, depression, mania, tangential thinking, extreme grandiosity, suicidal thinking, or frequent dissociative experiences. Other problems that may warrant hospitalization may include difficulty in concentrating or in completing routine tasks.

Perhaps the most important reason for making hospitals available for gambling addicts is the fact that gambling generates, during the early stages of abstinence, the same severe problems with craving as substance-based addictions. This was illustrated in research by Castellani and Rugle (1995), whose subjects came from the first—and, some would say, the most successful—inpatient program for gamblers. A large study compared consecutively admitted patients who had one of the following primary diagnoses: pathological gambler, alcoholic, or cocaine addict. These groups of patients were compared for differences on impulsivity, sensation seeking, and craving. Gamblers were found to be more impulsive and to have a more reduced ability to resist cravings.

In other words, gamblers acted more impulsively and gave in more to their cravings. Besides reflecting the specific nature of the treatment program being studied, these findings strongly suggest that inpatient services deserve a much larger arsenal of weapons for treating problem and addicted gamblers.

STAGES OF INPATIENT TREATMENT

Typically, inpatient treatment activities involve three overlapping, or not necessarily mutually exclusive, stages. Because of the reluctance of insurance companies to pay for treatment, the admitting diagnosis is often "laundered" as a mood disorder or a substance abuse problem. In truth, anxiety, depression, suicidal ideas, and substance abuse often do cloud the clinical picture, and we don't encourage outright deception. On the other hand, in the United States, a capricious and ruthless cohort of financiers who are immune from traditional tort liability by an act of Congress, have destroyed traditional mental health services.

THE INITIAL PHASE: STABILITY AND A NEW BEGINNING

In the initial phase of inpatient treatment, there are several goals. The first goal involves a systematic effort aimed at stabilizing the patient emotionally and, if necessary, physically. This may require extensive sessions of ventilation on the part of the patient, and the willingness of a highly caring staff to listen to the patient's evolving "story" or life narrative. Our belief, based on observing inpatients in a general psychiatric unit, is that unless a patient exhibits manic tendencies that interfere with the ability to participate in group activities, the patient should be encouraged to ventilate at any hour, even during the night. Often, during the first or second night, the patient begins to obtain insights into the seriousness of his or her disorder.

A staff that insists on a nonwavering policy of bedtime adherence not only infantilizes the patients, but also loses a valuable opportunity for therapeutic intervention that may never be repeated. The staff must make it clear that staying up late will not excuse a patient from daytime activities. However, examining a patient's sleeping cycles may provide diagnostic clues regarding the prevalence of bipolar disorder or depression. Most importantly, having someone available to discuss gambling recovery at any hour serves to model the role of meetings and sponsorship. In our observation (again, we have no firm data here), it seems to decrease the number of sudden terminations of treatment "against medical advice" ("AMA," in the popular parlance).

During this initial phase, evaluation for selection of medication is made, if medication is indicated. Many patients will benefit from an antidepressant, for reasons that are discussed later. However, antidepressants are not a panacea. Great care must be taken with prescription of the benzodiazepine class of anti-anxiety drugs, because, with the exception of buspirone, they tend to be addictive (Swinson, Antony, Rachman, & Richter, 1998). If a patient is manic, he or she needs to be treated with lithium, or an appropriate substitute, by a psychiatrist who has been optimally trained both in treatment of addictions and management of mania.

The importance of psychological examinations is discussed in Chapter 8 and in McCown and Keiser (2000). We also believe that a newly admitted patient should have a *comprehensive* physical, as well as a psychological examination. Aggressive lifestyles associated with gambling disorders frequently result in cardiac or hepatic problems. An advantage of a dedicated gambling unit as part of a free-standing hospital or medical center is that physician collaboration and emergency treatment are easier to obtain (McCown & Johnson, 1993).

Typically, at this time, the patient is oriented to the treatment program regulations. Patients (a label for people who have entered the medical system) seem to benefit from a highly structured schedule, with minimal initial confrontation. Gamblers with rebellious tendencies are at a higher risk to act out during this period. Their ways of challenging the rules, in some cases, can be quite brilliant. Good-natured consistent response is probably the best method of dealing with this behavior, which we have found most positively labeled as a developmental phase of recovery. One of our pragmatic rules regarding inpatient treatment is that the staff must have a sense of humor!

We recommend some degree of isolation and meditation during this first crisis-stabilization period (McCown & Johnson, 1993). We encourage patients to keep a journal and to begin writing their autobiographies (or telling their "stories"; see Thompson, Skowronski, Larsen, & Betz, 1996, for a discussion of this technique and the importance of coherent narrative generation). Also, at this point, patients will meet with a primary counselor, as well as their physician and the nursing staff.

For persons who are "addicted to excitement" (Zuckerman, 1999), a syndrome of physical withdrawal may be as intense as any that is routinely seen with addiction to pharmacologically active drugs. The subtypes of patterns may resemble alcoholism and its subsequent withdrawal syndrome, described by Zucker (1987). The withdrawal period in gamblers may be characterized by restlessness, irritability, and other symptoms of addiction, perhaps because of a similar role of autonomic arousal. The decision on whether to treat withdrawal with appropriate medications depends, too often, on the physician's attitudes, as we indicated in the previous chapter. We reiterate a maxim that we have found to be common among all successful addiction programs: In our experience, there is no reason to make persons suffer withdrawal symptoms based on a belief in the moral model. "Transferential sadism" is too common among practitioners who have not experienced recovery. It is also common among persons whose recoveries were characterized by a great deal of psychological and physical suffering.

What we do not wish to see is institutions that routinely punish during the initial phase. For example, a very well known substance abuse facility, with an international reputation, routinely detoxes patients "in a cold turkey fashion"—even patients who have serious medical problems. In our opinion, there is no ethical basis for this harsh treatment. The idea that pain is necessary in the most crisis-oriented and acute phase of recovery is a vestige of the moral model that deserves burial. There will be enough pain in the gambler's subsequent life without denying him or her appropriate medical and psychological interventions. Unpleasant treatment surroundings, poor food, wretched physical environments, and other facts of some aspects of hospitalization are simply not justified. Supportive therapy, often intensive, is necessary during this critical phase (Pinsker, 1997).

Phases Two and Three: Facing the Problems

Treatment in the next two phases continues as before, with the addition of strong psychological and educational components. The disease concept of gambling, along with the application of this concept to other substances, is taught at this time. At this stage, it may be important to provide personal financial counseling and a vocational assessment. A more intense exposure to GA typically occurs during this phase, along with development of a financial restitution schedule. Collateral involvement of family can provide both support and an opportunity to assess family dynamics.

During Phase Two, we believe there is a role for a healthy increase in confrontation. For people who have worked primarily with substance abuse, it may seem remarkable that resistance or denial is as intense in the dysfunctional gambler as it is in any other addicted person. Here, we ask the practitioner to defer to our clinical experiences, although we do possess data regarding this point. Although the patients included in the data represent a small sample and no matching of patient socioeconomic status was done, *the data indicate that denial is at least as severe in gambling disorders as it is for these two pharmacological addictions.*

Phase Three may involve the most intensive treatment. With all components in place, including family members, the patient confronts his or her addiction and plans an appropriate response. During this phase, a delayed depression often occurs. Depression and anxiety were measured concurrently on a daily basis for 21 days of inpatient treatment for 12 patients admitted to a hospital unit for gambling problems. Anxiety was found to be highest in the initial phase of treatment. It peaked within two days of admission. Subsequently, in what we refer to as Phase Two and Phase Three, anxiety decreased substantially.

Depression seems to take an abrupt leap upward about halfway through treatment. It dips abruptly at the onset of admission, perhaps because of the psychological and physical safety offered in the inpatient setting. It rises substantially, however, and remains high, in response to the advent of a growing sense of insight, which is not quite accompanied by the notion of hope.

Treatment during this phase is ongoing, even if the patient is in denial. We do not expect the patient to fully understand or accept the severity of the gambling problem. If legitimate insight does occur at this stage, all the better.

PHASE FOUR: STARTING A NEW LIFE OF FEELINGS

In the fourth and final stage of an inpatient treatment, the client forms a liaison with a GA home group. Patients with insight may also act as "counselors in training" for newer patients. Their schedules are structured for the next few weeks when they will be outside of the hospital. Finally, they are able to say goodbye to the staff and therapist.

For us, the fourth stage is not a set of arbitrary dates, nor is it the advent of insight into the disease concept. Instead, we are more interested in a different type of insight—specifically, an understanding that behavior can affect emotions in positive as well as negative ways. Our implicit theory here is that gamblers inherit or develop either alexithymia (difficulty knowing emotional states) or hypohedonia (a lack of hedonic capacity; Hamburg, 1998).

Lumley and Roby (1995) provide the most comprehensive data regarding alexithymia. When these researchers examined the relationship of alexithymia and pathological gambling in 1,147 university students, they found that about 3.1% of the students were pathological gamblers. Alexithymia was found in 31.4% of the pathological gamblers, compared to 11.1% of controls. Furthermore, both affective and cognitive aspects of alexithymia were associated with gambling problems. This relationship was independent of depression. Unpublished data we have obtained on 76 GA members suggest that half demonstrate alexithymia, and another one-quarter show moderate depressive symptoms without alexithymia, but tend to be symptom minimizers (McCown & Keiser, 2000).

To us, the most important insight a hospitalized gambler can gain is the very intangible link between psychological states and overt behaviors. Either because of inborn vulnerabilities or a developed lack of sensitivity, hospitalized problem or addicted gamblers do not respond to emotional situations the way others do. Although they cognitively realize that their behaviors affect their moods and symptoms, they fail to recognize this fact emotionally. They lack psychological mindedness. The final stage of inpatient treatment occurs when these patients are able to realize that feelings can cause behaviors, and behaviors can cause feelings.

How do we tell whether a patient has achieved this stage? This is where the art of being a clinician comes into play.

This treatment framework can be supplemented by a variety of other adjunct methods. These include a plethora of behavioral therapies, especially those based on extinction. They may also include the cognitive restructuring discussed in later chapters. However, the major therapeutic tool is the therapeutic group, with its dynamics and its gentle but realistic confrontation about the course of gambling disorders (Posthuma, 1999). Because of the group's unique role, and because of the magical attachment that many gamblers will have with the institution associated with their recovery, return visits are discouraged for a period of several months. Instead, attendance at GA is strongly encouraged.

CHAPTER 6

A Multiphasic Model of Outpatient Treatment

What was it about my treatment that made it work? Nothing particularly, but then again, maybe everything in general. Something clicked somewhere and it never did before. That's the thing about treatment. Some parts work for someone, some parts work for someone else.

—Ron R., recovering gambler

IN THE previous chapter, we made it clear that we prefer to be able to employ the therapeutic "luxury" of inpatient treatment with some clients. In the modality of inpatient treatment, the therapeutic team can employ discrete but flexible phases of service provision. Among the numerous advantages of hospitalization, for both the staff and the patients, is the treatment of possible concurrent psychological problems (Becona et al., 1996). The therapeutic team can obtain a medical and psychological baseline and history (Morrison, 1997). Inpatient treatment also allows more thorough therapeutic work with difficult patients and their families (McCown & Johnson, 1993; Price, 1996). Ongoing supportive therapy may concurrently be administered, regardless of the clinical and treatment phases, because a professional therapist is available virtually at any time (Pinsker, 1997).

If inpatient services are delivered with compassion, and, indeed, with a bit of a sense of humor, we remain optimistic about the benefit of "the hospital" for chronic gamblers. Respectful humor may be even more important than the specifics of the inpatient programs (du Pré, 1997). The advantage of inpatient programs is that they allow tremendous emotional reconstruction, in a safe environment and in a comparatively short period of time. In particular, the losses associated with a lifestyle of gambling can be more rapidly facilitated through both individual (Pennbaker, 1990) and short-term intensive group work (Piper, McCallum, & Azim, 1992). Eventually, patients who undergo such treatment seem to establish "a beachhead," as one of our clients recently described the initial progress, "regarding the fact that I can live with an intimacy that doesn't involve wagering" (Prager, 1995).

We wish that the options for inpatient treatment were available for everyone. They are not, and they will not be in the immediate future, unless basic health care reforms mandate that society should pay for an increase in compassion. In this chapter, we attempt to integrate some of the techniques discussed in the previous chapter into a more flexible, yet theoretically sound framework. Based on clinical literature, empirical studies, theoretical models, survey research, and discussion with colleagues and experts in the field, we have composed a loose and adaptable representation of features of optimized outpatient treatment. This treatment framework can be administered in an individual or a group format, depending on the clients' needs. Many of the techniques that we highlight can be integrated easily into the phasic model described in the previous chapter, but the model is primarily designed around the limitations of outpatient therapy.

OUTPATIENT TREATMENT:
OPTIONS AND REALITIES

At one end of a theoretical continuum of gamblers are those whose problems will not improve unless they are hospitalized and receive intense therapy. At the other end of the continuum are persons who only need outpatient treatment. Their condition does not justify the expenses of 24-hour supervision. Another reality is that outpatient treatment may be all that is available. Our opinion—and we stress that it is only a clinically derived opinion—is that outpatient care is probably the treatment of choice if the client has not "hit low bottom." Ironically, the treatment is likely to be the same whether the client is very motivated or not motivated at all. Motivation may serve as a buffer for some of the influences that encourage relapse. When motivation is lacking, resources can be maximized and treatment can be tailored to foster a realization of the extent of the gambling problem.

Outpatient gambling treatment is quite different from outpatient substance abuse treatment. A key factor is that the client knows that there are no biological tests that can detect relapse. Consequently, even more than in outpatient substance abuse treatment, the client will try to control the therapy. Almost invariably, he or she will volunteer self-imposed limited periods of abstinence as evidence of self-control. As in the treatment of substance abusers, a skillful counselor can use these methods of denial therapeutically, reminding the client that "controlled gambling" is more difficult than he or she imagines.

A major disadvantage of outpatient treatment is that most outpatients are (wisely) trying to avoid particular people. In a locked unit, these untoward people—threatening creditors, loan sharks, and other figures from their past wagering—can be excluded by hospital security personnel.

However, there is ample evidence that patients can benefit from outpatient treatment. We can centralize the outpatient treatment as having a number of distinct phases, similar to those of inpatient treatment. Gamblers Anonymous (GA), if appropriate, remains a focal point. Other, more specific aspects are discussed below.

THE INITIAL MOTIVATIONAL INTERVIEW: THE BEGINNING OF OUTPATIENT THERAPY

Patients in a hospital system can be afforded the "luxury" of denial. Skillful clinicians and recovering group and community members may help slash through the carefully guarded path of personal and social deceptions that interfere with the process of recovery. Unfortunately, the highest risk for the failure of outpatient treatment occurs before the first session.

Only about 20% of those who initially make contact with an agency for treatment of gambling addiction will attend the first scheduled session (McCown & Keiser, 2000). Among this number, the attrition rate during the first four sessions is generally another 50%. Persons who perform program evaluations or manage clinical services need to realize that this situation is typical. They should not withhold funds or evaluate services negatively because of declining attendance figures.

The highest attrition rates are associated with "hot lines," which are presently in vogue. They are popular because they are inexpensive and they give the impression that executives in the gaming industry and their counterparts in state lottery offices and regulatory commissions are concerned about chronic gambling. The best thing we can say about hot lines is that they are cheap to maintain. They are only as good as the treatment sources to which they refer desperate gamblers. In Louisiana, two-thirds of all hot line clients call to inquire about daily betting results and winning lottery numbers (Westphal, personal communications, August 1998).

To reduce this attrition, decrease denial, and encourage continuation of treatment motivation, Miller and Rollnick (1991) have developed a technology that uses the initial interview to motivate clients toward behavioral change. A review of their specific and detailed methods is outside the scope of this book, but therapists and counselors working with any addicted population will find their approach well worth mastering. If a person is hospitalized for an extended period, the information needed for a motivation effort can be acquired slowly. An outpatient counselor or therapist has less time to draw out this information and convert it to a basis for the gambler's positive self-help. Learning how to motivate *while interviewing* is one of the most important skills an outpatient gambling counselor can acquire.

A second goal of the initial interview is to obtain a comprehensive history of the gambling problem. After the history is narrated, it is imperative to compare it with data gathered from family or friends of the gambler. Performing this task quickly is especially important if the gambler is receiving outpatient treatment. A spouse may exaggerate the pathological gambler's problems and their impact on the family system (J. Johnson & McCown, 1996). Conversely, the gambler may deliver a highly abridged version. Background and formal training in family systems and interviewing are essential for outpatient therapists.

When we work with family systems, we find it is useful at this point to introduce the concept of "disease," which allows that gamblers are not responsible for the onset of the disorder. Instead, biological and psychological factors have combined to put people who were already at risk past a breaking point. However, they are responsible for their recovery. An analogy to heart disease or cancer may be useful. Once a disease is identified, recovery is largely up to the person who has the disease, and his or her social network.

Two assumptions, shared by self-help groups and 12-step organizations, form an interesting approach:

1. The person who has committed the undesirable behavior is owed respect and dignity.
2. The success or failure of the recovery effort rests with the individual and his or her work environment.

Although total abstinence is the ultimate goal, it is rarely realistic. However, a relapse prevention model may help clients to feel better about themselves (Marlatt, 1991) and to learn not to ignore high-risk behaviors associated with relapse.

THE COMPLEXITY OF GAMBLERS: WHY ONE METHOD DOES NOT FIT ALL

We preface the remaining portions of this chapter with the statement that no one personality profile that is definitive of pathological gamblers has yet been identified (McCown & Keiser, 2000). This is true for a variety of addictions, as we have shown earlier. In Chapter 3, we noted that the personality variables and other shared and individual factors that contribute to disordered gambling are multifaceted and inherently complex. Meaningful subtypes of chronic gamblers can be identified, based on personalities, wagering opportunities, degrees of pathology, and recalcitrance of their problems. It remains controversial whether these subtypes have, as yet, generated clinically meaningful outcome differences. Furthermore, it is highly unlikely that a single type of "typical" pathological gambler will emerge from future studies. The paradox of gambling is that a multicausal series of processes is involved in the development of its abuse. Yet a fairly common prognosis awaits unbridled gambling addictions.

Even though the natural history of gambling suggests that it may have some universal treatment commonalities, we believe that treatment must be customized to the client's needs. This is the first commonality of successful outpatient programs. As with the treatment of alcoholism and other substance abuse disorders, gambling programs that "work," whether inpatient or outpatient, all seem to understand that individuals are different. They have different cognitive capacities, histories, family resources, instrumental assets, and idiosyncratic needs. Successful programs allow for individual differences.

Treatment providers may be reluctant to admit that not every addict, whether an alcoholic or a gambler, is governed by the same disease dynamics (Zinberg & Shaffer, 1985). Even if addictions have an underlying unity and share the same label, common sense tells us that treatments have to be tailored to individual needs. To borrow an example from neuropsychiatry, even though Alzheimer's disease (AD) may be a single disease, we do not employ identical treatments for every patient unfortunate enough to have this syndrome (Johnson & McCown, 1996). For some patients with AD, behavioral therapy may be most indicated. For others, family therapy or psychopharmacology may be necessary. Psychopharmacology for patients with AD may be subdivided into medications employed for anxiolytic effects, antidepression, antipsychotic effectiveness, or specific neurotransmitter replacement. In laypersons' terms, treatment is prescribed based on what the patient needs, and identification of those needs takes into account the patient's strengths and weaknesses. The treatment needs of problem and dependent gamblers are just as diverse.

OPTIMAL OUTPATIENT SETTINGS:
THE MYTH OF WHO AND WHERE

Although we prefer to treat gamblers in modalities that allow exposure to other gamblers, we realize that this is not always possible. As with other addictions, successful treatment for a variety of pathological gamblers has occurred in a number of settings. These include both inpatient and outpatient programs in which alcoholics, other substance abusers, and persons in general psychiatric and hospital wards shared virtually every imaginable therapeutic modality. Gamblers are variably treated by social workers, general addictions counselors, clergy, psychologists, general practitioners, psychiatrists, family therapists, and specialized gambling counselors or therapists. The particular therapeutic niches of those who treat gamblers are less important than their attitude, their quality, and their capacity to react flexibly and realize when treatment emphases need to be shifted toward other methods.

This chapter addresses some of the common pragmatic concerns that any clinician who treats gamblers will undoubtedly encounter. This is not a complete review of all different types of treatments and where they should be administered. Griffiths (1996b) summarizes the diverse treatment options that are available for gamblers. Instead, we continue here the previous chapter's discussion of what we have seen that seems to work (from our admittedly biased perspective). The model that we advocate more specifically in this chapter is applicable to either group or individual work, at various phases of the recovery process. The general process of gambling treatment is not limited to people with specific credentials. (Some procedures may require credentialing; for example, clergy usually do not prescribe medications.) As problems with gambling increase, the burden of treatment undoubtedly will fall on a wider variety of care providers, including nurse practitioners, school counselors, academic faculty, and recovering persons.

Successful treatment programs for gambling are administered in a number of locations: mental health centers, private practitioners' offices, traditional medical centers, pastoral counseling centers, college counseling centers, and the general clinical spaces of health maintenance organizations. Schools, churches, employee assistance offices, substance abuse clinics, storefronts, taverns, and the Internet are often sites of informal treatment programs.

Questions concerning *who* and *where* are less important than the manner in which treatment is administered. In addition to possessing a sense of humor and cognitive flexibility, effective treatment providers are intensely self-critical. They constantly analyze their own work, their own paradigms, prejudices, and conceptions. They balance theory with pragmatism and are always open to new methods of treatment. Their values often show no distinctly similar patterns, but, in our opinion, they are united by their way of viewing the world. They see life as a complex, ever changing set of systems that defy simple explanations. They respect both individual differences and cultural variations. Their personalities may vary dramatically on traditional measures of openness, neuroticism, extroversion, agreeableness, or conscientiousness, but competent therapists possess a "confident humbleness" regarding their wisdom, capacities, and incessant need to improve their work. Whether these attributes can be taught in schools, modeled, or successfully mentored is a question for further research.

Newcomers to the field of gambling disorders commonly ask us: "Is your orientation primarily cognitive? Psychodynamic? GA? Behavioral?" They seem somewhat frustrated when we answer, "Yes to all."

We maintain this eclecticism because, too often, we do not know what makes people change. As Chapter 9 on chaos theory indicates, it is mathematically impossible to determine exactly *why* and almost always impossible to determine *when* people are likely to alter their addictive life courses. However, we believe that the possibility for successful treatment is optimized by the involvement of a number of therapeutic phases, plus emphasis on specific techniques during the diverse phases of the recovery process. This approach represents the desirability of employing a continuum of treatment, rather than a menu of unrelated treatment strategies and possibilities.

THE CONTINUUM OF TREATMENT: WHAT WORKS FOR US

We have defined this continuum of treatment as *multifaceted treatment integration* (MTI). It consists of sequential and developmentally related phases, based in part on observing what is successful for other practitioners. In other words, we are employing informed clinical experience, as discussed in Chapter 5, but our interventions are also grounded in the self/systems theories of L'Abate (L'Abate, 1994) regarding phases of addictions therapy. L'Abate and Baggett's caveat is important (L'Abate & Baggett, 1997):

> As long as practice is based on the personality of the professional helper, and the medium of exchange between the helper and clients remains the spoken word, it is virtually impossible to verify whether a relation between theory and practice is indeed taking place. Even though the person of the therapist and the spoken word are necessary to start and maintain therapeutic exchanges, they are not sufficient to help people change. Clients can be helped to change when all three media of exchange are employed: the oral, the nonverbal, and the written. If the professional helper operates as an artist, helping intuitively, immediately, and empathetically through verbal interpretations, reflections of feelings, commiserations, commentaries, rational understanding, and support, it will be difficult, expensive, and virtually impossible to see how the helper's actions are derived from any theory. (p. 295)

This statement is congruent with the premise of future chapters: Chaotic processes may be the most important aspect of behavioral changes. We presently do not know what maximally helps people change. We have hypotheses, informed clinical experience, clinical intuition and wisdom, and, occasionally, a few controlled studies. Still, the process of human change remains largely mysterious. All we can claim is that this model seems to work for us, providing a metaframework for a variety of treatments of gambling disorders.

The model that we are advocating in this chapter does not conflict with the stage-based treatment strategies of lengthier or more intense hospitalization or outpatient programs. Phasic descriptions define periodic regularities in progress. Treatment integration, as we define it below, includes an overriding clinical philosophy that is able to be "infused" into any treatment model, stage-based or otherwise.

MULTIFACETED TREATMENT INTEGRATION

In our experience, perhaps the most important intervention into gambling behavior is an *explanation offering multifaceted interpretation* of the causes and treatments of the behaviors in question. Medical, educational, correctional, and spiritual interventions are all usually framed within the disease paradigm. In other words, we tell a client that he or she has a disease and that the purpose of offering a variety of therapies is to enable the client's rehabilitation—medically, psychologically, morally, spiritually, and financially. After the rehabilitation process has made substantial inroads, we spend time attempting to find possible causes. Clinical experience suggests that the client is often both surprised and relieved when his or her problems are directly identified.

PHASE ONE: HOPE

When they are no longer battling with "insanity" but understand their problem as an identifiable disease syndrome, clients are empowered with the beginnings of an ability to change and to develop meaningful coping mechanisms. They begin to lose the helplessness of not understanding how to control themselves (Shapiro, Schwartz, & Astin, 1996). The cornerstone of this first phase, therefore, is the battle against helplessness and despair.

During the first phase, almost every program we have knowledge of presents the disease model of gambling. The presentation includes programs that are primarily cognitive-behavioral in their orientations. A number of alternative causes of gambling diseases may also be presented; the depth of the presentation depends on the clients' cognitive abilities. It is often helpful to stress the biology of addiction and its related behaviors (e.g., Comings, 1990), at least during this very early stage. This approach helps to reduce any stigma associated with recovery from gambling.

In addition to ascribing hope, successful programs emphasize that their initial aims are *primarily behavioral* (Tarlow & Maxwell, 1989). This does not mean that counselors or therapists are commited to philosophical behaviorism (Marlatt, 1998) or that therapists are ignoring other components of human behavior (Brickman et al., 1982). It simply means that we seek to *immediately* interrupt and prohibit the problematic gambling behavior "in its tracks," as one of our patients recently said. In imitation of the popular approach of Reality Therapy (Mickel & Liddie Hamilton, 1997) and similar theoretical approaches, we do not promote, demand, or even accept excuses for client failure during this phase of treatment. We believe that the client's dysfunctional gambling is usually outside of internal control, especially during an initial treatment phase. Instead, we are unrelenting in our observations and comprehensive in our assessments of gambling behavior, looking for cues that place the person under stimulus control.

An observation made by one of our students needs further research, but seems to resonate with almost every gambling clinician. We recently examined a set of data that revealed the amount of time that therapists had spent discussing with their clients or patients *whether* they had a problem. He found that clinicians who are very good at helping clients to frame their problems and to initially admit that their gambling is interfering with their lives are less successful as ongoing change agents. This holds true for clients whom they have "shepherded" through the initial stage themselves and for clients who admitted problems and were subsequently referred to them.

In other words, two opposite sets of skills seem to be necessary in treating gambling disorders. One group of clinicians is extremely good at promoting acceptance of dysfunctional gambling. Another group is extremely good at fostering ongoing maintenance of behavioral changes. These skills seem separate and distinct, yet are poorly understood.

The therapists' countertransferences may be responsible for these types of findings. Addicted patients tend to evoke in therapists strong feelings of either overinvolvement ("rescuing") or rejection. Some therapists may alternate between the two, placing the patient on a bizarre schedule of reinforcement.

Phase One involves acceptance and hope. Addictions counselors will recognize it as offering the first steps of 12-step work. During early stages of treatment, successful therapists usually do not confront defenses too aggressively or prematurely. Perhaps therapists who perform this task well—those who excel in breaking through the cycle of dependency

denial—have a different set of skills than those who are able to act to reduce addictive behaviors. Research regarding these and related topics has
now begun and should produce some interesting conclusions.

PHASE TWO: NEW PATTERNS AND BEHAVIORS

Next, we move toward identifying the common and the unique behavioral
and cognitive factors that lead to dysfunctional gambling. These include
cognitive distortions about the probabilities of winning, and the mistaken
self-statements that gamblers make when they are actively chasing
(Blackman, 1987). Such distortions may be important in the maintenance
of gambling behaviors (Brenner, 1990).

In this phase, we operate from a more "dynamic" stance, although
strict cognitive behaviorists might note similarities between our work
and relapse prevention in other addictions (Holtgraves, 1988). We seek to
identify the specific emotional states that cause gambling or cause the
cognitive distortions associated with dysfunctional gambling behaviors.
We try to find these patterns, even if the client is exhibiting alexithimia
or depression (problems that are quite common among gamblers during
this phase of treatment). The patterns may be linked to the client's long-
standing personality traits.

We often find that gamblers early in recovery are faced with more than
the loss of the activity; they face the loss of the fantasy. Because gambling
is based on the "what if" fantasy, gamblers can find themselves tremendously depressed by the realization that the miracle win isn't going to
occur. We liken it to the levels of grief experienced in the loss of any significant relationship. There is both the loss of the actual person and the
loss of the dreams, expectation, goals and sense of the future of the relationship that also must be confronted and grieved. Replacing the fantasy
with the harsh reality of the gambler's situation can be psychologically
and emotionally devastating. Whereas people in early recovery from substance abuse often feel somewhat better early on because they begin to
reclaim some of their health and abilities, for compulsive gamblers, the
opposite can be true. It may take months for them to experience a sense of
hopefulness in the face of overwhelming financial and relationship problems. When all one's hopes have been placed in the hands of chance—a
pull of the lever, a spin or the wheel or roll of the dice—learning true
hopefulness based on effort and responsibility can be a slow process,
both cognitively and emotionally.

We also delve further into our explanations of the possible biological
factors of addiction, including opponent processes and the role of alcohol,
attention deficit disorder (ADD), and other biocognitive deficits in fostering gambling problems. Client insight is encouraged but is not required
for facilitation of behavioral change.

During Phase Two, defense mechanisms are redirected and supported to promote continued treatment, abstinence, and long-term improvement of mental health. From a psychodynamic perspective (Paris, 1998), issues of omnipotence, narcissistic entitlement, and vacillation between power and intimacy are commonly encountered. Compared to Phase One, the treatment provider is less of an authority and more of a coach and pragmatic skills builder. Unlike a clinician who must cut through denial, we do not directly attack the client's primitive defenses. Instead, we employ them skillfully, strategically, and perhaps even manipulatively.

During Phase Two, we often appeal quite frankly to the client's pathological narcissism. It is common for the therapist to chide the client with such phrases as "Once you understand this, someone as smart [or good, or attractive, or sensitive, or Christian, or religious, or whatever the client believes to be true about himself or herself] as you will realize why gambling isn't helpful." The best phrase we have encountered is one we repeat to most of our clients: "Gambling just isn't *you.*" This implies acceptance—but not endorsement—of the client's narcissistic tendencies and need to be different. Our message excites the most primitive part of an injured personality—the part that says, "I am special." A skillful therapist, without lying and while remaining totally honest, says, in any way possible, "You can't be *that* special if you continue gambling."

During Phase Two, we furnish the skills necessary for continued abstinence. Usually, we set out behavioral and cognitive-behavioral tools, but our stance is based more on a psychodynamic paradoxical interpretation (Bütz et al., 1997). Our "metastance" recognizes that the client will experience emotional turmoil, crises, and extreme vacillations in commitment. Our message, however, remains strong as we challenge the basic narcissistic successes that the client has achieved. We reiterate: "You can be more successfully 'special' if you stop gambling. *You* are too smart for such self-harmful behaviors."

If the patient or client is maintained in the community during Phase Two, we do not recommend extensive confrontation. In an inpatient setting, the therapists and recovering community members may proceed more vigorously in tearing down the omnipotence, distrust, avoidance, fears of intimacy, and other dysfunctional defenses. On an outpatient basis, this zealous approach may encourage complete relapse and a much more intense pattern of gambling abuse.

PHASES THREE AND FOUR: CONSOLIDATING GAINS
AND GAINING MEANING

During Phase Three, the next systemic phase, we and our clients examine the role of social, work-related, community, and familial variables in the mutual causation of addictive gambling. Work and leisure issues are directly addressed along with present and past family issues (McCown & Johnson, 1993). The family is brought in, both metaphorically and physically, if possible. The gambler learns to recognize and admit the problems he or she has caused family members' social system, and why that system's response to the problems may cause an upward spiral of addictiveness (Ramirez, 1999).

Difficulties in dual disorders are also addressed (O'Connell, 1997). Many people with addictions, as we have demonstrated earlier, also have psychiatric difficulties. The clinical art at this point is to prevent the fostering of addictive behaviors, while encouraging the client to understand that the addiction alone has not necessarily caused his or her anxiety, depression, delusions, lack of intimacy, or whatever other symptoms are present. This is a most dangerous phase, because, previously, the client's ability to cope with uncontrollable feelings has been ascribed to the addictions. Here, we must impart to the client that a healing power is involved in the expressing of emotions (Pennebaker, 1990). A simple "mind over mood" belief, however, may foster a relapse because it encourages overconfidence (Padaskey & Greenberger, 1995).

During Phase Three, it is important to evaluate the patient for the possibility that he or she has two or more independent disorders, each requiring aggressive treatment. The emergence of increased anxiety or depression optimally requires a separate treatment regimen, with emphasis on cognitive behavioral treatments. We do not recommend the addictive anxiolytics as a treatment of choice for gamblers. However, we recognize that for clinical syndromes such as panic disorder, clinical judgment remains important. As in alcohol dependence, chronic use of benzodiazepines is usually contraindicated. The existence of any addiction does not reduce the dangerousness of depressive or psychotic symptoms. A psychiatric diagnosis independent of gambling-related problems is made only if symptoms persist during abstinence. Protracted cognitive impairments, such as memory deficits, disorientation, and evidence of confusion and poor judgment, require consultation with a neurologist and a neuropsychologist.

Posttraumatic stress disorder (PTSD) is also an important disorder to rule out (Briere, 1997). PTSD can mimic many psychiatric disorders, and can include symptoms of irritability, depression, anxiety, and frank psychosis. Notably, PTSD can be both a reaction to the experiences of gambling and a cause of association with gamblers. PTSD can complicate the ability to control addictive behaviors and demonstrate consistent self-control (Brister & Brister, 1987). In some cases, it can lead to blatant dependency (Bornstein, 1993). PTSD complicates treatment, but it should not displace abstinence as a major treatment goal.

Phase Four is the existential or spiritual/moral phase (Pargament, 1986). Not all clients can reach this phase because it involves an intensive reworking of the past, in order to resolve core conflictual themes (Book, 1998). In Phase Four, we also hope to give the client or patient the ability to find some meaning in the suffering associated with dysfunctional gambling. Often, this involves more extensive work with GA or special sessions with pastoral counselors (Richards & Bergin, 1997). This discussion may be outside our purview, since we are not experts in the distinctively personal areas of spirituality. On the other hand, we attempt to make the client realize that some good, whether personal or abstract, may come from former dysfunctional gambling behaviors.

Some people are able to turn the horrors of addiction into a process imbued with personal meaning, especially when they are allowed to construct a coherent and positive life story (Cramer, 1996). In Phase Four, the client is offered the opportunity of existential redemption. Gamblers who reach this stage of treatment are able to see their behavior as a choice they can make to provide their lives with meaning (Eisenbuch, 1977). By developing an alternative and genuine spirituality, problem and addictive gamblers find a meaning within their previous lifestyle and the freedom needed to abandon it.

SUMMARY

It is important to realize that our phasic model is not rigid. We may spend time working on family issues and then shift—for certain clients, and when it is relevant—to more cognitive issues. Exceptions are made for behaviors that foster an immediacy of gambling. When relapses occur, the focus of treatment shifts to immediately arresting the problematic behaviors.

Other techniques may be necessary for the special populations discussed in the following chapter. For example, more rigid treatment strategies are necessary for supervising persons convicted of gambling-addicted offenses. Provisional supervision of problem gamblers requires dealing with problems of compliance, employment, and substance abuse. Gowen and Speyerer (1995) note that a three-component treatment approach is necessary, consisting of (1) personal therapy, (2) individual financial counseling, and (3) attendance at Gamblers Anonymous meetings. It is also essential to monitor leisure activities and to obtain the cooperation of family members in treatment.

DYNAMIC TREATMENT METHODS: LINKING FEELINGS AND BEHAVIORS INTO INSIGHT AND UNDERSTANDING

Until fairly recently, classic psychodynamic and even psychoanalytic treatments were often viewed as treatments of choice for gamblers.

However, few studies show that classic psychodynamically oriented insight therapy is, by itself, specifically helpful. A large body of clinical lore and the beginnings of some consistent empirical research suggest that these techniques are appropriate for people who have characterological problems (Greenberg & Safran, 1987). This may be especially true when the clients' gambling appears to be related to dramatic events or to narcissistic injury. For example, Haustein and Schurgers (1992) believe that pathological gambling is an attempt at self-healing and conflict solving.

By *dynamic,* we do not necessarily mean "psychodynamic." We mean approaches that recognize the tangibility of human emotional states and their impact on subsequent mental and behavioral processes (Bütz et al., 1997). As we stated in Chapter 5, it may seem obvious that feelings influence behaviors. Surprisingly, to many people who suffer from addictive disorders, these very basic links have not been made—or, if they have been made, they are often selective. A person with a severe gambling disorder might not realize that the gambling accompanies depression but might use overeating or smoking as "remedies" for feeling blue. The goal of the dynamic phase is to provide sufficient insight into what is, for nonaddicts, a very obvious emotional connection.

"Denial" is ostensibly common in every addiction. For reasons that are poorly understood, addiction is too often characterized by a psychological "dysnomia"—an inability to see for oneself how severe a problem is. Oddly, everyone around the person can see the likely outcome of his or her behaviors, and this makes confrontation a possibility and a useful tool. It is often difficult for nonrecovering persons to understand the process of denial. It is illogical. It makes no sense. It violates all we know about human nature. Yet it is so common that it is often considered diagnostic. A recovering person may have more insight into the process of a lack of insight than a nonrecovering person will ever have, and this proves invaluable in any treatment program.

If the clinical treatment for borderline personalities can be taken as an indication of the treatment of gambling, the three framework transitions for treatment of gambling are rooted in psychodynamic thinking, theory, and treatment. The first framework was the most popular among practitioners until about 1970. It involved primary emphasis on supportive work. Therapists using this framework sought to limit regression, strengthen the client's defenses, and prevent transferential issues from becoming so serious that they interfered with other aspects of treatment.

During the 1970s, therapists shifted to a second framework involving more expressive features, within the relatively confined span of the psychotherapy session. Additional emphasis was placed on limit setting and neutrality. Currently, more analytically oriented therapists are likely to use briefer approaches, simultaneously providing limit setting and interpretation. More often, a theory of object relations and subsequent personality development is used as a framework. This type of treatment may be very attractive for therapists working with personality-disordered clients.

However, psychodynamic therapy alone is not our first treatment for "addictive personalities." These people have been referred to as multi-impulsive because insight-oriented psychotherapy (especially if based on psychodynamic therapies) is practically impossible while the person is actively gambling. Basic behavioral goals, including abstinence, have to be met before such therapy can be promoted. Following a period of abstinence, insight-oriented therapy may be highly appropriate, depending on the client's needs, strengths, and available resources.

Our initial and more limited goal in what we label as "dynamic therapy" is having the client recognize the role that emotions play in triggering both cognitions (cognitive mediated gambling) and "unconscious" gambling, which seemingly occurs without forethought. During this period of treatment, we are attempting to foster the growing realization that feelings count and are influential in gambling. If the client is particularly "psychologically minded" we may also attempt to draw upon the past as a cause of present feelings. This is helpful, though not necessary, at this stage.

We try to resist using the past as an excuse for continued behavioral dysfunction. For example, a client might realize that his or her dysphoria comes from severe abuse as a child (Foy, 1992). Often, this insight can be so overwhelming that it triggers a relapse. Too often, an insight-oriented clinician may tolerate such relapses, even if objective indexes of behavior indicate that the client is getting worse. For us, this approach rarely works.

Instead, we see insight as a gradually encouraged process, tempered with behavioral and cognitive progress that occurs in a semisequential fashion. Insight alone never supplements behavioral change. It may come before or after, and may be a cause or an epiphenomenon. Yet, once insight occurs, it often predicts powerful behavioral changes and indicates that the client's struggle toward abstinence may be able to become less intense. Because of insight, the client feels more in control of his or her behaviors. What is under control is less threatening and less likely to cause relapse.

CHAPTER 7

Working Strategies for Treatment Success: The Pragmatics of Therapy for Abusive and Addicted Gamblers

I had a choice. The judge said, "Treatment or jail. It's up to you, buddy." It wasn't a fair choice. They have some hellacious card games in prison. That's when it hit me I might be better off with treatment.

THIS CHAPTER highlights specific treatment strategies that have found some support in the scientific and clinical literature. Frankly, data regarding their efficacies are suggestive, at best. We, or our associates, have tried them all with diverse populations of gamblers. In our informed clinical experience, sometimes they work quite well. None, however, appears to work sufficiently well that it can replace traditional abstinence-based methods. This is our opinion, but it is based on experience and observation.

We prefer to use these methods as adjunctive therapies rather than core therapeutic processes. We do not believe that they constitute sufficient therapy by themselves, given our orientation toward abstinence. The methods integrate quite easily into either an inpatient or an outpatient setting. When they fail, a case can be made that one problem was a lack of training on the part of the therapist, or that the client had a strong belief that these methods were going to be ineffective. Failure of these techniques may then be a self-fulfilling prophecy.

Fortunately, we have a number of diverse strategies to supplement the core of gambling abstinence. They include behavioral, cognitive behavioral, and family treatments. (The latter are so important that we devote

136

Chapter 10 to them.) Our strategy is completely pragmatic: If one method doesn't work, try others until something does work. A very strong case is made for pragmatic clinical interventions, based on the unique factors of each case (Fishman, 1999).

BEHAVIORAL APPROACHES

The principal alternatives to treatment methods that challenge GA and AA have been derived from behavioral techniques and learning theory. These include the S→R Skinnerian principles (Skinner, 1953), which have gone somewhat out of scientific vogue, and the more theoretically complex neobehavioristic traditions highlighted in the once popular works of Clark Hull (1943). More contemporary approaches are based on social learning models of controlled drinking/gambling (Marlatt, 1998).

In the United States, unfortunately, that there has been little cooperation between clinical behaviorists on one hand, and proponents of abstinence-based treatment on the other. Behavioral therapy is an extraordinarily powerful tool that is useful throughout the therapeutic process, but especially in the early stages of recovery. Its emphasis on observable outcomes (e.g., "Did you slip or not?") is congruent with a 12-step model. Especially in the early stages, clients are encouraged to view abstinence in terms of immediate behavioral actions ("One day at a time . . .") and not to inadvertently encourage relapse by worrying about the future.

As one example of the usefulness of behaviorism, a variety of different aversion therapies have been impressive in a number of addiction treatment fields, and some have demonstrated an empirical use in the clinical treatment of gambling. The goal of aversion therapy is to produce an aversive reaction to gambling by establishing a negative conditioned response (Griffiths, 1996a). Gambling is usually paired with a negative stimulus to produce an automatic negative response before gambling can begin. Common aversive stimuli include: nausea, ice (cold pressor), and electric shock. Aversive imagery conditioning also appears to be effective. However, most studies that demonstrated the efficacy of any aversion therapy procedure, especially for gambling, have had limited sample sizes.

Operant or Skinnerian methods have also been used to modify behavior. There are few controlled studies, but the abundant single-case studies in existence claim this form of treatment is effective. Overall, as expected, reinforcement and punishment contingencies can be used to enhance program compliance. They enable many clients to escape the overwhelming immediacy of gambling urges by placing them less under the control of stimulus gambling behavior.

Thought stopping, which we use in our early phases, is highly useful in both an inpatient and an outpatient setting. The technique is described in the following case study.

John

John, a 38-year-old salesman, was being treated on an outpatient basis for a $1,000-a-week video poker gambling habit. As part of his sales job, he commuted by or near a number of video poker establishments. "Often," he noted, "I find them almost irresistible. It's like I lose my free will when I am around them."

In therapy, John was instructed that, indeed, gambling addiction overcomes will, but, through treatment, he could maintain initial control and keep from being overwhelmed. He was given 100 trials of imaginary (covert) sensitization, where he followed through a fantasy of gambling with thoughts of rotting corpses and human vomit. This worked for a while but was insufficient to keep him from a severe slip.

Following one "binge" in which he chased an initial $50 loss into a $600-plus deficit, John was more desperate. The therapist, who was well trained in behavioral techniques, devised a plan to pair John's initial thoughts of gambling with a loud, self-generated verbal instruction: "Stop, goddamn it!" John practiced this at home until he had experienced over 250 trials.

As John explains, the procedure was very helpful. "Every time I would start to even think about gambling, I'd yell at myself out loud. It worked pretty well. I had some embarrassing times, doing it in public, but I think people thought I had that disease when (sic) you can't help yourself swearing" [Tourette's syndrome].

John was able to continue working, and because he spent less time gambling, he actually increased his sales output, despite a few embarrassing episodes.

An artful man with a good bit of country pragmatism, John used this assumed diagnosis of Tourette's syndrome to his commercial advantage. "I think they felt sorry for me, you know, like when I'd be trying to take an order at a truck stop that had video poker, and they'd hear me swear. I don't think it hurt business. For variety, I used some other curse words. The only time anyone ever asked me, I told them I had an illness, and they didn't ask any more. Maybe they even ordered more because they felt sorry for me.

"One guy even asked me how my 'torniquette's disease' was, because he said his son had it, too. I think I made my sales quota on him alone one week!"

Although we didn't encourage the above adaptation, it is an interesting example of how people can turn behavioral deficits into advantages.

SOCIAL SKILLS TRAINING

Social skills training derived largely from attempts, in the 1960s, to use operant conditioning to assist psychiatric patients in the transition to community living. It was observed by many sources that these patients were lacking in specific abilities that were necessary to function among normal people. As a result, they were considered likely to relapse. A number of technologies were developed to teach these skills to schizophrenics and then to others, including children (Shure, 1993). A wealth of literature now links social skills deficits with a variety of behavioral disorders.

Social skills training with gamblers is based on the assumption that gamblers are deficient in social skills. These skills may be absent because the gambler, when young, spent valuable days chasing horses instead of romantic partners (Haubrich-Casperson & Van Niespen, 1993). Equally likely, the aberrant gambler has turned to gambling following periods of excessive stress. Gambling serves as a type of drug, but the gambler lacks the ability to relax and maintain social contact in more appropriate domains (Halpern, 1995).

The subset of gamblers for whom social skills training is necessary or effective is not clear. For example, John, a bit of a con (which he later addressed through GA), had very polished, even adroit social skills. However, some people have basic deficits in contemporary living abilities, such as how to look for housing, how to shop, and even how to open a checking account.

Social skills training involves a variety of approaches (Shure, 1993). Excellent sources are found in a number of structured and semistructured exercises. Because of the plethora of dysfunctions among gamblers, a "blanket" approach—for example, six one-hour sessions of social skills training—will be inappropriate for most gamblers in treatment. However, almost universally, gamblers in treatment can benefit from some degree of assertiveness training, to enhance their resistance to external pressures to gamble. Other social abilities need to be assessed and subsequently addressed, either individually or by treatment team members or therapists (Haustein & Schurgers, 1992). For example, an overbearing expansive gambler does not need the same social skills training as the shy and aloof person who gambles because he or she cannot make friends (Antonello, 1996).

Stress management is also a useful adjunct in therapy, either through simple training in relaxation or more sophisticated techniques, such as biofeedback. General relaxation training, a useful adjunct for almost any type of psychiatric and/or physical disorder (Comer, 1992), is strongly recommended, provided it is administered by a competent practitioner who believes that it is a key component in the treatment process. Workbooks or tapes marketed for the purpose of teaching nonclinical populations are usually not helpful for people with more severe problems. Even though the procedures of relaxation training may seem straightforward and automatic, they are enhanced if they are administered by a therapist instead of a computer program.

Opponents of behavioral techniques have argued that stress management often defeats the "incentive to change," as if autonomic overarousal was the client's only motivation to eliminate problem gambling. This is complete nonsense, bordering on clinical Puritanism. If anything, the early successes in being able to control one's extraordinarily aversive biological states lay a foundation of empowerment. Subsequently, this foundation will foster a greater motivation to change (Roth & Fonagy, 1996). The process of change will then become self-reinforcing, and the client will begin to gain healthy confidence.

Perhaps the best variety of relaxation methods includes those classified as Autogenic Training (Linden, 1991) or Self-Hypnoses (Fromm & Khan, 1990). These procedures use imagined exercises to produce mental and physical relaxation as well as physiological states that are directly opposite those of sympathetic arousal.

In general, however, despite their demonstrated efficacy in a number of areas, many behavioral techniques have gone somewhat out of vogue, especially in North America. The reason isn't entirely clear. The fault is not a simple lack of clinical effectiveness. Some of the strongest data in the gambling literature concern the fact that behavioral methods work. Perhaps they require from the therapist an amount of effort and training that is considered unusual. They are not the panacea that practitioners a generation ago thought they were, but they have a permanent place in the treatment of chronic gambling.

COGNITIVE TECHNIQUES

During the second phase of both inpatient and outpatient treatment, we concentrate on implementing "cognitive distortion corrections." These techniques, derided in the cognitive behavioral literature, are often effective for gambling disorders (Gaboury & Ladouceur, 1988). Excellent reviews of many of the techniques are available in several sources (Griffiths, 1996a, 1996b; McGuirrin, 1992; Walker, 1992). For example, individuals who behave without thinking about their gambling may profit from noticing the cues associated with gambling behaviors.

Cognitive techniques for reducing gambling are well known and amply documented (Walker, 1992). Initially, they have received excellent empirical support, but, like the entire field of gambling treatment in general, they need more research.

We now base our psychoeducational approach to gambling on many of the constant findings in the cognitive behavioral literature, regarding the incorrect assumptions made by gamblers (e.g., Letarte et al., 1986). The literature suggests a number of discrete treatment strategies that are useful for most gamblers and can be conceptualized as appropriate in any stage of treatment (Langer, 1975; Lee, 1971; Murray, 1993; Roth & Fonagy, 1996; Walker & Phil, 1992).

One concern that we almost always address in treatment is the concept of explanatory style, one of the best researched variables in the psychological literature. Atlas and Peterson (1990) found evidence that pessimistic explanatory styles predicted rumination following a lost bet. The rumination after a loss was, in turn, associated with track patrons' larger wagers on subsequent races. This resulted in a tendency toward less successful wagering, which the authors suggest may be a model relevant both for depression and for the development of pathological chasing behaviors.

Cognitive therapy—or its close ally, rational emotive therapy—may be extremely helpful in helping gamblers realize that their negative attributes result in a spiral of behaviors. For example, the tendency to react negatively following losses, which has been found in laboratory gambling research, is also associated positively with the tendency to bet more intensely and wager more money. Growing evidence suggests that when gamblers lose, they bet more. In fact, one "system" of betting that is common among gamblers is to double any bet following a loss. For example, if the gambler loses $5.00 on a hand of blackjack, the next bet must be $10.00. If they lose that hand, they must bet $20.00 and so on. Although the "logic" dictates that they will eventually win a hand, and therefore recoup their losses, the irrationality of this plan becomes apparent when one considers how quickly losses then accumulate and the losing streaks do occur which can quickly devastate the gamblers financial resources. This behavior can be interrupted by showing the gambler in treatment that it is part of a dysfunctional pattern. A cognitive behavioral theory of problem gambling often resonates with gamblers because they understand from experience that they are more likely to bet irrationally when they are upset (Sharpe & Tarrier, 1992).

As we have stated earlier, one of the most common occurrences that is associated with wagering anomalies, and hence with dysfunctional gambling, occurs when a "sure bet" is disrupted. Too often, problem gamblers respond by increasing their wagers (R.J. Rosenthal, 1995). Research from our laboratory, as well as advice in a number of "classical" books for gamblers (Quinn, 1987), suggests that unexpected losses are usually handled by a subsequent decrease in betting frequency. This pattern, however, is reversed in problem gamblers, who tend to bet more after a "sure" bet results in a loss. This behavior may represent a form of "chasing".

Again, problem gamblers can often relate to this behavior through their experiences. In addition to their habit's being successfully conditioned by a big win or other reinforcing variables, their negative emotions may have been necessary for the acquisition of problem gambling

(Dickerson, 1993). When these elements are combined with the character structure associated with pathological gambling, which may include sensation seeking and a wish for omnipotence (Blaszczynski & Steel, 1998), losses may predispose the gambler to the negative affect necessary for subsequent "chasing." Further research could assist the therapeutic community by pinpointing whether this negative affect causes a change in expectations regarding the subsequent chances of future winnings. It may act to distort future bets by simply causing an unwanted increase in cognitive and physical arousal that disrupts regular, planned behaviors.

Coulombe, Ladouceur, and Desharnais (1992) found that arousal alone is sufficient to produce cognitive distortions that can overestimate gambling results. Overestimation of the chance of positive results is a common cognitive distortion among gamblers (Griffith, 1996b).

Ladouceur, Sylvain, Letarte, Giroux, and Jacques (1998) have suggested that a potential treatment for reducing the frequency of gambling among gambling addicts involves having the patients verbalize the thoughts that occur during laboratory-controlled gambling sessions. It may also be useful for patients to make self-statements regarding gambling in a group format, and have other patients criticize them. This is especially helpful for narcissistic, expansive gamblers, though it is probably counterproductive for neurotic gamblers, especially in an outpatient setting (Paris, 1998).

More specific gamblers' errors in thinking can also be addressed during cognitive phases of treatment. Keren and Lewis (1994) have discussed two types of cognitive fallacies that gamblers frequently believe. The first is well known: the belief that random units exhibit a positive pattern. Some gamblers tend to bet on a winning number under the assumption that the number is somehow more likely to "come in." (We will demonstrate an intervention to help defeat this irrationality.)

The opposite cognitive distortion can also be found among gamblers. Problem gamblers will often believe that past events are not independent. Therefore, a certain number that recently "hit" may be less likely to come up again. These myths generate beliefs that certain gambling machines or lottery numbers are "not hot" or are "due to hit."

Keren and Lewis also cite experiments showing that people underestimate the number of observations needed for reliable detection of biased numbers. It is ironic that people who will dispute the accuracy of scientific media polls because of their small sample size will find irreproducible patterns in ten or twenty randomly numbered sequences. We have seen this phenomenon so often that we have labeled it the *phenomenon of self-referential truth*. Preliminary data indicate that this phenomenon correlates with Eysenck's psychoticism factor (Eysenck & Eysenck, 1985). To quote one client, "Screw what *you* think. If *I* see it, that settles it. That goes for gambling, too!"

Gamblers (until they enter treatment) score higher on measures of self-righteousness and report higher beliefs that their lifestyles are more "correct" than the general population (McCown & Keiser, 2000). Unfortunately, the world that they insist they "see" is tested by the reality of their wagers and usually proves to be completely wrong. Cognitive behavioral techniques may be helpful in reducing "self-referential truths" by elucidating the way that chance operates to distort cognitions and acquisitions of beliefs.

In an effective demonstration that we sometimes incorporate into our clinical work, we present to subjects an ongoing computer-generated string of random numbers. We ask them to find the "pattern," if there is any. There is no pattern in the numbers, yet the majority of problem-gambler subjects will insist that they have observed a definable pattern! Care is needed with this exercise; the therapist must be able to somehow "prove" that there is no consistently discernible pattern. For example, he or she may have to show the gambler in treatment the line in a computer program that says "Random Number Generator." This opens up discussion to the fact that even random data can have apparent patterns over the short run, and these often cause future mispredictions.

Occasionally, we are asked whether the goals of cognitive therapy implicitly endorse the hope of successful social and controlled gambling. We reply negatively. Cognitive techniques are tools to help gamblers see how irrational their behavior has been. We have never seen or heard that a person committed to abstinence lost that commitment by being treated with cognitive or cognitive behavioral techniques. Our first concern regarding their use involves the fact that many clinicians, especially psychologists, tend to use them alone and not as part of a total treatment package. At this time, based on our clinical experience, we do not recommend this course of action, but we are open to suggestions from the therapeutic community.

Our second concern involves the philosophical and empirical issue that humans aren't always rational, even when they know the rules. Cognitive therapies work best for people who are fairly rational. Most gamblers are not. This is discussed below.

INTEGRATING ABSTINENCE AND RELAPSE PREVENTION

Relapse prevention is the concept that cognitive preplanning can prevent relapse and that the client who examines cognitive processes can fruitfully use relapses. We try to present these concepts most gingerly. We want to empower the patient with the knowledge that he or she can control relapse, while simultaneously conveying the message that relapses are frequent and, for some addictions, inevitable. Nevertheless, relapse is not the end of the world. In the relapse prevention model, the patient learns from his or her relapses, making it less likely that they will occur again.

Persons who were not familiar with GA but have experience with AA may note that it is often difficult to integrate a relapse prevention model into the AA framework because of the abstinence violation effect (Marlatt, 1998). It is assumed at AA that once a person begins drinking again, he or she will continue until physical processes or legal interactions stop the activity. Relapse prevention, on the other hand, views relapses less negatively and attempts to use them as learning experiences for the client.

GA does not take such a negative view of relapse prevention or relapses. It seems to be understood that relapse may occur when gamblers get some disposable income again. GA seems more tolerant of relapse and relapse prevention. Slips are recognized as part of the rehabilitation process.

Relapse prevention acknowledges that a number of events or settings may have salient abilities to induce relapse. These can be external, like locations, or internal, such as feelings, powerful feeling that generates relapse is guilt (Greenberger & Padesky, 1995). Systemic behavioral relapse prevention is important because change is given priority.

IS COGNITIVE BEHAVIORAL THERAPY/RELAPSE PREVENTION A MAGIC BULLET?

Some practitioners, particularly psychologists, think the answer to this question is "yes." Often, these practitioners are striving to find a unified set of principles for therapeutic change (Goldfried, 1980). They reject the overly simplistic views of human behavior that were promoted by twentieth-century behaviorism (Buckley, 1989), and they would often prefer to have a set of causes of psychopathology that is amenable to the methodological rigors of behaviorism (Baars, 1986).

Our own bias is that the present emphasis on cognitive behavioral techniques, to the exclusion of other methodologies, is frankly a bit dangerous. It seems to reflect the fact that many practitioners, psychologists in particular, are ordered, rational people who themselves respond well to cognitive approaches. Rigid cognitive behavioral adherents ignore the growing literature from the evolutionary perspectives, which indicates that there are two parallel processing systems in human decision making: (1) a rational system and (2) an experiential system (Denes-Raj & Epstein, 1994; Epstein, Lipson, Holstein, & Huh, 1992). Under conditions of less structure, emotionality, or uncertainty, we may have evolved somewhat irrational thinking. If we reinforce rational behavior as the sole treatment strategy, we fail to realize that, much of the time, human behavior is guided by different rules than are operative in the safety of the therapist's office. Apparently, we have evolved to be irrational under many conditions.

Mobilia (1993) argues this point indirectly when she presents data to describe gambling as a "rational addiction," not different from economic behavior in other fields. Economic gambling demand equations, which hypothesize that gambling is an addictive behavior, were derived from the theoretical model of rational addictive behavior. Using data from parimutuel betting at horse tracks from 1950 through 1987, Mobilia examined the effectiveness of changing the takeout rate on gambling behavior. The methodology and results are outside of the realm of this discussion, but in general, her results supported the hypothesis of the model—that gambling is a rational addictive behavior.

In particular, significant intertemporal linkages were found in patterns of gambling, confirming the assumption of clinicians and others that gambling is indeed addictive. On the other hand, future events were found to have a significant impact on current gambling. This implies that individuals are not behaving totally irrationally, despite the fact that they demonstrate addictive behaviors. Studies such as these yield evidence that therapeutic appeals to only the rational parts of the brain will not always be effective in preventing problem and abusive gambling patterns.

RECOVERING-GAMBLER COUNSELORS AND THEIR ROLE IN COGNITIVE THERAPY

During the first phase and especially during the second phase of treatment, we like to introduce persons in treatment to peer-based, or recovering-gambler counselors. Often, the recovering-gambler counselor can empathize with or share experiences that are difficult, at best, for a nonrecovering counselor to understand. The question of whether it is necessary to have recovering addicts as counselors is controversial. To date, there is no good empirical evidence to address this point. Either way, when asked this question, the therapist faces a dilemma. If he or she says, "I too have a gambling problem," then a client may say, "How can you help me? You're no better than I am." On the other hand, if the therapist makes it clear that he or she does not have a gambling problem, the client may say, "How can you possibly understand me?"

Honesty is the best policy for inquiries like these. A simple analogy to surgery may be helpful. A surgeon does not have to have experienced cancer to be able to help treat it successfully. However, a surgeon must have special expertise regarding the body. Similarly, therapists and counselors are experts in certain aspects of human behavior. It may also help to point out, after responding honestly, that such questions help deflect attention away from the client's gambling problems and toward other concerns. Finally, the use of cotherapists, especially in groups, makes this excuse more difficult for clients to defend.

It is of the utmost importance that recovering people have adequate clinical skills (Egan, 1975). A guarantee for therapeutic failure is to award someone credence to do anything clinically, simply because he or she is recovering. Problems are numerous, and there is a tendency to myopically view all problems as caused by gambling. Furthermore, any untreated personality disorders may be magnified in such persons. Adequate clinical skills are necessary for successful work with other problem gamblers.

ADDITIONAL TREATMENTS AND
CONCERNS: MEDICATIONS

We are somewhat less sanguine about the use of medication than some of the recent clinical articles, but a medication evaluation is almost always necessary. Medications are clearly indicated if the patient is psychotic or manic. Patients who only abuse gambling when they are manic usually do not relate well to the stories in GA. (We have no data regarding how well they do without GA.) We assume their major problems involve medication compliance, as is typical of many bipolar patients (Comer, 1992).

Medications may also be helpful in managing anxiety or depression. Aside from this, some clinical case studies suggest that the selective serotonergic reuptake inhibitors (SSRIs) may be helpful in reducing the core symptoms of gambling (Kalat, 1998). Yet there are problems with medication use that are often overlooked in today's biologically oriented treatment regimens.

Our clinical experience indicates that there are higher attrition rates where medications for gambling disorders are routinely used. (An exception, of course, is the benzodiazepines, which are often highly abusable.) Patients looking for an excuse to terminate treatment may do so because they do not like the "feel" or the side effects of medication. These side effects are usually innocuous, but perhaps as part of the addictive process, they seem particularly likely to be noticed by addicts. In every phase of therapy, the decision whether to "stay on meds" may become the major issue, distracting from other topics that should be more fruitfully addressed. One advantage of the present situation regarding medication administration is that it may reduce ill-founded and distracting expressions of false concerns during therapy. The clinician can simply advise the client to discuss these issues with his or her prescribing physician, and politely refuse to talk about medications.

We have also seen good and occasionally outstanding results with the SSRIs. Issues concerning medication become more complex at this point; dopamine forms a critical link for all reward, including opiates and sedatives (Brick & Erickson, 1998). Data are beginning to suggest that a number of disparate impulsive symptoms may cluster together in the same person

(Coventry & Brown, 1993; McCormick, 1993). Furthermore, this person may have deficits in his or her reward systems that seem to be dopamine-mediated, as we have earlier indicated. What is remarkable is that these symptoms respond at all, in varying degrees, to SSRIs (Stein, Hollander, & Liebowitz, 1993). These drugs, despite occasional chemical differences, work primarily by blocking the reupdate of serotonin (Zuckerman, 1999), which allows for better neural transmission. Even newer drugs, such as nefazadone (Serzone) and mirtazapine (Remeron) are more selective in their action on the serotonin synapse; for example, nefazodone blocks 5ht2a receptors, while augmenting other serotonergic action. This results in reduced anxiety and sexual performance difficulties. Mirtazapine increases noradrenergic and serotonergic neurotransmission via a blockade of central alpha 2 autoreceptors. It also selectively stimulates the 5ht1 type receptor and blocks 5ht2 and 5ht3 type receptors.

The role of serotonin in the dopaminergic loops still remains unclear. Data clearly indicate that the effects of SSRIs are not limited to depression but also seem to have some effectiveness with disorders traditionally labeled as "impulse control." These include gambling, chronic shopping, bulimia, and, perhaps, shoplifting (Becona et al., 1996). This suggests that the so-called "addictive personality" has a low bioavailability of serotonin, among other substances (McCown & Keiser, 2000). With this deficit would also come frequent episodes of moderate depression, possibly accompanied by alcohol abuse, or use of other drugs, and a desire for exaggerated sensation seeking, because such experiences temporarily increase serotonin (Zuckerman, 1999). There may be an underlying continuum or two-dimensional space that characterizes impulsive behavior.

Controlled studies of the effectiveness of SSRIs and other antidepressants are only in their nascent stage. Our experiences are that they help some people quite well, most people only slightly, and many, not at all. Again, this is merely our clinical experience. SSRIs impress us as being less helpful in controlling disordered gambling behavior than they are in breaking through the ubiquitous denial that accompanies addictions. Again, this is merely a clinical observation. Further research is desperately needed.

BIOFEEDBACK: A USEFUL SUPPLEMENT

Previously, we mentioned biofeedback as a useful treatment method. Biofeedback has largely gone out of vogue, for reasons that are outside of the scope of this volume. Therefore, a brief review may be in order. In the 1960s, Neil Miller and several other scientists shocked the scientific world by illustrating that autonomic functions could be controlled through operant methods. Previously, it was believed that only voluntary muscle control benefited from operant training. Thus began 35 years of biofeedback training and application, with insufficient expenditures aimed at research.

Data are fairly consistent that general biofeedback, such as that using skin response or muscle tension, is no more effective than general relaxation treatments. However, we do not underestimate the power of the latter procedure! Biofeedback has had extensive use for patients who cannot relax or who do not know whether they are tense or relaxed. We find it is most helpful for clients whose relapse is prompted by "unconscious" or unrecognized anxiety or physical pain. It may be especially useful for people who have the "illusion of mental health"—people who clearly are impaired but do not recognize that they have seemingly obvious problems, such as anxiety or panic attacks.

Perhaps more promising for the treatment of addiction is a specific type of biofeedback: *EEG biofeedback.* This term refers to at least three separate therapeutic modalities, and each is associated with its own medical or mental health disorders and frequency range in the human EEG spectrum. Alpha biofeedback, the best known type, involves conditioning of EEG activity between 7 and 13 Hz through visual or auditory feedback. It may acknowledge the role of meditation or deep relaxation and is relatively easy to perform. Many of the popular "relaxation machines" that were available a decade ago were crude monitors of alpha EEG waves. Yet there is little good evidence that the degrees of relaxation from EEG activity are better than those obtained through meditation, deep relaxation, or even exercise.

A second form of EEG biofeedback, commonly referred to as beta biofeedback, was developed from operant conditioning, primarily on cats. It involves training in the middle- to high-frequency range (12–20 Hz). It seems to reduce motoric excitability and to restore cortical stability in general, perhaps by increasing the release or blocking the reuptake of GABA, the major inhibitory neurotransmitter in the brain.

The third form, alpha-theta neurofeedback, deals with the lower- to middle-frequency range (4–12 Hz). Data suggest some effectiveness with chemical dependency/alcoholism, depression, and posttraumatic stress disorder (Peniston & Kulkosky, 1989). Its effectiveness may come from its ability to produce transient states during which physiological tone is quieted, regardless of the emotional content being processed by the client. This might provide a window of time and/or psychological capability for delayed frustration and nonreward that a client would not otherwise be able to generate. This type of biofeedback seems especially helpful for "multi-impulsive" personalities—people who have impulsive behavior in a number of different areas in their lives.

To date, there are no controlled studies on EEG biofeedback and gambling, although we hope to follow this route soon. Presently, we have treated patients with this modality as an adjunct. The treatment follows the protocol of Peniston and Kulkosky (1989), involving 15–30-minute sessions, with baseline and follow-up measures. Anecdotal results have been satisfactory and generally align with Peniston and Kulkosky's findings regarding alpha-theta brainwave training in alcoholics. Gambling abstinence has been maintained by one patient for five months and by another for 13 months. (The latter patient has refrained from support through GA attendance because "I hate the whole fucking thing concerned with GA.")

With our current body of knowledge, it is impossible to compare the treatment effectiveness of EEG biofeedback with other components of ongoing services and GA attendance. Ethical concerns limit random assignment of patients to GA versus non-GA modalities. Still, it may be one of the more promising modalities to emerge in recent years. This is especially true if a comprehensive theory is able to link alpha-theta resynchronization to seronergic and dopaminergic deficits that would likely encourage gambling and other impulsive behaviors.

PRAGMATICS OF THE TREATMENT OF GAMBLERS

SCHEDULING CLIENTS

Scheduling of the chronic gambler is one of the most important problems faced by therapists who treat gamblers. It is also one of the first problems encountered. The first indicator that an individual may have an addiction often occurs when the prospective client calls and requests to be seen immediately. Sometimes, these individuals will plead with the therapist to be seen at once, even when the therapist's schedule is completely full. When the client's motivation seems genuine, the therapist is often in an uncomfortable position regarding schedule changes to facilitate an emergency first session (McCown & Johnson, 1993). Too often, the therapist gets burned because the client fails to show up for the "emergency" session. If therapy ever does begin, the therapist carries the memory of having been manipulated.

Our model of chaos theory, presented in Chapter 9, and its relationship to addictions suggest that motivation may wax and wane during the therapeutic process. As we state in later chapters, a change in complex behavior is most likely when a system has reached a critical point. With this in mind, we believe that individuals who seek help for gambling problems should receive a face-to-face evaluation as soon as possible. Unfortunately, this evaluation often involves nothing more than a referral to a GA meeting. We simply do the best with whatever resources we have.

A second question regarding scheduling is: How frequently should gamblers be seen? This remains controversial, even in the most structured outpatient programs (McCormick, 1994). To our knowledge, there are no data that suggest that it is helpful to see gambling outpatient clients more frequently than the standard once-a-week schedule, unless they are in crisis. More frequent intervention may increase dependency and actually decrease the amount of thought and work accomplished by the client between sessions. It may also distract from the major method of support and perhaps of treatment—GA. Again, this is simply clinical conjecture; it lacks sufficient empirical support.

FEES

A major source of contention with gambling clients is the payment of fees. Financial matters are difficult for most therapists to discuss (McCown & Johnson, 1993). They pose an even greater challenge when the persons being treated have been financially irresponsible and may have lost their jobs (Maurer, 1994). They may also place a low priority on responsible behavior, such as paying bills on time (Retzlaff, 1995). Nothing depresses a therapist more than to work intensely with a difficult abusive gambler who subsequently fails to meet the basic financial obligations for services received. Late payment or nonpayment constrains a therapeutic relationship very quickly, and the client may use the inevitable tension as an excuse to justify abruptly quitting treatment (without paying) (Rockland, 1992).

Too often, we have seen clients attempt to pay fees that they owe private practitioners by returning to gambling to make that one "last great score." Consequently, when a large fee has been building up over time and is suddenly paid off in full, a wise therapist should probably conclude that the client is gambling to pay his or her therapy bills! A therapeutic approach that emphasizes eight time-limited series of immediate goals may make treatment of these patients more practical than immediate commitment to longer-term therapy. It can be stated to these clients that such an arrangement may help them decide whether treatment is mutually workable and *affordable*. Behavioral patterns that clearly interfere with future therapy, such as missing sessions or showing up intoxicated, can be cited to the client as appropriate grounds for termination. These patterns may also be signs that interaction between the two parties would not be productive. During this period of time-limited therapy, the therapist can help the client to prepare for continued 12-step work and to deal with any problems involving other attendees at GA.

It should be stipulated that the client must make responsible provisions for fee payment. If fees that the client can afford are not paid within a specific interval, the therapeutic contract can be renegotiated or postponed until the client's financial behavior is more responsible. Those clients who participate in GA's "pressure relief group" can include payment of treatment fees in their new budget. If married or living with other family, others may be notified regarding fees and other policies of the therapist so that they can help assure that the gambler meets his or her obligations.

A consistent policy regarding fees should be articulated clearly in advance and should itemize charges for late cancellations, emergency sessions, between-session telephone calls, and case management. It is wise to discuss these policies directly and to give a signed copy of them to the client, so that there can be no claim that he or she did not realize what the therapist would be billing. Inability to pay a bill may be an excuse for a relapse. Therapists who work with impulsive gamblers must realize that they will necessarily write off a number of accounts receivable from their clients. This is simply a fact of therapy and should not cause undue distress.

HOT LINES AS A METHOD OF TREATMENT ENTRY

Hot lines are in vogue. They are inexpensive, and they can give an appearance that the gaming industry and the state regulators are concerned about chronic gambling. The best thing we can say about hot lines is that they are cheap.

They are only as good as the source to which they refer. In Louisiana, two-thirds of all callers to hot lines are inquiring about betting results or the winning state lottery numbers. We have no evidence that they are a helpful resource, and much evidence that they exist to assuage the guilt of public officials and the gaming industry.

PARTIAL HOSPITALIZATION PROGRAMS

Very frequently, we are asked to discuss the viability of partial hospital programs for persons who are problem or addicted gamblers. Traditionally, partial programs, as they are designated in the psychiatric literature, involve a five-hour to eight-hour daily treatment regimen. The client sleeps at home at night. They are much cheaper than full hospitalization because they reduce the need for a full hospital staff to be available around the clock.

Partial hospitalization programs are useful in the rehabilitation of severe mental illnesses, and they reduce the cost of alcohol rehabilitation. But evidence regarding their efficacy with drug therapy is questionable.

Day treatment programs for chronic gamblers are not particularly advisable; ample gambling opportunities are available during evening and night hours. Unlike chemical dependency units, where drugs can be used to make abused substances unappealing, no magic bullet is available to help a gambler through the evening.

A major advantage of inpatient treatment—safekeeping of the person from the outside environment—is negated by partial programs.

Entrepreneurial therapists will, without sufficient justification, attempt partial hospitalization programs. In our view, such programs have the disadvantages of both inpatient and outpatient treatments with none of the advantages associated with intense isolation from environmental cues and dangers.

ONGOING DYNAMIC THERAPIES: THEIR ROLES AND LIMITS

In our experience, additional therapy—generally, long-term, psychoanalytically oriented therapy—is often sought by people recovering from various addictions. This is especially true when:

1. The addict has a middle-class lifestyle.
2. The addict has achieved a few years of abstinence, but some psychological problems are still evident.
3. During the period of addiction, the addict performed behavior that he or she now regards as shameful.
4. Other people whom the addict knows have had successful experiences in long-term therapy.
5. The addict has achieved a degree of financial stability.

The desire for long-term therapy is perhaps as fundamental to early twenty-first-century North Americans as is the desire to stay healthy. In our opinion, long-term therapy is invaluable for helping people "fix what is broke and avoid breaking what ain't," to quote a rural client of ours. Such therapy may be supportive (Rockland, 1992) or exploratory (Roth & Fonagy, 1996). Long-standing personality issues are often salient in recovering people. Paris (1998) discusses useful methods of triaging and treating some of this "baggage."

Insight-oriented group therapy is becoming less common (Benard & MacKenzie, 1994). This is unfortunate, because a group of recovering people in an insight-oriented modality can produce powerful behavioral changes that supplement 12-step work (Book, 1998). One of the authors (McCown & Keiser, 2000) describes group work with addicts who have exhibited prolonged recovery. Although working with these patients or clients does not produce the immediate and gratifying life changes that abstinence and the early stages of recovery produce, an insight-oriented therapist can help the recovering person achieve a level of social competence, inner peace, and self-awareness that facilities life-long self-healing (Bohart & Tallman, 1999).

In our experience, classic individual psychoanalysis remains contra-indicated for recovering gamblers. Psychoanalysis was pessimistic about the likelihood of recovering from gambling problems. Freud (1929/1950) believed that gambling is like a sexual orgasm, and its uncontrollable urges are similar to those of repetitive masturbation. Previously, we related a clinical account of a patient who used similar terms. This patient, however, achieved a level of abstinence that probably would have surprised Freud, and he no longer thinks of his behavior as being sexual.

Psychoanalytic theory also depicts gambling as an attempt to resolve conflict with authority figures (Galdston, 1968). Herman (1967) believed that gamblers were engaged in masochistic behavior, punishing themselves to appease internalized parent figures. Few of our clients have been able to accept this interpretation. We prefer more cognitive terms. It is often more useful to emphasize the complexities of the concept of Self (Guidano, 1987), rather than the classic tripartite model of personality advocated by the classic analysts.

UNSUCCESSFUL TREATMENTS: LEARNING HOW TO COPE, AND REWARDING ONESELF

For a therapist who works with gamblers, one of the most gratifying moments comes when a client, several years after an apparently unsuccessful treatment, begins paying for these long past services. A brief note usually accompanies the payments. The client states how well he or she is doing. Often, an apology is enclosed, and a statement that the therapist helped the client to "plant a seed." When this happens, the therapist is often at a loss to imagine what he or she could possibly have done to effect the beginning of a change process that sometimes proves to be quite dramatic. It is best not to worry too much. According to chaos theory, people sometimes change for reasons that are unpredictable. The therapist should be glad that he or she is credited for being part of the process.

LEGAL ISSUES

Unfortunately, programs that treat gamblers may be held to a higher standard of service provision than other treatment programs for clients with different diagnoses. Therapists, and programs for gamblers, must realize the inherent legal dangers involved.

In any form of clinical intervention—therapy, diagnostic assessment, consultation, or even a simple referral—potential legal issues are always present and must be considered. In a situation where a client's gambling behavior has been identified, certain specific legal issues may complicate the handling of the case. Therapists treating gambling patients are accountable to some degree, under ethical or case law, and they need to understand this duty in their particular jurisdiction(s). In some situations, a duty to warn overrides client confidentiality.

Although no direct physical danger exists, clinicians cannot fail to wonder whether they may be liable for not warning a family of a compulsive gambler that its life savings are in danger of depletion or loss. If, in the course of therapy for compulsive gambling, a clinician becomes aware of the client's problems, can the clinician be held liable when the client is no longer able to afford basic living expenses? If a family member starts a guardianship proceeding to protect the client's assets, are the records protected by standards of confidentiality and privilege? These complex legal questions have not been answered satisfactorily.

Assuming that many, if not most, voluntary gambling clients present some danger to themselves (due to high suicide rates) or to others (through criminal behavior to secure money) then, in theory, nearly all gambling clients should legally be the subject of some type of warning. Ludicrous as this idea may seem, it points out the need for duty-to-warn guidelines within the community. The importance of detailed written documentation must always be remembered, even when the clinician is busiest.

CHAPTER 8

Assessment of Gambling and Gambling-Related Psychological Disturbances*

I've met gamblers who operate on adrenaline and I've met them that operate on a big yawn and a beat-up set of rosary beads. We're not the same, regardless of what you counselors think. When you try to lump us all together, you make us want to prove that we're different. For us, that's usually gambling.

—Susan H., gambler with five years of abstinence

Why do you need any assessment if you claim they all have the same disease? Don't you know what you are doing?
—Clinical supervisor, managed care company, 1999

GIVEN THE dearth of research regarding gambling, it is not surprising that there are comparatively few assessment tools to measure the intensity of gambling problems and subsequent behavioral changes. The changes are directly associated with problem gambling or with methods of measuring treatment outcome. The absence of assessment tools is in marked contrast to the array available for a practitioner who is interested in measuring depression. Over 65 reliable and valid instruments are available, most of them in published form.

This chapter reviews a number of contemporary instruments that are presently available to assess gambling. In later sections that are perhaps

---

*This chapter is coauthored with Ross Keiser, PhD, Professor and Director of Clinical Training, Northeast Louisiana University.

most relevant to psychologists, we discuss the use of traditional psychological tests for assessing initial psychopathology and subsequent improvement of persons with problem gambling behaviors.

DIAGNOSTIC INSTRUMENTS FOR DIRECTLY ASSESSING GAMBLING BEHAVIOR

The most widely known instrument for the general screening of gambling disorders is the South Oaks Gambling Screen (SOGS). This brief but comprehensive assessment tool was introduced to practitioners in 1987 by the pioneer gambling addictions researcher Henry Lesieur and his associates (e.g., Lesieur, 1989; Lesieur & Blume, 1993). A substantial body of data suggests that the SOGS is both valid and reliable. It can be used for initial screening and for confirming a diagnosis or diagnostic impression. It is the major instrument used in prevalence studies by epidemiologists who attempt to assess the severity of gambling problems. Its results are highly correlated to *DSM-IV* diagnoses derived from more extensive structured interviews. The SOGS is also the most popular instrument for research. It works well in English-speaking countries but is also available in most European languages and some specific Native American dialects. Outstanding results have been obtained using a Spanish version.

As a final advantage, the authors of the SOGS have allowed it to be freely used by researchers and clinicians, as long as items are not revised or the name is not changed. The spirit of scientific cooperation of Lesieur and his associates should be applauded!

Its many advantages recommend the SOGS for novice practitioners as well as experienced researchers. For example, it is easily scored. It has a reading level appropriate for tenth or eleventh graders, which is very useful, given the prevalence of teen gambling. Ladouceur (1996) has used it with students as young as 11 years, in a widespread study and with excellent results. It seems especially useful for research on college students. It uses an easy-to-understand cutoff method of scoring. A score of three or more is equivalent to a "potential pathological gambler"; a score of five or more indicates a "probable pathological gambler." Interpretations are straightforward and do not require complex algorithms or sophisticated training.

Despite its popularity, the SOGS has serious detractors, especially in the academic community. One criticism concerns the number of false positives it may produce. (False positives are people who are labeled as having a diagnosis when in fact they do not.) To an extent, this outcome may be "site-specific." For example, we have observed that the SOGS produces more false positives in southeast Louisiana, an area where, compared to the rest of the nation, there are cultural differences regarding the appropriateness of gambling as a leisure activity. It may also overdiagnose minority and ethnic groups, such as Asian Americans, who may participate in low-stakes gambling because other entertainment options are not afforded to them. Lesieur and Blume (1993) addressed many of these concerns in their 1992 revision of the SOGS and their use of a companion instrument for spouses and significant others.

Other criticisms include the fact that the SOGS fails to consider the frequency of gambling; instead, it emphasizes the intensity. (We do not believe this is a substantial criticism.) In some studies, the SOGS is not sensitive to problem gamblers who are not actually addicted but may be "teetering on the fence." If true, this is a deficit, because this group could benefit most from aggressive intervention. Finally, as noted above, the SOGS has been criticized for a lack of clinical utility in administration. Uncooperative clients can make it unwieldy or make its results uninterpretable. Future researchers need to remember this point, inasmuch as the SOGS and other semistructured tests do not contain reliable scales or validity measures.

Despite these criticisms, the SOGS remains the most popular research and clinical instrument for the assessment of gambling-related disorders. At present, it remains the "gold standard" of psychodiagnostic instruments for the measurement of gambling disorders. It is relevant for both clinicians and researchers. Additional research may help to fine-tune a more definitive diagnostic instrument.

The Massachusetts Gambling Screen (MAGS), a less popular and newer instrument, was developed largely by researchers at Harvard University (Shaffer, LaBrie, Scanlan, & Cummings, 1994). This brief clinical screening instrument can yield an index of nonpathological (NPLG) and pathological (PLG) gambling during a 5- to 10-minute survey or interview. It is useful for both adults and adolescents.

The MAGS was validated with the *Diagnostic and Statistical Manual of Mental Disorders,* Fourth Edition (*DSM-IV*; APA, 1994). Initial data for the MAGS were obtained from a survey of 856 students in three Boston-area high schools. In its initial study, the instrument correctly classified 96% of the adolescent gamblers.

Our own data suggest a high test–retest reliability for this instrument, but a somewhat shaky factor structure. It may be that both the MAGS and the SOGS are *differentially* sensitive to diverse aspects of the gambling experience. Each may tap a different subset of problem gamblers, as suggested by data from our research group. In college students ($N = 322$), we found correlation of only .54 between two of these measures, suggesting that while there is indeed some overlap of construct, there is also a great deal of variance that is not common. (Psychometrically oriented readers might also note that this correlation should probably be attenuated to remove method variance from a paper-and-pencil test.)

Two attempts have been made to construct extremely brief screening inventories regarding potential problem gambling behaviors. Westphal and associates (Westphal & Rush, 1996), at Louisiana University Medical School in Shreveport, have constructed the "Felt Guilty/Kept Betting" scale, which asks two questions:

1. "During the past year, have you felt guilty about the way you gamble or what happens when you gamble?"
2. "Have you ever spent more time or money than you intended gambling?"

The reliability and validity of this instrument for populations outside of those for which it was normed are not clear. However, it appears to be a very useful screening inventory, although perhaps erring on the side of false positives. It seems to be especially helpful for telephone studies of gambling, a difficult area in which these researchers have excelled.

A prior attempt to construct a very brief questionnaire is the "Lie/Bet" questionnaire. It also asks two questions:

1. "Have you ever felt the need to bet more and more money?"
2. "Have you ever lied to people important to you about how much you gamble?"

Again, psychometric properties are unclear. The science of test construction makes it much more likely that longer tests will be more reliable and valid. On the other hand, brief screening devices such as these are useful for epidemiological research, public health campaigns, and primary care screenings. We have found a correlation of only .45 ($N = 384$) between the "Lie/Bet" and the "Felt Guilty/Kept Betting" instruments, which suggests that they may tap different aspects of the problem-gambling experience and continuum.

One of the best known measures is not a traditional psychometric inventory at all. It is the Gamblers Anonymous "Twenty Questions" (Gamblers Anonymous, n.d.). According to GA, affirmative responses to seven or more questions may indicate a problem with gambling. An advantage of the 20-question inventory is that it taps some of the phenomenological knowledge of gamblers. It talks about issues that problem gamblers experience. Besides having appropriate face validity, it works superbly as the basis of a motivational interview.

On the other hand, this inventory has no clear factor structure. We have repeatedly factor-analyzed it and found between two and seven factors on various occasions, with results dependent on the various populations sampled. Moreover, all of the questions are not equally weighted. For example, question 15 concerns gambling to escape worry and trouble. This item should probably not be as heavily weighted as question 20, which concerns contemplation of self-destruction as a result of gambling. The clinician is in somewhat of a quandary when a person answers in the nonproblem direction for most responses, except question 20. How is this to be interpreted?

Technically, we would be forced to say that the person who answered in this fashion did not have a gambling problem. On the other hand, common sense tells us otherwise. The "instrument" may be more suited to weighting by alternative test construction methods, such as Rasch scaling or other Item Response Theory methodologies. This is a question for future research. Meanwhile, we continue to use it, primarily because it resonates quite well with people who have gambling problems.

ASSESSMENT TOOLS SPECIFICALLY DESIGNED FOR ADOLESCENTS

We have previously discussed the MAGS (Shaffer et al., 1994). Our clinical impression is that it works well for adolescents. Other instruments have also been designed especially for adolescents. The Texas Council on Problem and Compulsive Gambling (1996) has adapted the Gamblers Anonymous "Twenty Questions" to make them specific to the unique gambling patterns of adolescents. The Council states that this tool can be used to determine whether a young person has a problem with gambling; however, it freely admits that this tool is not a psychometrically valid diagnostic instrument, but might be useful in working with adolescents in the assessment stage. Affirmative responses to seven or more of the questions may indicate a problem with gambling, but the problem of weighting the items remains.

A more psychometrically sophisticated instrument based on the "20 questions" has been constructed by a group at Louisiana State University Medical Center (Westphal & Rush, 1996). It is based on the SOGS, but it also measures other abnormal or deviant behaviors. It has been used extensively in Louisiana and appears to be both psychometrically adequate and clinically useful.

Winters et al. (1993) have designed a psychometric instrument that is based on the SOGS but is particularly relevant for adolescents. The scale was administered to 1,101 adolescents (aged 15–18 years) as part of a statewide gambling survey. Study results indicated that the scale had moderate internal consistency reliability and was significantly related to alternate measures of problem severity for male subjects. The authors are careful to note that since not enough is known about adolescent female gamblers, care needs to be taken when using any instrument with this population.

Given the severity of the problem, it is not surprising that several research groups are working on devising parsimonious scales to measure gambling disorders. One is based on Item Response Theory (IRT), a mathematically sophisticated procedure for scaling the value of test items. Because extensive computations are required, these procedures became practical only with the increasing availability of computers. With IRT-scaled items, the assumptions regarding the appropriateness of comparisons across groups and ages are more easily made. Furthermore, with the use of computer-assisted assessment, IRT-scaled items can be administered in a very brief period, making them more appropriate to the often transient attention span of young people.

COLLEGE STUDENT
GAMBLING INVENTORY

Regarding college students, the only formal diagnostic tool that we have worked with is the College Student Gambling Inventory (McCown, 1997). This is a paper-and-pencil instrument with high internal consistency (*alpha* = .89) and high test–retest reliability (.85 for three months). It has been used in a number of studies, mostly in Louisiana, and appears to have adequate concurrent and predictive validity. The internal consistency of this scale is .87 ($N = 832$), with a test–retest reliability of .81 over a one-month period.

Hutton (1998) showed that the test–retest reliability and correlation of this instrument with symptoms of anxiety and depression could be increased by administration of this test through computer methodology. He cites literature that states that, for socially proscribed behaviors, people will admit more potential deviance to a computer than to a piece of paper, even if the former has identification and the latter does not.

Table 8.1 reproduces the questions composing the College Student Gambling Inventory. This inventory may be freely copied as long as it is not distributed for financial gain and is not altered.

FAMILY ASSESSMENT

We are aware of only one assessment device commonly employed with families: Lesieur and Blume's (1993) South Oaks Leisure Activities

Table 8.1
College Student Gambling Inventory*

1.	I've spent more money than I planned to on gambling.	1 2 3 4 5 6 7
2.	Gambling cuts down my study time.	1 2 3 4 5 6 7
3.	I feel I can't have a good time when I go out unless I gamble.	1 2 3 4 5 6 7
4.	I have felt guilty over gambling.	1 2 3 4 5 6 7
5.	I gamble to relieve stress.	1 2 3 4 5 6 7
6.	I gamble longer than I initially planned to.	1 2 3 4 5 6 7
7.	I worry about my gambling.	1 2 3 4 5 6 7
8.	I feel my grades would be better if I didn't gamble.	1 2 3 4 5 6 7
9.	I'd have less financial problems if I didn't gamble.	1 2 3 4 5 6 7
10.	I'd have more spending money if I didn't gamble.	1 2 3 4 5 6 7
11.	When I lose at gambling, I don't want to quit until I win money back.	1 2 3 4 5 6 7
12.	I borrow money to gamble.	1 2 3 4 5 6 7
13.	I worry about owing money to people because of gambling.	1 2 3 4 5 6 7
14.	I feel that gambling makes a good evening even better.	1 2 3 4 5 6 7
15.	My friends gamble.	1 2 3 4 5 6 7
16.	My family or friends think I gamble too much.	1 2 3 4 5 6 7
17.	Sometimes I gamble in secret, so no one will know I am playing.	1 2 3 4 5 6 7
18.	Sometimes I run short of money because I've gambled too much.	1 2 3 4 5 6 7
19.	I feel I would have a better social life if I didn't gamble as much.	1 2 3 4 5 6 7
20.	I gamble when I know I should be studying.	1 2 3 4 5 6 7
21.	I have had a strong urge to gamble.	1 2 3 4 5 6 7
22.	I have enjoyed gambling.	1 2 3 4 5 6 7

*The computerized version of the College Student Gambling Inventory is available from Danny Hutton, MS, Instructional Technology, School of Education, Strauss Hall, University of Louisiana at Monroe, 700 University Avenue, Monroe, LA 71209.

Screen (SOLAS). This instrument appears very promising but may lack sufficient empirical research for routine clinical work at this time. It is definitely not recommended for the assessment of gamblers' difficulties in the absence of other data.

More popular among recovering people is the Gamblers Anonymous questionnaire: "Are You Living with a Compulsive Gambler?" This somewhat informal questionnaire does not claim to possess sophisticated psychometric qualities. It was not designed for reliability or validity, but it is helpful in reducing the denial experienced by families. To date, it has not been factor-analyzed. Our clinical impression is that it is a useful instrument to provoke self-reflection regarding codependent and enabling behavior among gamblers' significant others.

Other family therapy instruments that have different purposes but are often relevant to the problems of gamblers and their families are reviewed by L'Abate (1994). L'Abate is a well-known family therapist who has consistently recognized the importance of systematic assessment prior to and during family intervention. Inasmuch as family pathology is closely related to gambling behavior, practitioners might do well to administer one of several diagnostic inventories to the entire family system. This may provide a baseline to assess eventual change.

TRADITIONAL PSYCHOLOGICAL TESTS

Traditional psychological testing—a comprehensive battery of objective and projective tests—has never been particularly popular with persons who treat addictions—gambling or otherwise. One reason may be that personality factors are considered secondary to the "real" problem, the disease of addiction (McCown & Keiser, 2000). However, as we have seen in previous chapters, the development and maintenance of gambling behavior are multifaceted and involve a complex skein of genetic, environmental, learning, and personality factors, as well as chance. Therefore, we believe that a systematic psychological and psychosocial evaluation is central to successful treatment interventions.

The following sections discuss our research findings with popular psychological instruments. Clinicians using the same instruments may wish to pool data, to develop a larger and more valid normative base. Such persons are urged to contact the authors for participation in this collaborative effort.

The Minnesota Multiphasic Personality Inventory (the MMPI-2)

Perhaps the most popular of all psychometric instruments is the MMPI and its recent revision, the MMPI-2 (Meyer & Deitsch, 1996). We routinely use this instrument, and we collaborate with other investigators to obtain data. In our research with the MMPI-2 ($N = 387$), we have found two clearly distinct clusters of chronic problem gamblers existing across different sites. These clusters account for about 56% of all people in treatment. A third cluster appears in some gambling populations, but not all.

The first cluster is marked by persons who score in elevated directions on Scales 1, 2, and 3. They generally score in the below-normal or "depressed" ranges on scales 9 and zero. They appear to represent an anxious and sympathetically overaroused group of persons who gamble primarily to distract themselves from their miserable internal states. Classic descriptions of such people without gambling problems depict

Assessment of Gamblers

A brief description of some clinical measures

MMPI-2

The MMPI-2 is a true-false test consisting of 667 items. Designed for adults, there is also an adolescent form, the MMPI-A. There are a multitude of scales, subscales, and profiles associated with various characteristics. There are ten basic scales, numbered 1 through 0, and three basic validity scales. These are interpreted both individually and in combination with other scales. The names of the scales date from the original norming groups in the 1930s, and should not be taken literally. Also, the scales are not fully independent, many sharing items with other scales.

Scale	Traditional Name Validity Scales	Clinical Correlates
L	Lie	Naive defensiveness, denial, refusal to admit faults
F	Frequency	Openness to admission of faults, faking bad
K	Correction	Subtle defensiveness
	Basic Clinical Scales	
1	Hypochondriasis	Concern with health and body issues
2	Depression	Dysthymia, low self-esteem, discontent, pessimism
3	Hysteria	Denial, naivete, somatic concerns, neurotic defenses
4	Psychopathic Deviate	Antisocial attitudes and behaviors, anger, hostility
5	Masculinity-Femininity	Traditional sex-role interests, activity/passivity
6	Paranoia	Suspiciousness, interpersonal dissatisfaction
7	Psychasthenia	Anxiety, agitated depression, obsessiveness, poor concentration
8	Schizophrenia	Psychotic ideation and symptoms, alienation, dysphoria
9	Mania	High energy and activity, distractibility, flightiness, amorality
0	Social Introversion	Shyness, alienation, social discomfort and avoidance
	Some Supplemental Scales	
Es	Ego Strength	High scores tend to indicate good candidates for therapy
A	Anxiety	Inhibition, maladjustment
R	Repression	High scores tend to suggest disinhibition
MACR	MacAndrews Rev.	Generally interpreted by using a raw score, rather than a T score; correlates with substance abuse
O-H	Overcontrolled Hostility	Correlates with a high degree of control over emotional expression, often seen in assaultive individuals

them as having a host of neurotic or autonomic disturbances, with little insight and even less energy. Depression frequently dominates their presentation, but they may deny these symptoms, especially if their F scale (a validity measure) is elevated. About 30% of people we have treated show this cluster. Women and video gamblers are disproportionately represented in this group.

The second type of profile involves elevations on scales 9 and (possibly) 4, and a low scale 0. This suggests a classic profile of a serious table gambler. About 26% of people we have interviewed meet these criteria: They are likely to be male; they gamble at tables, including poker games and games of chance where there are dealers; and they gamble for higher stakes. The 4/9 pattern is very common among gamblers with antisocial personalities (but also with graduate students!). Classic 4/9 gamblers may be forced into treatment if they are young, uneducated, and of lower intelligence. Otherwise, they are usually "too sophisticated" to believe they have a problem. This is especially true if there is an elevation on the validity scale K.

More cognitively sophisticated persons can also have this profile. When they seek treatment, it is usually for depression or for very serious financial and legal problems. For example, serious securities speculators usually do not get treatment until their world, including their finances, collapses. People who have embezzled money for risky ventures often have this profile.

Usually, a 4/9/2 pattern is seen in response to failing to score the "big win." It represents depression, which is usually acute but then goes away the next time the gambler succeeds. However, the prognosis for persons with an elevated 2 may be better than for others with a similar profile who are experiencing little dysphoria. An elevation of scale 7 is also frequently seen. People with a 4/9/7 pattern almost always have a substance abuse problem as well, and this makes treatment much more difficult (McCown & Keiser, 2000).

As we have noted, a third cluster representing elevations on scales 6, 7, and 8 has emerged in some studies but not in others. The basic pathology here appears to be related to misconceptions about the world and a failure to understand the basic laws of probability. These problems may be largely culturally based and are more likely to occur among the poor or other socially deprived groups. In our very limited experience of administering the adolescent MMPI to teenagers with gambling problems, we have seen an elevation in this direction in about half of the cases. However, this number is well under 50, and no firm clinical conclusions can be drawn from this preliminary pattern.

Other patterns have been more rarely observed, but they warrant attention because they may involve complicating factors that potentially interfere with traditional gambling treatment. The 2/4/7 pattern is common among passive aggressive persons (Meyer & Deitsch, 1996), and, in our experience, among alcoholics who also have gambling problems. These people tend to be fearful of treatment and may become worried enough to sabotage any treatment efforts. They may be very meticulous regarding religious issues, but will use gambling as an escape from otherwise rigid lifestyles. Anecdotal accounts suggest that this profile is more common among Southern fundamentalists who have gambling problems, but we do not know whether this is true.

In general, the prognosis for the 2/7 gambler is fairly good; psychotherapy is probably also indicated. The prognosis becomes less favorable the more the 4 is elevated. A high point 4 is generally a negative treatment indicator, regardless of the other elevations. However, the clinician who treats a gambler with a 2/7 profile does well to seek supervision regarding the inevitable obstacles to treatment such a person will present: frequently forgetting appointments, showing up late or on the wrong day, and always neglecting to pay fees!

Rarely will people with problem gambling behaviors show a 4/3 or 3/4 profile. People with either of these profiles tend to be very aggressive and angry, often with their spouses (McCown & Keiser, 2000). They may also be avoidant personalities who, beyond amusing themselves with gambling, do not have any other method of entertainment. Inhibitions about gambling may be suddenly overcome with a flood of positive feelings that seem to desensitize reasoning processes. Actually, this pattern is more common in spouses of gamblers than in the problem gamblers themselves.

A Spike 9 profile is similar to a 9/8/6 profile. For gamblers, it occurs when they develop problems that involve odd or eccentric and fantastic theories. Their judgment is typically poor. In chronic gamblers, a Spike 9 profile is likely to indicate drug abuse and antisocial tendencies, along with gambling. These people tend to bet on practically anything. Mania must also be ruled out, as is specified in the *DSM-IV*.

The content scores of the MMPI may also be of some value. Anxiety is often elevated in avoidance gamblers; their symptoms include low self-confidence, distractibility, and sleep problems. These people are likely to feel pessimistic and depressed or perpetually stressed. They often will show withdrawal during attempts to avoid relapse.

Persons who score high on the obsessive content scale ruminate odd thoughts and may be especially prone to gambling if the bizarre mentation scale is elevated. These people believe in magical thinking, are obsessed with the idea of luck, and search for signs that it is their lucky day. For example, they may be convinced that they need to gamble because they are in a lucky phase, as indicated by a horoscope or other idiosyncratic "informer." For example, they may cruise a casino for long periods of time until they "feel" their lucky slot machine or card dealer has been identified.

It is also useful to examine the low self-esteem and work interference scales. We do not have data to determine whether negative treatment indicators relate to success in therapy or in 12-step groups, but this work is continuing.

Persons who score high on the MacAndrew Scale (MAC) usually represent risk-taking, outgoing, assertive gamblers who gamble for self-stimulation. They frequently are similar to people who demonstrate disinhibitory sensation seeking (Zuckerman, 1979). These people generally prefer table gambling because it is more exciting and involves more social contacts. When they do play the slots, they play erratically and with the highest-stakes machines they can find. The MAC seems to be a good predictor of gamblers' inability to quit while ahead. Perhaps it represents the purest measure of potential disinhibition on the MMPI-2 (Meyer & Deitsch, 1996).

We must emphasize that the MMPI-2 is useful in the manner described above only for elucidating the problems of people who have a confirmed diagnosis of a gambling disorder. It is not a diagnostic instrument of gambling behavior per se, nor is it a screening instrument. We must stress that no "dedicated MMPI gambling scales" have been discovered to date. The MMPI alone produces too many false positives. Although the MMPI can't be used solely as a diagnostic tool, it is useful in planning treatment to address particular issues, patterns and needs that emerge in the results. For example, if there is a high level of depression noted in the pattern, that should be a focus of treatment. *Therefore, it should be used in suspected problem gamblers only after a diagnosis is confirmed and the clinician desires insight on the specific problems of the gambler in treatment.*

The Rorschach Test

Until very recently, there has been little interest in the Rorschach for addictions research and treatment (McCown & Keiser, 2000). However, this attitude is beginning to change, now that the Rorschach is clearly on a firmer empirical basis.

Like the MMPI-2, the Rorschach has at least two clusters of discriminants among problem and addicted gamblers. These seem to represent one group of people who are underaroused and gamble for sensation-seeking purposes, and another group who form a pathologically over-aroused subset for whom gambling is primarily a distraction from internal dysphoria. There is no evidence that these clusters are related to the severity of the problem at hand. They are only replicable subtypes with treatment implications.

On the Rorschach, it is common to find the following pattern among "low arousal" gamblers: a high number of space responses, adequate human movement, excessive active movement, generally good form quality, an elevated affective ratio, and generally low shading or texture, indicative of little self-perception (McCown & Keiser, 2000). On the other hand, narcissism is usually evidenced by the larger-than-usual number of pairs and reflections. In gamblers who are thrill-oriented, ES, the Rorschach variable, is often less than the variable EA; these people are feeling less stimulation than they are actually experiencing. This is usually a negative treatment indicator. An elevated FM score, especially FM > M, is also common with impulsive gamblers.

Among high-arousal gamblers, it is common to find elevated V, Y, and, consequently, DEPI and S-Con. Coping resources may also be impaired. Low W responses, common in this group, indicate that the clients' aspirations are generally lower than their abilities. These responses are typical of people who, even for a few minutes, want the chance to purchase the dream of "getting something big for nothing," as one client described the desired reward.

Isolate R, the isolation index, attempts to describe the desire of the individual as isolated and withdrawn from other people (Exner, 1991). The lower the number, the less withdrawn the person. This number is often elevated for solitary gamblers and low for underaroused gamblers. A large number of isolate R suggests that the person will not do well in self-help or traditional 12-step groups.

Elevated C and CF > F are commonly found for both underaroused and overaroused gamblers. The affective ratio indicates that these clients are psychologically receptive to emotionally provoking stimuli. The normal values range between .47 and .75. Lower values are often associated with solitary gambling—usually, with machines, bingo, or horse racing. A high value is often seen in people who go on gambling binges and may report either an amnesic response or an analgesia (an extreme high) following these episodes. The Rorschach variable ES is generally low in many gamblers, which probably indicates a generalized low tolerance for any type of stress and frustration. Gamblers are caught up in a vicious cycle: They gamble to relieve stress, but are stressed because they gamble.

m, which seems to represent biobehavioral response to uncontrollable stress (McCown, Fink, Galina, & Johnson, 1992), may be elevated in either type of gambler, depending on the situation. A low ES and an abundance of *m* usually indicate a person who is caught up in the cycle of chasing, described in Chapter 3. Gambling becomes simultaneously reinforcing and stressful; it is associated with both relief and further losses. Elevation in the number of *m* responses in a person with a higher ES is, of course, rare. It would indicate that the gambler has experienced temporary stresses

The Rorschach

The Rorschach has gained a wide and well earned notoriety due to problems in interpreting so-called "projective" tests. However, with John Exner's *Comprehensive System,* this test can be a reliable and valid test. Test results from examiners not using the *Comprehensive System* should probably be discarded without consideration.

The Rorschach consists of ten pictures of inkblots, to which the subject responds to the question, "What might this be." The verbal responses are coded (often called, mistakenly, scored) in order to reduce the unlimited variety of verbiage to a discrete number of variables which can be statistically manipulated.

The variables of the Rorschach are generally interpreted by comparing various frequencies and ratios to those of norm and sample groups. In general, some of the most common and useful codes and concepts are as follow:

Code	Name	Clinical Correlates
R	Responses	High—productive or obsessive Low—rigid, withholding
L	Lambda	High—rich protocol Low—meager protocol
EB	Erlebnistypus	A ratio: weighted to left, introverted, to the right, extroverted
D	D Score	Adjustment: minus scores indicate overwhelming stress
Adj. D	adjusted D	Chronic Adjustment: removes situational stress from D Score
EA	Experience Actual	Amount of coping resources available
es	Experienced Stimulation	Amount of stress experienced
2	Pairs	Indicates self interest and ego-centrism
r	Reflections	Narcissism
FD	Form Dimension	Introspection
Mor	Morbid Responses	Sense of self damage or inadequacy
Fd	Food	Suggests dependency
P	Popular	Conformity
X+%	Good Form Quality	Accurate perceptions
X-%	Poor Form Quality	Inaccurate perceptions, psychopathology
M	Human Movement	Intelligence, planning
FM	Animal Movement	Stress, internal stress
m	Inanimate Movement	Situational stress
y	Diffuse shading	Situational stress
V	Vista	Negative introspection
C'	Achromatic Color	Pessimism
T	Texture	Need for affection
S	Space	Opposition, divergent thinking

Ratio	Traditional Name	Clinical Correlates
2AB+Art+Ay	Intellectualization	Use of intellectualization as a defense
Isolate/R	Isolation Index	Use of isolation as a defense
H:(H)Hd(Hd)	Interpersonal Interest	Object relations
3r+(2)/R	Egocentricity Index	Self Centeredness
Blends/R	Complexity Index	Complexity of thought
An+Xy	Anatomy and XRay	Fear of harm
SumC'; WSumC	Constriction Ratio	Freedom of emotional expression
Sum6	Sum Special Scores	Cognitive slippage—frequency
Wsum6	Weighted sum six	Degree of Cognitive Slippage

Constellation	Traditional Name	Clinical Correlates
SCZI	Schizophrenia	Psychosis
DEPI	Depression	Distress (note: this shows upset, not clinical depression)
CDI	Coping Deficit	Inadequate Personality
S-CON	Suicide	Potential for self harm
HVI	Hypervigilance	Suspiciousness, mistrust
OBS	Obsessive Style	Rigidity

that have not been incorporated into his or her cognitive schema. High-stakes gamblers who experience a string of bad luck may show elevations in *m;* this Rorschach variable appears acutely sensitive to situational factors. In fact, *m* is one of the few variables that can be experimentally manipulated in the laboratory by arranging for a series of gambling losses.

In combination with an elevation in the number of space responses, a high affective ratio often indicates a tendency toward antisocial behavior (Meyer & Deitsch, 1996). These people are at risk for committing crimes to pay for their gambling. Usually, there are corroborating data from the MMPI-2, such as an elevation in Scale 4. Although this is more common in underaroused gamblers, it may also occur in overaroused gamblers who have chased too long.

When Mp is greater than Ma, the gambler is likely to be suffering from the "Snow White Syndrome" of denial. As a defense against problems, this client will often withdraw to a personal fantasyland to await a magic person or experience that will carry away the problems. The client has little acceptance of responsibility, and little genuine self-direction is present. However, this type of person often functions extremely well in GA, because his or her dependent needs are transferred to the group.

Similarly, an elevated texture response indicates that the person is ready for the group work involved in recovery. A high number of texture responses (T > 4) indicates people who are likely to develop strong dependencies on 12-step programs. Texture responses of 0 are often found in people who were ordered into treatment by a court and are not interested in behavioral change. Clients who score between these extremes probably have the best prognosis. Excessive meeting dependence can lead to abrupt relapse if a meeting is missed.

A low Zd score is found with both types of gamblers; it indicates a haphazard style, possible carelessness, or a tendency toward depression or anxiety. It is pathognomonic only when a low Zd is combined with a high (> 115) IQ. This pattern seems to be common in gamblers who are about to "bottom out" (McCown & Keiser, 2000).

Regarding "magic ideation gamblers," discussed above as a potential third group, clients who have M- on their protocols are often at risk for having peculiar ideation. They frequently believe in a variety of types of sleight of hand, but are usually able to delay gambling until they feel that an external influence has made them lucky. Typically, the W Sum scores of people in this range are greater than 6, almost always indicating at least an occasional degree of cognitive slipping. This type of person may also produce a low F+% score, which often indicates inappropriate logic and poor judgment capabilities. People with these low scores do not usually see the world as the rest of us do. They believe strongly in the magic and vagaries of luck. Often, they do best with religiously proscribed injunctions or authoritative pronouncements.

The 16 PF

The 16 PF (Personality Factor) test is a paper-and-pencil measure of 16 correlated traits of personality that are found in nonclinical and clinical populations (Cattell, 1989). Data regarding gambling and discrete patterns found with the 16 PF are limited. This is especially true in the fifth or newest revision of this instrument, which in many ways resembles a new test more than a revision (Meyer & Deitsch, 1996).

Our experience suggests that table gamblers tend to have elevations on scores A, F, and H, and low scores on N and Q2. Their tough-mindedness is also indicated by low scores on I, M, and QA1. Lack of self-control is indicated by high scores on F, a low score on G, a high score on M, and a low score on Q3.

More anxious, usually solitary gamblers have low scores on A, F, H, and, especially, Q2. They are usually prone to more anxiety, as indicated by elevation of L, O, and Q4, and a low score on C. Usually, there is a

The 16 PF

The 16 Personality Factor Questionnaire (16 PF-5) is the most recent edition of this true-false test. It is much like the MMPI in format. However, it was designed to measure normal, rather than pathological individuals, from ages 16 through adult, and has only 185 questions. In addition to 16 primary factors, there are 5 "global" or secondary factors.

The factors are expressed by 10-point scales, and each represents a continuum, such as warm vs. reserved. High scores (over 7) indicate the terms on the left, i.e., Warmth or Reasoning, while low scores (3 and below) reflect those on the right. Average scores (four through seven) show a relative balance on the traits.

16 Factors

Scale	Name	Opposite	Clinical Correlates
A	Warmth	vs. Reserved	Sociable vs. aloof and rejecting
B	Reasoning	vs. Concrete	Able to abstract, mentally flexible vs. rigid
C	Stable	vs. Reactive	Ego strength and maturity vs. Irritability and upset
E	Dominant	vs. Deferential	Tough, independent, and independent vs. needy
F	Lively	vs. Serious	Enthusiastic vs. introspective, intro- vs. extra-vert
G	Rule-Conscious	vs. Expedient	Conscientious and responsible vs. unreliable
H	Socially Bold	vs. Shy	Friendly and open vs. constricted and shy
I	Sensitive	vs. Utilitarian	Aesthetic and empathic vs. tough and realistic
L	Vigilant	vs. Trusting	Suspicious and jealous vs. relaxed and trusting
M	Abstract	vs. Grounded	Intuitive and imaginative vs. practical and sensible
N	Private	vs. Forthright	Socially astute and aloof vs. open and disclosing
O	Apprehensive	vs. Self-Assured	Insecure vs. confident, especially in the social sphere
Q1	Open to Change	vs. Traditional	Impatient vs. staid
Q2	Self-Reliant	vs. Group Oriented	Independent vs. dependent
Q3	Perfectionistic	vs. Tolerates Disorder	Over-controlled vs. identity diffusion and impulsive
Q4	Tense	vs. Relaxed	Anxious and tight vs. relaxed

Second-Order Factors

Scale	Name	Opposite	Clinical Correlates
QI	Extraversion	vs. Introversion	Outgoing and independent vs. group-dependent
QII	Anxiety	vs. Dynamic Integrity	Guilty and anxious vs. high ego strength
QIII	Tough Poise	vs. Sentimentality	Realistic and decisive vs. emotional and flighty
QIV	Independence	vs. Subduedness	Hostile and self sufficient vs. dependent and passive
QV	Behavior Control	vs. Sociopathy	Group conforming vs. rule rejecting

struggle of some type for independence from an authority figure, as indicated by elevations on scales E, H, L, and Q. However, in normal subjects, these scales usually all correlate positively. Ambivalence toward independence may be indicated by a mixture of high and low scores on these scales.

Again, none of these instruments is sufficiently sophisticated to discriminate persons with gambling problems from persons with other psychiatric or psychological disorders. Instead, these instruments are most useful for determining treatment planning, including the psychomedical necessity of inpatient treatment and the presence or absence of Axis I or Axis II pathologies that can complicate treatment (Magnavita, 1997).

PERSONALITY DISORDERS

Well over 60% of gamblers may have personality disorder (McCown & Keiser, 2000). The Millon series of personality instruments, while outstanding (Retzlaff, 1995), is usually too expensive to be used routinely with indigent patients (Ogles et al., 1996). This is an unfortunate reality of contemporary mental health services. Millon's work is masterful; his diagnostic instruments have an artistic flair, in addition to their clinical capacity to discriminate successfully. They are, however, simply too expensive. And, just as unfortunate, gamblers with problems severe enough to warrant treatment usually are included in this group of patients who do not receive state-of-the-art diagnostic assessment.

Because of the affordability and free-per-use cost, we now routinely use the Personality Disorders Questionnaire IV, Revised (PDQ 4 R; Hyler et al., 1990). This instrument is especially helpful because it is self-administered and can show change over a period of time. Subjects tend to disclose more with this instrument than they would in a clinical interview. Unfortunately, little is known about the sensitivity and specificity of this test for gamblers. Still, information regarding personality disorders is important for clinical use and for research purposes.

A variety of personality disorders may be identifiable from any of the three disorder clusters in the *DSM-IV*. Their relationship to the severity of a person's gambling and to the possibility of recovery is only now being fully appreciated. Personality disorders may not cause gambling problems, as we stated in earlier chapters. Instead, they may arise in response to chronic gambling behaviors. Whatever their origins, their existence complicates treatment and usually warrants longer-term therapy, including supportive individual therapy (Pinsker, 1997).

THE THEMATIC APPERCEPTION TEST AND THE THEORY OF MOTIVES: BEYOND ASSESSMENT AND INTO THEORIES OF CAUSATION

Murray's Thematic Apperception Test (McClelland, 1987) may be very useful for determining both some possible etiological factors and the potentially successful treatment strategies associated with gambling. This is true, however, only if thematic material is scored quantitatively and for motivational content (McCown & Keiser, 2000). We do not refrain from the excellent work being conducted in this domain regarding object relations. However, we have not yet been able to integrate it into a gambling treatment paradigm.

McClelland, Atkinson, and their research associates (e.g., McClelland, 1987) have conducted extensive research in the psychology of motivation. Their major focus has been on how individual differences in the strength of human motives are to be measured, especially thought or fantasy. The number of articles published by these researchers and their associates exceeds 1,000, yet few are actively cited by today's scholars. This is truly regrettable because these authors have managed to link areas as diverse as Freudian theory, Hullian mathematical learning postulates, biological psychology, and the now very fashionable area of narrative and personal construct psychology.

A motive, according to McClelland (1987), is a largely unconscious cause of spontaneous behavior. Motives, according to McClelland and his once prolific research group, are important for predicting what people will spontaneously do, whereas values are more important for determining what they will cognitively decide that they should do.

Five major motive systems have been examined in detail: (1) Achievement Motives (n Ach), (2) Power Motives (n P), (3) Affiliation Motives (n Aff), (4) Avoidance Motives (n Av), and (5) Intimacy Motives (n Int). Several of these will be discussed below. The Need for Power (n P) will be emphasized because it has the most impact on causation of addictive behaviors.

Individuals high in n P are more sensitive to power-related stimuli than to neutral stimuli, as demonstrated by a variety of experiences. For example, they recall more peak experiences that are described in power terms. Persons who score high on the need for power resemble those with serotonergically based depressive symptoms (McCown & Keiser, 2000). Often, they are unhappy and impulsive. In laboratory tasks, they tend to bet excessively in large amounts. Individuals high in the need for power can appear powerful by collecting symbols of power or prestige (McClelland, 1987).

Although we have stated that extroversion correlates negatively with slot play, alcohol, which causes a state similar to extroversion, may increase gambling incentives and motives. It has been found (in men, but not yet in women) that those who are forced by a laboratory situation to feel inadequate about life's responsibilities often drink to feel more powerful. We have recently replicated this finding with gambling. It has also been found that drinking increases power concerns and decreases inhibitory thinking.

Related to this is the tendency of gamblers, as they drink, to go through a biphasic process: Moderate drinking is associated with fantasies about the social good that could be achieved with the winnings. Heavy drinking, however, is associated with fantasies that are more significantly concerned with personal power. In the heavy drinker, losses are seen as a deep deprival of personal power, causing strong motivation to continue to play (or to chase). In this manner, although extraversion is related to less play, it is related to more persistence.

Subjects who are high in the n Ach prefer being personally responsible for performance results (McCown & Keiser, 2000). In this way, they feel satisfaction when they do something good. As a rule, subjects who are high in n Ach tend to prefer moderate risks to very short or very long odds. Furthermore, they prefer gambling that involves some upscale skills, such as poker or sports handicapping.

Subjects who are high in the n Ach may be especially susceptible to sports betting, because they need frequent feedback regarding their performance success. Often, they will bet just to show that they are right. Consequently, they scan their environments for opportunities for gambling, and they frequently test new theories. They tend to disagree with magic, ideas of luck, or trusting in superstition. At the racetrack, for example, subjects who score high in n Ach are much more likely to buy and study a racing form than persons who score low on this motive.

Therapy for persons who score high in the n Ach involves allowing them to meet these needs in other areas, including those that involve increased social interest. In fact, for persons who are high on n Ach, this alternative activity is frequently most effective.

Persons who are low in n Ach tend to avoid receiving feedback regarding their performance. As a result, they often avoid realizing their losses but quickly recognize their winnings.

Another motivation is relevant to our discussion. Some people have strong fears of failure. These fears can be measured in fantasy or other tests. The causes of fear of failure have been highlighted. In essence, they are as follows: A parent says, "You must be better, but I know you can't."

Parents who were rigid and mean tended to produce children with a strong fear of failure.

Persons who experience fear of failure have a tendency to gamble with either the lowest or the highest odds available. They may, for example be attracted to nickel blackjack machines, because there is less chance that they will run out of money, especially if they play at a slow pace. They may also be attracted to gains of chance that have extremely high stakes but very little chance for winning. In this way, there is little self-criticism for failure.

There is strong evidence that people who have a high n Aff actually have a strong fear of failure or rejection. These people are poorly identified by traditional psychological tests. On self-report measures, they deny fear. People who mention only desirable qualities in themselves also score very low in admitting to anxieties. They deny they are anxious, but they behave as if they are anxious. They have, to use the felicitous phrase, the "illusion of mental health."

Unfortunately, the assessment of motives requires a trained practitioner, usually at the doctoral level (L'Abate, 1994). Motives cannot be assessed by using objectively standardized and computer scored paper-and-pencil tests. Motives are largely unconscious, and they require methods of assessment that tap into fantasy (McClelland, 1988). However, different motives can drive different people to the same behavioral ends. They warrant radically different treatments. The field of addictions in general, and of gambling in particular, might do well to incorporate motivational theory into its assessment.

DYNAMIC MEASURE OF SYMPTOMS

It is very important to present a gambling client with a dynamic portrait of his or her symptoms. We do not wish to get into the area of whether recovery from addiction involves the possibility of symptom substitution. However, when people gamble, they often experience initial symptom reduction, and then a subsequent, often fierce rebound. When they quit, they may experience event- or time-related anxiety and depression. It is often helpful to get a snapshot of this process, both for treatment planning and for measuring the directions of therapeutic change.

To do so, we use one of the brief measures of psychopathology. An example is Johnson's (1994) Symptom Survey 77, a brief inventory designed to measure symptoms that change in psychotherapy. These include traumatic stress, depression, anxiety, body complaints, and substance abuse. The inventory also has two validity scales, indicating whether the tendency of the client is positive or negative. The SS 77 can be administered repeatedly, without harm to validity (Hutton, 1998). Its brevity makes it a good device for following progress, and may make it clinically useful for impulsive persons. Research from our laboratory has shown that visual feedback is significantly related to a lack of attrition in psychotherapy for impulsive people (McCown, 1994). Instruments such as the SS 77, which can generate visual feedback and chart symptoms, may be effective in keeping clients in treatment.

A slightly longer version of the SS 77, the SS 88, is being piloted. This instrument measures gambling symptoms as well as manifestations of anger, and the symptoms measured by the SS 77 inventory. This new instrument may be useful for showing clients how their urge to gamble increases or decreases, depending on their response to mental states or internal dynamics. This technique of dynamic assessment was pioneered by Raymond Cattell (Cattell, 1990), but, to date, has had limited clinical application. One reason might be that the visual graphics of such a program have been too difficult to conveniently manage.

However, with the advent of fast personal computers, several different perspectives on the patterns of symptoms can be shown. For example, using rather common software, it is now easy to show a correlation or delayed correlation between gambling and anxiety. A client who has several weeks' data can test personal hypotheses regarding anxiety—for example, anxiety during one week may lead to gambling behaviors worth rating during the following week. In this manner, clients can decipher their own patterns of behavior and become aware of trends that otherwise would influence relapse.

Life stress, symptoms, and the urge to relapse do not appear in a linear and identical fashion for all clients. They are individual, and they combine in individual manners to produce idiosyncratic results. Therefore, any individual clinical idiographic pattern, analyzed with computers, may be the most helpful tool of all for determining what the client may do in the future. Such methodology may be most effective in predicting immediate relapse. Fortunately, with today's technology, such idiographic causal portraits can be generated, provided enough data may be obtained.

When a client has excessively high gambling urges, he drinks very little but is depressed. When the gambling urges decrease, so does the depression, but this is countered by an increase in alcohol and drug use. This in turn is related to an increase in gambling, which inevitably results in more depression. This complex causal picture represents the *causal dynamic* of symptoms in the patient. In this case, the symptoms were recorded, at weekly intervals, over four months. The pattern was not clear to either the therapist or the patient. This line of thinking is congruent with that of Abraham and associates, who argue that visual displays of complex data are much more appropriate for those of us who lack the formal mathematical sophistication to appreciate equations regarding our own behaviors.

NEUROPSYCHOLOGICAL AND INTELLIGENCE TESTS

In Chapter 4, we discussed the fact that many people who have gambling problems do not have sufficient intelligence to be able to determine that the laws of probability are not on their side. In Chapter 9, we argue that a number of neuropsychological deficits may also place people at risk. For example, a subgroup of gamblers may show fronto-orbital deficits associated with an inability to develop insight. Others may have memory deficits, especially if there is a history of substance abuse or head injury. Other types of brain injury may be related to an inability to respond to social cues or magical thinking. At least minimal levels of socialization and cultural intelligence are needed to understand the laws of probability. It is unlikely, for example, that persons who are developmentally disabled would have as easy a time with understanding probability as a high school graduate.

If there is reason to suggest that levels of intellectual functioning are deficient, an IQ test may be helpful in designing a treatment plan.

The number of neuropsychological tests may also be indicated. Brief neuropsychological batteries for adolescent and adult gamblers have been developed by McCown and Keiser (2000). This is essentially a normative computerized database, using item response theory (IRT) to maximize the "hit rate" of detecting people whose neuropsychological problems may be related to problem gambling. Research in this area continues at a rapid pace, aimed at both prevention and treatment planning.

AN EXAMPLE OF TESTING FOR A PROSPECTIVE CLIENT

The following Psychological Test Report is taken from a patient's records (with identifying information removed). This is an example of how a variety of psychological tests can be extremely valuable in treatment planning. This patient sought treatment at a partial hospitalization program for problem gamblers (strike one against him and his chances of staying abstinent!). Because he was willing to pay cash, he was very attractive to the hospital administrators, who pressured him to remain in the hospital. The question was: Could he benefit from partial treatment, or did he need a less, or more, restrictive environment?

Name: Roger Bently   Admit Date: 6/12/9X

DOB: 11/22/57   Med. Rec. No:

Date of Evaluation: 14 June, 199X

Requesting Party:

Procedures: Clinical Interview
              Records Review
              Wechsler Adult Intelligence Scale, Revised
              Categories Test
              South Oaks Gambling Screen
              Minnesota Multiphasic Personality Inventory, 2nd Ed.
              Rorschach Comprehensive System
              Thematic Apperception Test

Reason for Evaluation

Mr. Bently was evaluated at the request of the treatment team in order to help establish a differential diagnosis and treatment plan. The specific question was to rule out a primary Axis I disorder.

Brief Background

Mr. Bently is a 39-year-old white male who is married and has five children. They are recently separated. He has an MBA degree from _____ in _____. He is an independent corporate financier who admits to alcohol abuse, tobacco, and frequent cocaine use. He uses these substances "when I'm feeling bad . . . you know like when I lose at gambling or blow a big financial deal." He denies prior gambling treatment and he denies inpatient psychiatric treatment. He has been in marital therapy, and has been taking antidepressants. He denies legal problems.

Prior to treatment, Mr. Bently had placed over $159,000 of his clients' money in a number of highly speculative venture capital outlets, including two "very shaky" start-up companies. He lost over $120,000 but was not fired by his employer because "they know that when I get a handle on things I'll make it back." He also states that "I guess I am just a start-up addict. . . . I like to take a buck and turn it into $20. I like the quick return, the cash infusion just before they take (a company) public. You can make a fortune that way—it's a bigger rush than coke. . . ."

Mr. Bently states that he has had a long history of betting. "I started as a kid . . . you know pitching pennies in the city." In college he wagered on "just about anything I could get my hands on . . . I was good, too. I paid for my tuition pretty much from gambling." Following a year as a truck driver "where we had some butt-kicking poker" he reentered the university world. During this time he did not gamble "except the horses, you know, but that's not really exciting because there's not enough action."

While in his late 20s, Mr. Bently decided he could make more money as an entrepreneur. He put together a firm specializing in helping companies about to go public "get that final push. . . ." This included comprehensive services ranging from financing to public relations and corporate publicity. For several years he was very successful and began to receive payment in future stock options, a legally questionable activity. When this behavior came under close scrutiny, he sold his company and returned as a top employee. During the past several years, he has made some obviously poor investments, although "some of them, they were real long shots and they made a lot of money. . . ."

He is seeking treatment because he is afraid that his love of blackjack and casino table games—which involves all of his weekends—is interfering with both his marriage and his work. "I don't really have the time to put into either one, so I have to make a choice."

At the time of the testing, Mr. Bently was taking multivitamins, Prozac, Mylanta, and Tagamet. For more information, the interested reader is referred to his chart.

Behavioral Observations and Interview

Mr. Bently presented for his evaluation in an appropriate manner. He was cooperative with the procedures, and was friendly and extraordinarily personable. Mr. Bently seemed to enjoy talking to the examiner, and gave consistent, if aggrandizing answers. His mood was appropriate, though at times he appeared too eager to ingratiate himself. Mr. Bently was well oriented. He gave complete answers. He had a normal affect, being generally cheerful. His language was not remarkable. He had apparently good remote memory, and good recent memory. He denied suicidal and homicidal ideation and intent. He also denied symptoms of obsessions or compulsions. He denied hallucinations and delusions. Mr. Bently did state he was depressed on admission, but that he is not very depressed now. There was no evidence of manic depressive illness, either in presentation or by history.

Results of the Testing

On the South Oaks Gambling Screen, Mr. Bently received a score indicative of a probable gambling-related disorder.

On the WAIS-R, Mr. Bently received an IQ of 119, which falls at the upper end of the Above Average range. There was no significant difference between his Vocabulary and Abstraction sections. On the Categories Test, the patient scored at an appropriate level for his intelligence, with no evidence of preservative errors or interference.

On the MMPI, Mr. Bently answered the items in a manner which appears invalid. He had a defensive response (K = 80) set which is likely to mean that he is trying hard to maintain an appearance of adequacy and self-control. He is also likely to be rigid with accompanying limitations in personal insight. Despite this, he showed clear evidence of antisocial tendencies, marked by an inflated ego (Pd = 72, Ma = 65) which may have suffered some depression due to his recent loss of status at work and financial losses. He also admitted to work and marital problems, particularly to infidelity.

On the Rorschach, Mr. Bently provided 21 responses of sufficient complexity as to allow for interpretive statements to be made. It appears that many of his behaviors will be formulated with little concern about social acceptability. It is likely that he perceives his environment as threatening, demanding, and ungiving. Because of this perception, and his unconventional approach to avoiding his environment, he is likely to be perceived as eccentric or deviant.

Mr. Bently expends very little effort in trying to organize his perceptions. Rather, he decides how he wishes things to be, and then accepts that as how

(continued)

things are. He shows no tendencies toward introspection or self-examination. Much of this is related to a basic narcissistic style. His subsequent oppositionality exacerbates this situation. This inflated sense of self-worth tends to dominate his perceptions of the world. As might be expected, he tends to be more involved with himself than most other people. His self-image appears to be based on imaginary rather than real experiences, with himself in the center of whatever stage his imagination is able to create at the time he wants gratification.

In terms of his relationships with others, Mr. Bently tends to view them as objects to be used, rather than as individuals with whom to have mutually meaningful interactions. Of course, the general failure of this approach leads to anger and frustration, which he easily projects onto others.

There is no evidence of thought disorder or suicidal ideation on the Rorschach.

On the Thematic Apperception Test (TAT), Mr. Bently showed very strong needs for power, which he perceives as being largely unmet. He has a low need for achievement, common among people who want "something for nothing" out of life. Needs for affiliation and intimacy are also very low. However, he does have a genuine fear of failure and of making mistakes that can be socially criticized.

Summary

Mr. Bently lives in a lavish but hollow ego that he takes constant measures to defend. These efforts may cause some interference with his ability to utilize his cognitive capacity. One of the ways he sees himself superior to others is that he believes he can outsmart the rest of the world. When he fails to do this, as indicated by unsuccessful financial deals or losing streaks at the gambling table, he becomes depressed. This depression is fairly transitory and is negated by successful financial or gambling activities, which reaffirm his narcissistic self-worth.

Because Mr. Bently is highly narcissistic, he will resist therapy which will require any genuine insight or changes on his part. While he will initially seem to be a gratifying patient, as he introspects a great deal, he will become quite frustrating, as his introspection will probably become grandiose. He will subsequently reject any interpretations that may suggest a lack of perfection on his part. Then, he may quit treatment abruptly.

Diagnostic Impression

In addition to the gambling disorder, which has been addressed by the team, the following diagnoses are warranted:

Axis I: Major depression

Axis II: Personality Disorder, NOS, Mixed Personality Disorder with Narcissistic and Antisocial features.

Recommendations

1. Mr. Bently could benefit from a long-term, intensive 12-step affiliation, such as GA. However, there is little evidence at this time that he has sufficient insight to benefit from a partial hospitalization program.
2. Mr. Bently could benefit from ongoing marital therapy, perhaps with additional awareness on the part of his therapist of his gambling disorder.

3. At this time there is little evidence that he could benefit from insight-oriented psychotherapy or supportive therapy. He can benefit from therapy aimed at helping him confront his gambling disorder.

4. Because the patient does not admit to dysphoria over gambling (except on the SOGS), behavioral or cognitive behavioral therapy for gambling would likely be of little value at this time.

5. The patient may benefit from weekly testing with the SS-77 to show to him how his symptoms are changing through time. He has the intellectual capacity to draw conclusions from data; it may be possible for him to gain insight into his behavior by comparing his symptoms, his behaviors, and the environmental demands.

6. This patient is clearly depressed. Although there is no evidence that he is suicidal, this depression warrants treatment.

7. In my clinical opinion, partial program treatment is not indicated. An inpatient treatment might provide sufficient capacity for the patient to experience successful confrontation regarding his addictive behaviors. However, he is likely to terminate such a program. He may be very likely to continue gambling during the evenings if placed in a partial program.

Thank you for this interesting referral. I hope these observations are of assistance in treating this individual.

The patient was judged by the treatment team of outpatient experts to be ready to enter a partial hospitalization program. However, testing clearly indicated that he was not prepared for intense therapy of any type, and history proved the testing correct.

In case the reader is wondering how accurate the report was, this one was right on target. In this case, the patient quit marital therapy after two sessions, stating that he needed a "better" therapist. He attended one Gamblers Anonymous meeting, but decided it was for "losers . . . not people who are on top of the world." For a while, he managed to maintain a façade of success with antidepressant medication, but this only reinforced his grandiosity. During the next few months, he put several million dollars of his company's venture capital into a dubious Internet gambling project. His losses were so heavy that he quit abruptly, shamed by the fact that he was not "up to my regular genius." He eventually returned to seek treatment, though he copiously avoided both inpatient and partial programs. Eventually, he found that Gamblers' Anonymous was, although not completely suitable for him, "at least tolerable." His major complaint about GA was "all those gigantic egos in there that have failed. It just makes me sick to be in a room full of losers. . . ."

In what sounds to those without experience in this field as a grotesque parody, the patient states: "It's a shame GA can't be up to my standard of people. For God's sake, they don't even wear decent suits there, I mean the business types." However, he does now admit that he is not at GA to socialize. "I gambled with inferiors for a long time, so I might as well get help with them." His narcissism obviously remains intact. As we write this, he is still abstinent of gambling and of psychoactive substances.

CONCLUSION

Psychological testing may have a valuable place in the treatment of chronic gambling problems. Although empirical research tends to refine the predictive validity of psychological tests for abusive and addicted gamblers, present-day and well-normed psychological tests can help establish some potential problem areas that are likely to arise in the treatment and post-treatment of this very desperate population. Psychological assessment is a technology—a skill based heavily on empirical findings and extrapolated to novel situations. The interpretation of psychological tests, while not an art, is based on experience and requires the clinical wisdom discussed in Chapter 2. Without this expertise, the treatment team providing assessment and weighing interventions for persons in treatment for gambling-related disorders is missing a major therapeutic ally.

CHAPTER 9

Chaos Theory, Gambling, and Addictions: Speculations on New Methods of Nonlinear Treatment[1]

Picture this . . . you walk from machine to machine. There's no pattern. You drop coins in, maybe hit the tables for a while. It's random. But what's drawing you is fate. It pushes you, tugs at you, makes you go you don't know where. And out of all this chaos comes Lady Luck, shining her eyes at you. Suddenly you're hot. You can't lose. The whole time, what you thought was chance was really Luck. Then you know what the crazy pattern was all about.

—Susan T., problem gambler, during first clinical interview

One of the great challenges to both sciences and philosophy is to provide a rational account of the uncertainty we perceive in events of daily life. Classical probability theory offers one such approach, but it is riddled with many well-known epistemological flaws and paradoxes.

—Mathematician John Casti, 1992

IF THIS book is judged to present a novel approach to the treatment of gambling, it is contained in this chapter, which is based on our previous research and treatment of families in crisis and families with excessive stability (Bütz et al., 1997; J. Johnson & McCown, 1996; McCown & Johnson,

[1] The late Mrs. J.B. Lesley provided funding for some of the research in this chapter. Research facilities from the Nathan Kline Institute for Psychiatric Research were instrumental in this project, as they were for a number of others of the authors' in the area of chaos theory.

1993). We have applied analogue models from the multidiscipline science of chaos theory to problems of chronic dysfunctional gamblers. We believe that this approach may hold one of the many keys for the treatment and prevention of dysfunctional gambling. First, however, we must explain the beautiful, simple, but also infinitely complex ideas associated with contemporary concepts of chaos.

AN INTRODUCTION TO CHAOS THEORY

During the past 30 years, a quirkily eccentric scientific course has evolved into an entire paradigm for viewing complex behavior. *Chaos theory* is the name given to the collection of physical science and mathematical theories expressing the dynamic properties of nonlinear systems, especially systems in transition (Casti, 1992). In approximately the time it took for Einstein's special theory of relativity to be widely accepted, chaos theory has made the transition from a fringe movement to orthodox, mainstream science (Beltrami, 1993). Indeed, some commentators have argued that chaos theory represents the third great scientific revolution of the twentieth century, a scientific innovation of the same magnitude as relativity theory and quantum mechanics.

Briefly, chaos is said to exist when a set of data from a system can be mathematically modeled, yet can only be predicted in advance with very limited, if any, success. When researchers speak of "finding chaos" in a particular set of data, they mean that the data show evidence of underlying nonlinear causality, usually in contrast to either linearity or true randomness. There are many implications of chaos theory, but among the most important is the apparent paradox of phenomena that are simultaneously completely causally determined but essentially still most entirely unpredictable.

Chaotic processes are now known to be found in the irregularity of a dripping faucet, the flow of eddies in a stream of water, turbulence in the air, the pattern of smoke rising, and the spread of epidemics and forest fires (Tufillaro, Abbott, & Reilly, 1992). Chaos theory has also been applied to economic systems, including the stock market and, to a lesser extent, to biological systems. Problems in population ecology, in particular, have been fruitfully elucidated with an extremely simple model from chaos theory.

Regardless of the domain involved, the same kinds of processes occur repeatedly, across different media, time frames, and size scales. Chaos has now been discovered at many levels of measurement, from the macro level of movements of bodies in the solar system to the micro level of the movement of wave particles in the quantum world.

Although chaos theory is relatively new, its concepts are traceable back to the ancient Greeks. More recently, in the early years of the twentieth century, the French mathematician Jules-Henri Poincaré offered mathematical proof that the behavior of very simple systems could be complex and, in fact, quite literally unpredictable, even if their entire histories were known in advance (Cvitanovic, 1984). In 1928, Balth van der Pol, a Dutch engineer, developed a mathematical mode of an oscillating electronic valve based on Poincaré's dynamic topology, providing the first application of what is now known as chaos theory.

However, only since the advent of high-speed computers have researchers possessed the technical capacity to fully explore the implications of nonlinearity in data. A discovery relevant to this goal was made by Edward Lorenz, a meterological researcher at the Massachusetts Institute of Technology, who was studying weather patterns by creating models in his computer (Gleick, 1987). Accidentally, Lorenz found that when he changed the input of an equation by a mathematically infinitesimal degree, his computer produced results that varied much more widely than had been expected. In other words, a minute difference in the original situation magnified itself hugely over time. Lorenz postulated that apparent turbulence in nature could be partly explained by this "sensitive dependence on initial conditions" (Gleick, 1987). He called this dependence the "butterfly effect," derived from the idea that weather in New York, for example, could eventually be changed by circumstances as minute as the flapping of a butterfly's wings in China. The butterfly effect is now widely evoked to explain natural limits on our ability to accurately predict the weather.

Mitchell Feingenbaum, working at Cornell University, found that, in a surprisingly large number of natural systems, a sequence of order followed by turbulence eventually results in a new state of stable predictability (Loye & Eisler, 1987). By entering values repeatedly into a formula, he discovered that, within diverse systems that appeared chaotic and random, there emerged certain predictable patterns of order. In the late 1960s, Steven Smale was one of a number of other scientists who explored the behavior of nonlinear systems. He theorized that all systems in nature are continually changing over time. Like Feigenbaum, Smale concluded that these changes progress from order to chaos, and that the resulting chaotic state had its own rules of structure and order.

THE UBIQUITY OF CHAOS

By the late 1970s, scientists from many disciplines—with the surprising exclusion of the behavioral sciences—were beginning to investigate chaos. Biologists, and ecologists such as Robert May, looked at seemingly unpredictable changes in global populations of plants and animals. Mathematicians Benoit Mandelbrot and James Yorke were among those who focused on the stages of chaos and disorder toward which all mathematical, physical, and natural systems seemed to move. More complex still is the recent work of the Belgian scientist and Nobel laureate Ilya Prigogine, whose interest initially was in a class of chemical reactions that seems to violate the second law of thermodynamics. Prigogine (Prigogine & Stengers, 1984) discusses the idea that order comes out of chaos in the form of feedback loops within a system. He believes that this order is a state of self-generated dynamics, and he has done much to advance the mathematical models applicable to such systems. Prigogine's notion that chaotic systems have the innate capacity to "self-organize" from this feedback remains one of the most controversial but exciting aspects of chaos theory.

CHAOS AS A NEW PARADIGM IN SCIENCE

Chaos theory is not so much a set of findings as it is a new paradigm that has been useful in analyzing behavior as diverse as helical motion and the dynamics of the spread of disease. Most of the assumptions of the chaos paradigm are easily understood, despite the fact that some of the mathematics behind their proofs is formidable for most persons who lack an extensive mathematical background. Of principal interest to students of chaos are systems that receive feedback for determination of future behavior, such as a tropical storm front, or two people interacting in a conversation. Usually, these systems are best expressed mathematically by differential equations. Traditionally, a differential equation is "solved" by finding a function that satisfies the differential equation (Tuffilaro et al., 1992). A trajectory is then determined by starting the solution with a particular initial condition. For example, to calculate the prediction of a comet in 20 years, we need to measure the comet's present position and velocity, write down the differential equation for its motion, and then integrate the differential equation, starting from the measured initial condition. Before the work of Poincaré, it was believed that any nonlinear system would always have a solution if we were clever enough to find it.

Poincaré's work, however, showed that this view is mathematically wrong. No matter how clever we are, we will not be able to write down accurate equations that solve or predict many nonlinear systems. One reason is that many complex systems are highly sensitive to initial starting conditions, which cannot be controlled completely or predicted in advance. Hence, slight alterations in feedback or in the values of initial states may have extreme and literally unpredictable effects (Devaney, 1992). Subsequent research has shown that this is especially true when the system is undergoing a transitional phase of instability, a period when it is most vulnerable to slight perturbations (Abraham, Abraham, & Shaw, 1991). Although we may speak "probabilisitically" about the behavior of such systems, chaos theory demonstrates that it is mathematically infeasible to make long-term, accurate predictions of many complex nonlinear systems (Waldrop, 1992). The more unstable the system is, the less accurate our predictions regarding the system's future behavior are likely to be. We can describe the general shape of the behavior or illustrate its range graphically, but we cannot actually predict it with accuracy.

Chaos versus the Linear Model: Challenging Assumptions

These inherently unpredictable systems contrast to linear systems, which are much more familiar to behavioral scientists. In a linear system, the outcome of an equation is linearly proportional to the variables inputted into the equation. When we use techniques such as multiple regression or the analysis of variance, we are employing the *linear model* as a useful approximation of reality (Cattell, 1982). Examples in the behavioral sciences occur when we hypothesize that a given experience, a personality variable, or perhaps a certain neurotransmitter has a specific and proportional effect on human cognition or action. Often, we may even complicate the equation by predicting interactions between independent variables. However, such models are still linear and are mathematically very simple.

In theory, we should be able to make perfect predictions from linear methods, provided that the specific model we have developed is both accurate and appropriate to the phenomenon being studied. Much of the history of the behavioral sciences can be seen as a quest for more accurate linear models. For example, when we design a study hoping to find better predictors of violence than in previous research, we are attempting to alter our model to find variables that account for more of the variance. Most behavioral science research conducted today is reflective of this strategy. The overwhelming sentiment is that our models are good, but we have not been clever enough to optimally use them. Only very rarely will behavioral scientists conclude that linear models are inappropriate for the phenomena being studied.[2]

---

[2] Occasionally, simple nonlinear functions (such as $Y = X^3$, a common function in physics and life sciences) are employed as more appropriate mathematical models of human or animal behavior. Analyses using polynomial modes (squares, cubes, and cross-products of the original linear variables) are now available on many commercial statistical packages. Time series analyses using the popular methods of Box and Jenkins, Lisrel, and nonlinear regression are all gaining slowly in popularity, perhaps attesting to a realization that many of the phenomena of the behavior sciences are not appropriate for simple linear analyses. Yet, even these techniques are only applicable to very stable systems over short periods of time. Most systems in nature are better modeled by differential equations. Such systems, as Poincaré showed, always have the capacity to generate the unpredictable behavior we now call chaos.

DETERMINISM, WHOLENESS, AND CHAOS

A tenet of chaos theory is that there are often hidden patterns amid apparent randomness (Gleick, 1987). Unexplainable occurrences, formerly believed due largely to "chance" and "error variance," are looked at as potentially ordered phenomena (Moon, 1992). What appears disorganized, formless, and unpredictable is often found to contain an identifiable underlying structure, though typically the pattern cannot be predicted in advance. Such an observation may require input of up to several thousand data points before it is discovered. Another important insight has emerged from the new science of chaos: Complex behavior is not necessarily the result of many interacting variables. Even a simple system—one with as few as three variables—can, under certain conditions, demonstrate extremely complex and unpredictable behavior (Ruelle, 1991). Despite this unpredictability, it is important to remember that chaos theory remains entirely *deterministic*. Although fundamentally unpredictable, chaotic phenomena are not random (Stewart, 1990). This last point is the most anti-intuitive, and, not surprisingly, a conclusive demonstration requires a considerable background in mathematics, although a simple illustration is available in the popular book by Gleick (1987).

Chaotic Attractors and Nonlinear Behavior

In its departure from traditional science, chaos theory argues that the dynamics of systems are more important than their constituent parts (Goerner, 1993). Rather than viewing the world as a collection of physical events and properties, chaos theorists note that the universe is composed of systems whose dynamics intersect and interrelate. What appears disordered in these systems often emerges as an underlying pattern of complexity (Gilgen & Abraham, 1993). Borrowing heavily from research on turbulence (an area of mathematics called classical dynamical theory), chaos theory employs the notion of an *attractor*, or a mathematical force directing the behavior of a system. Most systems that are described by the linear model can be shown to have a fixed-point attractor. An example drawn from the physical sciences is the temperature of a glass of water placed outside on a summer day. The water will eventually settle at the same temperature as its surroundings (i.e., a fixed point) without subsequent fluctuation. In the language of chaos, traditional personality theory often assumes that personality constructs function as fixed-point attractors, forcing behavior toward a particular stable end point.

The number of studies suggesting the existence of chaos in topics traditionally studied by the behavioral sciences is growing daily. In psychology, for example, chaos theory has been applied to phenomena as diverse as schedules of reinforcement (Hoyert, 1992), levels of neurotransmitters (King, Barchas, & Huberman, 1984), and Jungian psychology (Bütz, 1992).

HUMANS AS COMPLEX SYSTEMS

The contention of this chapter is that humans and most human functions are complex systems. In certain circumstances—for example, when behaviors are associated with the so-called septo-hippocampal nervous system—change may occur linearly, a fact first observed by Eysenck in the late 1940s (Eysenck & Eysenck, 1985) and much touted by private managed care groups that endorse the "dose response" theory of psychotherapy. The mistakes of neobehaviorism and its application to psychotherapy were to believe that the simple dose response curve seen in extinction applied to all types of psychotherapy. Bütz et al. (1997) suggested that the family and family interactions represent a clear example of chaos theory that can be applied to the clinic.

If humans are complex systems, then problems with human gambling behavior are also complex. Hawkins and Hawkins (1998) have suggested that findings from chaos theory may be usefully applied in the field of chemical addictions. McCown and Keiser (2000) give an example of how nonlinear systems theory can be used to treat a gambling problem. Bütz et al. (1997) depict several methods in which chaos theory can be used to develop novel treatments for formally intractable problems. Bütz (1996) has suggested a number of other implications of chaos theory for psychology and psychotherapy. However, before we begin an excursion into this fascinating and new area of potential treatment, we must explain a bit more about the hidden order lurking beneath disorder.

FINDING CHAOS

Classical dynamical theory has recognized a number of types of attractors, including those we now call chaotic. An attractor may consist of a circle, called a limit cycle, if there is periodic behavior that never reaches an end point, such as a pendulum that swings eternally in a gravity-free environment. Classical attractors can also take more complicated forms, like a donut shape called a torus, if two systems are coupled together. An example of an application of a torus attractor is the motion of a pendulum driven by a motor. Each of the above attractors exhibits regular, stable, and predictable behavior. However, such behavior is rarely encountered in nature.

In contrast, a chaotic system displays a different kind of trajectory through space, one that moves erratically on an ever changing path

(Abraham & Shaw, 1992). This is called a *strange attractor*. Strange attractors come in many different shapes, depending on the nature of the system (Tufillaro et al., 1992). The first class of strange attractors identified was named after Lorenz and was initially used to describe patterns of turbulence in weather. It looks a bit like the wings of a butterfly, or perhaps a Rorschach card. Strange attractors mathematically capture the deterministic orderliness underlying a chaotic system. Although the specific trajectory may not be predictable, the parameters of the overall shape are bounded and delimited. Essentially, a strange attractor reveals the process dynamic of a chaotic system as it unfolds over time. The behavior of any system can be mapped as a trajectory through phase space, according to critical input variables called control parameters. Phase space consists of all possible states of a system, given one's control parameters. The trajectory represents the movement of the system over time.

Another way to visualize the irregular structure of a chaotic system is to analyze its *fractal composition*, as it is frozen in an instant in time. In other words, a cross-sectional slice through a chaotic attractor will reveal fractal architecture. Fractal geometry is a branch of mathematics named and described by Benoit Mandelbrot (Abraham & Shaw, 1992). Fractals are dynamic shapes easily created on a computer by taking the same mathematical formula and feeding its output back in as input, again and again. By assigning certain colors to ranges of numbers, this simple, recursive process is easily visualized, producing extremely complex and entertaining shapes called fractals. Every fractal may be described mathematically by a number known as its fractal dimension. This number captures the degree of irregularity in the shape.

Fractal dimensions are fascinating because they describe the degree to which an irregular shape falls between ordinary Euclidean dimensions. For example, the Euclidean dimension of 1 represents a straight line. A broken line—which occupies more space than a point but less than an unbroken line—may be represented by a fractional dimension of .6101, as in the case of Cantor Dust. A squiggle line wending its way through a plane, as in the case of a coastline, may be represented by a fractal dimension of 1.5287. Similarly, a piece of Swiss cheese, existing somewhere between a two-dimensional plane and a three-dimensional solid, might have a fractal dimension of 2.678. The higher the fractional number, the more complex the shape, essentially indicating a greater degree of randomness or disorderliness. Despite being bounded shapes, fractals can be infinitely complex. Fractals exhibit a remarkable property called *self-similarity*. This means that if a small section of a fractal is magnified, it will eventually reproduce the whole shape, either identical to the original or approximately so, depending on whether any degree of randomness is introduced into the formula. Examples of fractals encountered in daily life include the meandering boundaries of rivers (Bütz et al., 1997). Riverfronts, like mountains, oceans, capillaries, and sometimes, even family systems, are fractal in nature.

Fractals are very useful for modeling the kinds of complex, irregular shapes we see around us in everyday life, both inorganic and organic. The shapes of clouds and mountains, the irregularity of coastlines or electrical discharges, and the growth of some crystals, are all fractal. Each of these shapes displays the property of self-similarity across different size or time scales, also known as scale invariance. Fractals are particularly likely to occur at boundary points, the nonlinear remnants of chaotic forces shaping an environment. Fractal algorithms are especially useful for modeling the growth and evolution of dynamic processes.

In human physiology, fractal structure is evident in the branching patterns of ducts, the lungs, the small intestine, blood vessels, and the dendrite structure of some neurons. Fractal branches or folds in organs greatly amplify the surface area available. This facilitates absorption in the intestine; distribution and collection by blood vessels, bile ducts, and bronchial tubes; and information processing by the nerves. Partly because of their redundancy and irregularity, fractal structures are robust and resistant to injury. Fractal structures also appear easy to encode genetically, thus maximizing the given amount of information a gene can impart to the body.

A Technical Diversion: How Do We Identify Chaos?

Fractals as evidence of chaos can be identified by a number of procedures, including visual inspection. Sprott and Rowlands (1992) have suggested a very conservative set of procedures involving the search for chaos in time series data. They suggest a systematic staged effort of (1) visual inspection of all data; (2) various mathematical transformations, if appropriate; (3) removal of linearity and polynomials; and (4) statistical tests for determination of chaos. Because these procedures are not familiar to most behavioral scientists, they are described below in some detail.

Following these methods, a number of other, more specific procedures can be implemented, including calculation of the Lyapunov exponent, the maximum entropy method, Hausdorf's D, and correlational dimension analysis. Procedures are further described in Casti (1992), and computational software is available from Sprott and Rowlands (1992). Although some procedures are more accurate than others for determining the dimensionality of chaotic processes, sample size is also a consideration. In general, the correlation dimension is preferable where the data have high dimensionality (i.e., where they have low-order chaos or are close to random). On the other hand, Hausdorf's *D* is probably preferable for relatively minor series.

Sensitivity to Initial Conditions

Chaos is most likely to occur in systems undergoing specific transitions. Although we defer to other authors to outline the mathematical complexities involved (Casti, 1992), systems are likely to experience *bifurcation* at specific points in time. Such bifurcations represent the transition from relatively stable and linear behavior to periods of chaotic oscillation.

Areas where bifurcations occur are called *phase transitions.* These transitional occurrences are not the result of magical processes or randomness. Instead, they are due to the nature of complex nonlinear systems, where feedback about former behavior is used to adjust future behaviors. Casti (1992) describes the mathematics and practical assumptions of these transitional points in detail. His books are strongly recommended for a user-friendly introduction to nonlinear systems in transition.

Phase transitions occur, in large part, because systems are particularly sensitive to tiny variations in feedback. This is called "sensitivity to initial conditions." Subsequent research has shown that unpredictability and sensitivity to initial conditions are especially likely to occur in complex systems that are undergoing a *transitional phase of instability* (Abraham et al., 1991). Although we can speak "probabilistically" about the behavior of complex systems, chaos theory demonstrates—as Poincaré did, almost 100 years ago—that it is mathematically infeasible to make long-term, accurate predictions of many complex nonlinear systems (Waldrop, 1992). *The more unstable the system, the less accurate our numerical predictions regarding the system's future behavior are likely to be* (Casti, 1992).

Furthermore, instability is most apt to increase the effects of unpredictability when the system is at a critical point of transition. We can describe the general *shape* of the behavior graphically, or illustrate its general and probable range, but we cannot predict any complex system's behavior with accuracy (Abraham & Shaw, 1992). Complex systems, as Poincaré showed, always have the capacity for generating the unpredictable behavior we now call chaos.

GAMBLING AND SENSITIVITY
TO INITIAL CONDITIONS

A principal analogy from our endeavors in applying chaos theory to gambling has been the discovery that transitional points in the recovery process are positions where people are most sensitive to initial conditions.

This was noted independently by our colleagues in the alcohol field, Hawkins and Hawkins (1998). In other words, at specific and identifiable critical periods in the process of recovery, problem gamblers may be extraordinarily influenced by very small events, which may have extreme and unpredictable implications for future functioning. *At these critical points, therapeutic intervention is most important.* Hence, the GA/AA concept of bottoming out is crucial; people who are in sensitive positions are highly sensitive to change. This is why it is so important to "grab the addict" in a period of motivation.

Patients should not be wait-listed because their effective motivation often wanes. The maximal likelihood for behavioral change occurs when patients can be accommodated immediately. Outsiders often believe that addicts' desire for immediate treatment is a behavioral sample of their inability to tolerate frustration. Actually, it is much more complicated, but also much more simple. This is just an example of an outlier point from an attractor or set of attractors. The probability for maximal change is magnified if immediate services are available. Waiting lists help almost no one.

USING CHAOS THEORY
TO EXPLAIN RELAPSES

A useful theory regarding relapse is derived from chaos theory and is based on a notion developed by chaos theory and, later, by Stuart Kauffman (1993). Systems can display incredible stability for long periods of time and then begin to bifurcate and react chaotically. This may explain why relapse prevention is an ongoing, even lifelong pursuit. Systems sometimes self-organize to higher levels of fuctioning, but sometimes they do not. This explains, we believe, how some people "pull themselves out of their own addictions" while others cannot. This has nothing to do with the weakness, or technically, the seriousness of their disease. Instead, it depends on the complex equations that govern the likelihood and direction of bifurcation.

Hawkins and Hawkins (1998), who examined this point in detail, believe that perturbations in systems that are sensitive to initial conditions can explain both relapse and the desire to recover. Their model is actually quite parsimonious. It suggests that multiple systems affect the recovering individual. Their combined impact cannot be specified in advance, as advocates of chaos theory understand. Instead, they can be seen in retrospect and analyzed. The implications of their hypotheses are that we can never successfully predict relapse with much confidence. We can, however, provide logical and scientifically valid reasons regarding why relapses did occur, if indeed the patient "slipped." Moreover, even prolonged periods of extreme abstinence from alcohol, gambling, or other addictions may be punctuated by periods of a return to an unsteady state or disequilibrium.

In this sense, both AA and GA are right. Abstinence needs to be taken one day at a time. Long-range predictions about the behaviors of complex systems are mathematically impossible to make.

EVIDENCE OF CHAOS IN GAMBLING BEHAVIOR:
BRAIN WAVE FUNCTIONING

As we stated in Chapter 7, lower levels of EEG activity in the left frontal lobe are associated with relapse in recovering alcoholics. This is not surprising; we have also discussed the fact that EEG biofeedback may be a useful adjunct for people with cognitive impairment. However, continuous treatment is probably necessary in order to prevent relapse. Like occupational or physical therapy for a chronic disease, treatment needs to be ongoing.

More recently, we have found evidence of chaotic processes in the EEG wave analysis of gamblers. Here, the discussion becomes more technical and is reported elsewhere in greater detail (McCown & Keiser, 2000). However, the major relevant points are particularly exciting for people who work with chronic gamblers.

Jausovec (1998) illustrates that there are significant differences in the EEG waves between gifted and average students, in tasks representing mental processing speed, working memory, and active reasoning. These differences were nonexistent when the same students were under conditions of resting. However, when mentally stressed, there was less evidence of chaos in the brighter students. The differences were most pronounced over the frontal brain areas, especially for tasks involving working memory.

In Jausovec's very interesting article, an extreme change was observed with individuals who were involved in cognitive activity. Gifted individuals, in comparison with average ones, displayed less mental activity. Although this has been demonstrated with other models, the conclusion drawn in many previous studies has been that the speed of mental processing is related to intelligence. However, Jausovec concludes that there is less deterministic chaos in brighter persons. The conclusion drawn was that processing speed is not the main reason for differences in mental abilities. Instead, it is the amount of chaos.

EEG alpha activity has been investigated in a number of studies and found to be deficit in some, but not all, substance abusers. To our knowledge, this has never been tested in gamblers. Fourier analysis (e.g., alpha power) obtains alpha EEG measures. Recent progress in nonlinear dynamics has provided algorithms for quantifying chaos using experimental times series (Jausovec, 1998). Research using ongoing samples of EEG obtained through sleep, for example, shows less chaotic activity, compared to mental activity. However, the relationship between EEG power measures and measures obtained by nonlinear analysis—such as Lyapunov exponent, correlation dimension, or Kolmogorov entropy—are still unclear.

We compared the EEG data of 31 persons who had exhibited problem gambling behavior with those of 30 matched-age/race subjects who had no history of addictions. Persons were excluded if they drank more than three drinks a day or had a history of head injury. Neither education nor intelligence differed significantly between the groups.

During tasks that do not require viewing gambling-related stimuli, there is no difference in chaos in brain functioning. However, when viewing stimuli regarding gambling—namely, a five-minute vignette promoting wagering—there was substantially more chaos in the group of recovering individuals. Moreover, there was a negative relationship between the length of recovery and the amount of chaos. This is evidence that some gamblers remain sensitive to initial conditions for some time, even during the recovery process.

Data from other sources (McCown & Keiser, 2000) have suggested that changes in the prefrontal area of alcoholics can predict relapse. We argue that this is a function of increasing chaos, or sensitivity to initial conditions. Persons who are sensitive to initial conditions react nonuniformly to tempting stimuli. For example, they may be able to watch a gambling advertisement on television and feel the sudden impulse to gamble. Yet, sometimes, they will not experience these impulses. This reaction is impossible to predict in advance.

For persons in the early and even the middle stages of recovery, there may be an extreme sensitivity to initial conditions. Given what we know about chaos theory, this means that a person might view gambling-related material a large number of times, and once, for no apparent reason, be filled with irresistible impulses to gamble. Some people may never overcome their sensitivity to initial conditions regarding addictive materials.

To summarize, what we're arguing here is that these people are displaying a potential sensitivity to initial conditions that varies in an unpredictable manner. This helps to explain why relapse is unpredictable—a well-known phenomenon in addiction. All one has to do is go to a GA or AA meeting to hear tales of how a person who was relatively secure in abstinence "slipped." The so-called addictive personality may be someone who has a neural net propensity to remain sensitive to initial conditions at specific, unpredictable points. Hence, this person is always relapse-prone. Whether neural biofeedback may be useful in reducing or helping these neural nets to reorganize is not known.

Great care needs to be taken, regarding this methodology and these findings. There is considerable disagreement in the literature regarding different methods of sampling EEG waves in their relation to deterministic chaos. However, with these limitations in mind, we argue that evidence indicates that gambling is associated with chaotic thinking regarding gambling stimuli. Because of this, we strongly recommend abstinence, rather than controlled gambling, a sentiment that is echoed in the self-help communities and has been reiterated throughout this volume.

THE OPPONENT PROCESS MODEL

A more limited model of particular aspects of nonlinear system functioning may be especially useful in explaining some of the unique problems associated with gambling. The *Opponent Process Theory* was advanced by the well-known behavioral psychologist Richard Solomon and his associates during the 1970s and 1980s. Solomon's (1980) research culminated in an elegantly simple, yet conceptually rich schema with broad explanatory powers. This model has little in common per se with the dynamical chaos that we have discussed previously. However, later in this chapter we will suggest a way in which this new hybrid discipline of chaos can complement the Opponent Process Theory and assist the therapist in explaining and treating some of the perplexing aspects of abusive gambling and other addictions.

The Opponent Process Theory provides a useful elucidation for the often curious pattern of responses to strongly pleasant and unpleasant experiences alike. The theory also explains why many experiences that are initially unpleasing eventually become very acceptable. Solomon (1980) begins the theory with a nod to an obvious feature of psychology. He notes that for almost every intense action in the body, especially in the nervous system, there is usually an *unequal* reaction. This unmatched reaction typically involves reciprocal processes, which generally mirror the initial action. The reciprocal reaction usually varies in both intensity and duration from the action that it follows. One example is the routine activity in the sympathetic nervous system, which occurs quickly and in response to immediate threats in our environment. This action is eventually countermanded by much slower activities of the complimenting parasympathetic nervous system. The parasympathetic system responds slower, and in general, acts in an opposite direction from sympathetic activity. Parasympathetic tasks include the slowing of the heart and a gradual increase in the rate of digestion. These are "opponent" activities that are the converse of those evoked by sympathetic responses. They act to return the body to its steady state of homeostasis.

The example of the sympathetic and parasympathetic systems illustrates a general tendency that exists for many responses in the body and brain. Every physiologically intense state, Solomon (1980) says, is naturally accompanied by its homeostatic opponent state. Opponent states share a number of characteristics, regardless of what bodily or mental system they match or oppose. Initially, they are much "narrower," or less intense than the opposing states that evoke them or cued them to occur. They usually activate rather slowly, at least at first. They also react more gradually than the states that they counter, as if they were somehow sluggish.

Through the passing of time, these temporal attributes tend to change dramatically. Opponent states cease to be as "shallow," nor are they as slow to occur. Technically, Solomon (1980) says, they can be said to grow in intensity and decrease in response latency.

Solomon (1980) believes a general principle is common to the perception of all physically intense stimuli. The initial physiological state evoked by the stimulus, called the *A State*, usually occurs acutely and quickly. At first, and customarily for quite some time, there is little in the way of physiological counter response. In other words, the *B State* is initially trivial. It is commonly insignificant or forceless and very slow to activate.

However, the B State does not always remains so diminutive. Subsequent exposures to the stimulus that evoked the state cause the potential for the B State to increase very rapidly. In time, as part of the body's homeostasis, the opponent state, or B State, becomes potentially larger. It decreases in latency and becomes more intense or "deeper."

A key to Solomon's theory is awareness that the A State does not routinely change through the passage of time or from repeated exposures. The body initially responds to intense stimuli in an unchanging fashion, regardless of how many exposures it has experienced. To use the terms of learning theory, there is no habituation of the A State. There is also no growth of the A State. The B State, however, does change dramatically through time and experience. An important part of Solomon's theory is that B State is hypothesized to become potentially larger every time the A State is evoked. Eventually, Solomon argues, the B State's opponent processes, or properties that countermand the initial A State, become so intense that they essentially overpower or cancel out that state entirely.

Solomon believes that this process is quite common. It occurs for all physically intense stimuli that the body experiences. The natural history of repeated exposure to any intense stimuli is that they lose their intensity because of the organism's tendencies to develop opposing states. At this point, the A State may be so overshadowed that it is hardly noticed. Instead, what becomes conspicuous is the organism's opposing response to the initial stimulus. This simple model has immediate applications in the field of addictions.

As an example, consider nicotine dependence. Smokers often fondly recall that a cigarette brand or specific dose previously produced an euphoric rush or high. This euphoria is part of the nicotine-induced A State that the smoker experiences as pleasant. However, the capacity to obtain a pleasant feeling does not routinely last. Habituation to the nicotine occurs rather quickly. Solomon says that habituation is a process in which a B State, the physiological opposite of the initial euphoria, cancels out the euphoric effects of the A State. Eventually, the A and B states are approximately equal in strength. They neutralize each other. At this point in a smoker's history, a specific dose of cigarettes that produced euphoria now produces little, if any change in positive feelings.

As discussed earlier, exposure to the A State of any stimulus changes the parameters of its opponent B State. This means that simple exposure without learning or other experience is sufficient to make the B State become increasingly longer, reduced in latency and greater in opponent intensity. The body's natural response to intense stimuli, Solomon argues, is to counter the stimuli with progressively strict measures. As one example of this tendency, drugs that might make people initially euphoric eventually tend to have an opposite effect.

Application of the opponent process theory to substance abuse and other addictions deserves additional particular attention. In every addiction, Solomon argues, the first exposures or phases of exposure are characterized by an intense and usually pleasurable A State. The homeostatic B State is initially sluggish and shallow. As a result, the first few times someone uses a drug or gambles to excess, they often experience more extremely positive feelings than they will throughout the rest of their addiction history. The A State that is evoked acts as if it is unopposed. The high is intense and tends to be very long lasting. This results in the first dramatic rush that abusers are never quite able to overcome or to experience again.

The second phase of addiction, the process of stimulus habituation, is characterized by a B State that increases in intensity duration and frequency of onset so that it cancels out some of the hedonic properties of the initial A State. This A/B balance is theorized to be the mechanisms behind the decreased capacity of the drug user to experience a high or of the gambler to get the emotional charge that used to accompany wagering. Therefore, drug users usually expand their dosages and gamblers increase their wagers, all in a quest for the initial intensity that is proving elusive.

Stimulus tolerance, a further stage of addiction, occurs when the A and B States are of approximately equal duration and intensity. In this situation, the use of a substance or of an addictive experience such as gambling usually triggers both the primary affective state, or an A State, and its opponent state, the B State. These are triggered approximately simultaneously. As we recall, the potential for the A State does not change in intensity throughout a history of being evoked or through time. However, the B State certainly changes and becomes less sluggish. This is true because repeated exposure to an A State results in earlier onset of the opponent B mechanisms. Eventually, the net hedonic effect is zero. A person feels little or nothing from a formerly enjoyable addiction.

Exposure past the point of tolerance to any hedonically intense stimulus results in an even greater B State. In this case, the hedonic value of A-B eventually becomes negative. Thus, stimulus administration once habituation has occurred causes an even greater B State. Solomon (1980) has suggested that this process is the explanation of drug or stimulus craving. A person may gamble to experience a rush. She feels good for a few minutes, only to be overcome with the antithesis of the excitement that she craved. This may include feelings of anxiety, frustration, and boredom. Through the process of repeated exposures, gambling ceases to evoke much in the way of pleasurable feelings. Instead, it provokes negative moods and a craving for the initial feeling of an unrestricted A State.

Since the removal of the B State is best accomplished by the physiological antitheses-namely the A State—an individual will often seek to re-administer the A State stimulus to gain escape from the noxious B State. However, exposure to the A State while the B State is still attempting homeostasis results in an intensification of the B State upon subsequent exposures to the A State. In other words, exposure to the addictive stimulus results in the growth of the B State. This causes further withdrawal symptoms and tolerance. An example that is evidentially understandable to many college students: when you drink to eliminate the symptoms of a hangover (the B State), you boost your alcohol future tolerance.

This model can explain how gambling can be so addicting and can often seem clinically indistinguishable from other powerful addictions. Developments in neuroscience since the 1980s further clarify the impact of opponent processes and may offer biological underpinnings. Gambling is a special case of opponent processes, where the potential for addiction is potentially greater than with other behaviors or with many drugs. During the initial or early gambling history of an individual, two hedonically intense stimuli, one pleasant, and one unpleasant are occurring at the same time. One is the dopamine related reward response occurring primarily through the nucleus accumbens and probably involving dopamine subreceptors D2 and D4. The rewarding aspects of gambling probably occurs directly in the pleasure center of the brain, the same site where heroin and cocaine apparently are active. This is the source of the initial thrill of gambling and the rush that accompanies the first few hundred or thousand times a person wages.

In addition, gambling also routinely evokes negative feelings, usually the intense emotions of wagering anxiety. These emotions trigger a separate A State. (We can and do display A States and B States to unpleasant stimuli, as well as pleasant stimuli.) Initially, the A State associated with gambling anxiety is interpreted as being unpleasant. On the other hand, the anxiety of gambling induced by the A State is also associated with an opponent process response of counter anxiety. In other words, the anxiety generates its opponent B State, which is pleasant. This pleasant response is probably mediated by at least two neurochemical mechanism, either by a GABA-ergic response or a more systemic release of beta endorphins. These neurotransmitters act at several locations in the brain. One is probably at the nucleus accumbens to provide an "after effect high that is phenomenologically different from the initial euphoria of gambling.

Even after an initial habituation to the effects of the A State, the heavy gambler now has the anxious excitement associated with different aspects of gambling. This produces a B State, which is very pleasurable and grows through time in an expected manner. As a result, specific wagering and gambling related experiences that one would not typically find otherwise enjoyable, like chasing after lost wagers, begin to generate a different quality of euphoria. Eventually, chasing becomes rewarding in itself, regardless of how much money is lost. At this point, the gambler rarely displays emotion. He or she simply reacts quietly to the B State generated by the opposite of anxiety.

In summary, the heavy gambler evidently has at least two distinct addictive processes working against her or him. On one hand, there is the reward from dopaminergic circuits that is initially due to the pleasant excitement generated relatively early in the gambling career. In time this fades and is overcome by a B State that is associated with boredom, frustration, and agitation. However, the initial anxiety associated with gambling also generates a B State. The second addictive process is the opponent response of anxiety, which is probably mediated by both serotonergic and beta-endorphins. Not surprisingly, gambling ranks along with sexual addiction and perhaps certain thrill-seeking activities like shoplifting as the most difficult addiction to treat.

CONCLUSION

We believe that chaos theory may represent the next major paradigm in psychotherapy. It is particularly relevant to the complex systems involved in addictive behaviors. Chaos theory, like any competent theory, helps us better understand the phenomena at hand. Unlike other theories in the traditional behavioral sciences, however, chaos theory states that we are inherently limited in what we can predict about human behavior. This may be one of its most appealing aspects. The future is determined by the interaction of complex forces operating in unpredictable ways. No accurate predictions can be made for more than a few moments into the future. This is congruent with the experiences of millions of people who have attended 12-step groups. Abstinence, indeed, is a process of "one day at a time."

CHAPTER 10

Family Systems Therapy: Treating the Patient and the System

Family values are the strength of the nation. . . . When the family is strong, there aren't going to be any social problems in this country. Abortion, drugs, gambling . . . they'll all disappear as soon as we straighten out the family. And that's the God-ordained way the world works.
—Conservative Republican candidate for U.S. Congress, 1998

Family? I think I sold them off for groceries last year.
—Skid-row gambler in Las Vegas, 1998

THE FAMILY systems approach to behavioral change in people with gambling disorders is usually not thought of as the treatment of choice. Although there is literature to indicate that family therapy may be an effective treatment of gambling, there is also evidence that practitioners are reluctant to use this modality (Maurer, 1994). There are probably several reasons for this reluctance. First, many practitioners who treat gambling-related problems do so largely with theory derived from a self-help orientation. They may have been trained to be excellent counselors, but usually are not family therapists. Despite the fact that they may have learned the importance of families and family dynamics through 12-step groups, they have little formal training in the theory or methods of contemporary family therapy (L'Abate, 1994). When they attempt the often-dramatic techniques employed by family therapists, they will likely generate a poor client outcome, largely because they have not had the proper training or supervision. Consequently, they may grow reticent to treat a family, even if numerous family problems are blatantly obvious.

Nevertheless, there are several good reasons to use family therapy. Wildman (1989) notes the increasing tendency of gambling experts to cite family factors as important for the treatment process. Lorenz (1989), in the same issue of *The Journal of Gambling Behavior;* devoted specifically to family therapy and family problems associated with abusive gambling, noted that interpersonal conflict is the most frequent reason for a compulsive gambler's relapse. Family members often contribute to the relapse because of their own needs or shortcomings. Five case examples illustrated the ways that family members contribute to relapse. Among them were: fear of rejection or of sexual intimacy, the need to be needed, and financial control. The Lorenz article contains excellent treatment suggestions.

A nascent empirical literature regarding family pathology and gambling is beginning to emerge. Ciarrocchi and Hohmann (1989) measured the family environments of 67 male pathological gamblers (34 of whom were also alcoholics) and 73 male and 53 female nongambler alcoholics. Male alcoholic gamblers reported significantly more conflict and less personal independence than controls, and male nonalcoholic gamblers reported less independence and intellectual/cultural (IC) orientation. Male alcoholic nongamblers reported more conflict and less independence, IC orientation, and active/recreational (AR) orientation than controls. Female alcoholic nongamblers also reported less IC and AR orientation than controls.

Unfortunately, this chapter does not add to the empirical literature, nor is it a "how to" guide regarding detailed techniques for a comprehensive family therapy of gambling. Instead, it aims to be of use to practitioners who have some training or experience in family treatment. We hope to generate sufficient interest in this class of science.

This pattern occurs so commonly in the history of psychosocial intervention that it barely warrants discussion. When data do not support the use of theoretically derived interventions, the interventions tend to be used until something better comes along. Practitioners are encumbered with producing behavioral changes, even if the process that produces the changes is not fully understood. By the 1960s, a "cult of personality" was firmly entrenched in psychotherapy. It remains firmly in place, to this day.

HARD APPROACHES TO FAMILY DYNAMICS AND THERAPY

The common sentiment among family therapy theorists of almost any orientation is that the individual being treated for a behavioral dysfunction, traditionally labeled the identified patient, impacts on his or her family. Furthermore, this causality is assumed to be mutual. However, family therapists often proceed with a stronger set of theoretical assumptions. The "hard" approach to family systems and therapy assumes that the family dynamics are the *cause* of the identified patient's behavior. As advocated by such theorists as Solvadore Minuchin and Jay Haley (L'Abate, 1994), the strong version of the family therapy hypothesis states, in essence: "Cure the family of their dysfunctionality and the symptoms of the identified patient will subsequently vanish" (Johnson & McCown, 1997).

A shibboleth of structural/strategic approaches, as well as Bowenian and other prominent paradigms in family therapy, is that individual symptoms emerge in response to more global, broader family system problems and dynamics. This idea seemed extraordinarily radical when it was advanced in the 1960s, but it is actually a fairly conservative assumption, derived from traditional functionalist sociological theory (McCown & Johnson, 1993). Symptoms, according to these theorists, have positive functions. Usually, these functions involve maintenance of family cohesiveness or other necessary or desirable family processes.

As attractive as this theory is to practitioners, there is actually little evidence to suggest that it has broad utility. In some cases, family dynamics clearly and almost uncontrovertibly directly act to promote gambling problems. The case below, altered in enough detail to make it unidentifiable, is one of the most noteworthy cases of family "ennoblement" and enmeshment that we have ever seen.

Ms H and Her Mother: A Dysfunctional Dyad

This identified patient in the family system is a 20-year-old Caucasian female with a history of multiple substance abuse. She began drinking alcohol heavily at age 12. This resulted in suspension from school at 15 and expulsion at 16. At 16, she also began using both cocaine and heroin, which she no longer uses because "what you get on the street, you don't know what it is . . . like it killed some of my friends." She now drinks about a fifth of whiskey every other day, and she reports that she is "shaky" when she stops drinking. However, she denies having a drinking problem. She has been referred to the therapist by her mother, following her mother's complaints. "My daughter has gotten so impulsive and obnoxious that I can hardly live with her. And she is too immature to live alone."

Her mother, who also does not work, supports Ms H. Ms H tried working and going to school but states that "I just don't fit in." She and her mother spend the day watching television and buying lottery tickets, as well as going to a local casino "about every other day or so." Ms H admits that at times she supplements her income by selling cocaine. "I used to do it, and it really [messed] me up. I just want to stay away from that _____." She solicits drug sales "mostly at the casino. You get someone who just won big—you know, like a jackpot, and you can get anything from him or her. I don't rip them off or anything. I mean I want to, but I would feel real bad about that."

Ms H denies a gambling problem, but notes that on "several occasions— well, maybe more than a few" she has "dropped" more than $1,000 into poker machines in one evening. She almost always goes to the casino only at her mother's invitation. "That way I can get really _____ up and party. It gets Mom out of the house, too. It's one of the few things we do together." She has borrowed money "from a whole lot of boyfriends" to pay for gambling debts.

Ms H has attempted several periods of abstinence/sobriety; the longest lasted four months. During these periods, she reported that she was constantly anxious and depressed. She has not gone without daily gambling in at least three years. "I might quit some day when my mother stopped driving me, you know, like she would have something better to do. I guess I would play the lottery, though."

Her mother formerly drank heavily. However, she has been alcohol-abstinent since she became pregnant with Ms H. Her father was "never in the picture. . . . I never knew anything about him and I don't ask. That's the family message. I've heard he was a drunk, but I don't know." Ms H notes, "It's like my mom wants me to be drunk or something. . . . I mean, you know, like if I want some beer or something she'll go buy it for me. She says it's because she doesn't want me driving drunk, but it's like she wants to take care of me or something . . . you know what I'm saying?"

Ms H has never attended any self-help groups. "I know what they do from watching TV. All they are is a bunch of whiners who feel sorry for themselves. _____ that! Anyhow, I could quit drinking whenever I want." As for insight, Ms H denies she presently has any substance abuse problems. "I used to, really; I mean, I was strung out. Now, I'm just trying to get by—you know, not think about things that bother me a lot. I know it sounds silly, but when I drink I feel powerful." As for any potential gambling problems, "It never crossed my mind that anybody would think that's a problem. It's just something to do. Something for fun, sometimes."

Her long-term plans are "I don't know . . . maybe go to college or something. . . . I really want to be a singer and have my own TV show. . . ." Her mother, who is now quite financially secure, due to some exceptional investments of her own parents, has offered to pay for Ms H's singing lessons as long as Ms H remains living at home.

Two years ago, Ms H's physician tried to get her to enter a substance abuse program. However, her mother talked her out of it "at the last minute. She just started to cry and get all crazy, like she would die if I ever left. So I quit on my own, at least for a while."

Ms H's immediate goal is to get pregnant. She states matter-of-factly: "Mom had it pretty bad for a while, until Granddad made some money. She put up with a lot when we were poor, not having a man and all. I know she wants to be a grandmother. That would make us a real family."

Even the most vituperative critic of a strong family therapy approach would have to admit that the relationship Ms H has with her mother is pathological. The two of them need treatment. It is evident to almost anyone, except family members, that the mother in this system has a strong interest in continuing her daughter's addictive behaviors, including her gambling. Why? We don't really know. We would imagine it has something to do with the mother's meeting her own needs for companionship and thrill seeking through her daughter's behaviors. In cases like this, family therapy might proceed by confronting the mother, allowing the family to experience a crisis, and then intervening to reestablish an appropriate set of family behaviors.

Hard family problems such as these are common among families with multiple difficulties. The major defining characteristic is the ongoing denial of the major symptoms that are present. For example, a wife may be in therapy for her gambling problems, and the therapist decides to bring the husband in for assistance in evaluating his wife's problems. Despite the fact that the wife may have a several-thousand-dollar-a-month gambling habit, the husband may claim that it is "no problem" or that he "didn't notice" the falling bank account or rising credit card balances. Invariably, in these cases, one family member colludes with another for mutual gain.

Despite the fact that we do not have substantial data, we assert that "hard" family dysfunctionality cannot be addressed by focusing only on the individual in the family system who has a gambling problem. Invariably, another problem will emerge or the family will sabotage treatment. In this case, the problem is likely to be intensified because the family will grow resistant to treatment at a later date (McCown & Johnson, 1993).

TREATING HARD FAMILY DYSFUNCTIONALITY

In a previous volume, the authors and their associates discussed the family treatment of gambling (McCown & Johnson, 1993). Since that time, substantial anecdotal clinical reports have suggested that family therapy may be a treatment of choice for gambling disorders (Bergh & Kuehlhorn, 1994). Through additional experience, we have refined our techniques to the point where we now feel comfortable in suggesting appropriate theory and clinical guidelines for the use of family therapy in gambling treatment. It is, in our opinion, a sufficiently powerful tool that is appropriate for almost every client who has an intact family system. Very often, this involves destabilizing a family system that is invested in a pattern of dysfunctional coping.

The concept of the therapeutic destabilization of a family system is integral to family therapy and was common among the early family therapists. Although often necessary with "hard" systemic problems, these very powerful techniques need to be used with care. In traditional systemic approaches to family therapy, there are two reasons to disrupt a family's homeostasis. The first involves the possibility that such action will allow superior homeostatic processes to help the system. In other words, by temporarily disrupting the family, a superior level of functioning may emerge rather quickly. We have discussed these ideas at length elsewhere (Bütz et al., 1997) and have illustrated their application with a series of family narratives.

A second reason is to break down functional patterns that may have emerged either prior to or following gambling, but that act to discourage the gambler from seeking help. Often, the treatment of choice for breaking down such entrenched patterns of resistance involves interpreting behavior paradoxically. Why paradoxical interventions work is a matter of conjecture; *whether* they work is also occasionally questionable. What is not in question is that they have a dramatic and destabilizing influence on any family system. This can be seen in the following case study.

Don and Melissa

Don is a 57-year-old attorney and successful businessperson. Kay, Don's third wife, is 22 years his junior. They have been married for ten years and have two children, along with several other children from Don's previous marriages. Don and Kay are quite wealthy. Kay does not work outside of the home and is "hardly at home, because we have [hired] help."

Kay began treatment after she "became disgusted with myself." She states matter-of-factly, "All the money I waste on gambling I'd rather spend on myself. I know Don has all the money I need. But when I have to make the choice between a trip to Las Vegas and a few new outfits, I just get sick of myself when I think of all of the money I have wasted." Kay is also angry at herself for spending time gambling at a local establishment, rather than at a health club working out.

Although neither will admit it in therapy, Don has a mistress who is well known to and throughout the community. He usually spends time with her when Kay is either gambling at the local casino or is away. In fact, he is blatantly obvious about his relationship with the other woman; he escorts her to social and civic functions with little opprobrium. Kay particularly enjoys gambling in new venues, so Don has substantial time to spend with his mistress.

Therapy with this couple and a son from one of Don's previous marriages was proceeding poorly. Although the couple was very unhappy, they would ruin any attempts to change. Almost every therapeutic suggestion was derided in a most disagreeable tone. Don began spending more time with his mistress, and Kay began traveling more frequently to Las Vegas.

To break this dysfunctional pattern, the therapist introduced the radical concept of "prescribed gambling." Kay and Don's son were told to gamble as frequently as they liked, in as many places in town as they could. The therapist stated that Kay should be as proud of her gambling as Don was of spending time with his mistress.

For several weeks, Kay and Don's son gambled in every conceivable place they could find. This included tawdry truck stops, decrepit bars, and dangerous taverns. They gambled together with a fiery intensity, despite the fact that Don's son had never liked gambling before this intervention. Word began to circulate in town that Kay and Don's son were having an affair. This enraged Don, despite the fact that it was patently untrue.

Don also complained that Kay was "beginning to get a bad reputation." Kay and the therapist laughed, stating that Don already had a bad reputation. The therapist offered Don a cryptic interpretation, "If you are going to hell, you might as well travel together."

Abruptly following this session, Don lost interest in his mistress. He stated that he was "impotent with her." He then began spending more time with his family. Kay, sensing that she was being excluded from this family change, stopped traveling out of town. Within two weeks after Don's decision to stop seeing his mistress, she turned down a free gambling junket that she had won at a local casino. Following this, she rapidly lost most of her desire to gamble and all of her desire to leave town to wager.

Given the potential disruptiveness of many of the popular techniques in family interventions, the possibility for therapist-induced deterioration in client families is not a trivial concern. Therapists who perform potentially destabilizing interventions must do so with trepidation because they have little basis to assess the risk of interventions in advance. Yet, if a given intervention fails, a family is at minimal risk, provided it remains in treatment. A competent therapist can usually correct any adverse consequences from interventions. Additional interventions can be proposed and developed, with the goal of eventually targeting the family toward a desired course of action. One of the skills required in family therapy is determining whether the risk involved in destabilizing a family system is worth the potential benefit. When the risk is too great, alternative strategies should be pursued.

One alternative strategy for working with families such as these, which also tend to be both crisis-prone and treatment-resistant, has been discussed by us elsewhere (McCown & Johnson, 1992). This strategy is based on several components:

1. We attempt to lower, rather than increase, family tensions that may prompt early termination.
2. We prepare the family for more extensive individual and 12-step modalities by helping the enactment of minor changes.

3. We help the family to problem solve until they have demonstrated a commitment to ongoing therapy.
4. We encourage the family to accept appropriate responsibility for their likely early treatment termination.

Using this "gentle treatment" for "hard families" can often result in the substantial therapeutic gain encountered when a dysfunctional family's behavior is disrupted. However, it carries very little of the risks associated with more chaotic or provocative approaches.

THE SOFT APPROACH TO FAMILY TREATMENT

Due to the heterogeneity of factors associated with gambling, it is unlikely that the hard hypothesis will be of use in most treatment situations. The "soft" approach is not as specific in its insistence on family factors as the most important etiology. It argues that family factors may augment and foster individual dysfunctional behavior. The family is not necessarily the cause of the behavior we want to change, but the family is inherently involved in the maintenance of symptoms. At the very least, the family is so impacted and severely impaired because of the patient's symptoms that it also needs treatment.

The soft approach predicts that the mutual impact will eventually act to impair the family and its functioning. This outcome may benefit by use of a disease model, which attempts to avoid blame. An analogy with medical treatment is frequently helpful. Following a heart bypass operation, for example, a family will have to act together to make specific changes. If one of the family rituals involved going to a hamburger restaurant, a leaner form of celebration should perhaps be substituted. The individual patient has a disease that affects the entire family, so the entire family then interacts and reacts.

In this soft form of the treatment, we are assuming nothing regarding the causation of gambling problems. Although we strongly encourage family members to pursue 12-step participation (where they may learn about their culpability in fostering an addiction), in the soft model of family therapy that we advocate, we attempt to avoid direct family confrontation. Instead, we employ the strengths of the family system to help the patient avoid relapse and make a successful recovery. At the same time, we are able to evaluate and treat problems that other family members may have had because of the chronic gambler's previous and current behaviors.

Elsewhere, the literature has recommended potentially innocuous but powerful interventions for resistant family systems. These interventions can be applied to families with soft problems. For example, in a series of useful techniques, L'Abate (1997; L'Abate & Cox, 1992) advocated the use of structured paratherapeutic writing for many family systems. L'Abate illustrates how these collective techniques can be applied to specific problems that are likely to be encountered. Structured writing assignments rarely provoke family crises and disharmony. This class of interventions may also be a treatment of choice for families unlikely to return after the first session or two.

An example of a soft therapy treatment modality is illustrated in the following case study. Note that the therapist remains fairly direct, yet does not give direct advice. The therapist generally maintains a fairly neutral stance—attempting to avoid conflict, but also trying to get family members to generate their own solutions to their problems. This is a transcript of a small part of one of the sessions.

The Curtis Family

This family . . . includes a 24-year-old father, Jason, who has a history of gambling excessively, to the point where the family declared bankruptcy. The family therapist has been employed to help keep Jason from relapsing. Crystal, Jason's wife, age 22, initially demanded that her husband seek treatment when she thought he "was running around on me." She noticed that he spent increasing time away from home and was always broke. In a very emotional family session, Jason revealed that he did not have a girlfriend, but had, in fact, a gambling problem. Crystal's response was typical of spouses experiencing this phase of treatment. At first, they are relieved that their spouse is being faithful. Subsequently, they become enraged that the spouse is so "irresponsible" with family finances.

At this point, Jason has been abstinent from gambling for about six weeks. He does not attend GA; there is none near him. He is very afraid that he will slip. His wife, however, seems less concerned about this potential for relapse, despite the fact that she is still quite angry at her husband for losing thousands of dollars and for leaving her alone with the children.

THERAPIST (to wife): Crystal, how has it been going this week?

CRYSTAL (22-year-old wife): Okay. We're doing okay. Adam (the two-year-old) was sick so I got Jason to help me out. I feel like I have a husband again. He wouldn't help when he was gambling. That's what made me feel like he had some girl on the side.

THERAPIST (looking to Jason): You know, Jason, when you were gambling, you were never home.

JASON: Yeah, it is like I have a new family. I like it. I really do. If I could just be sure that we wouldn't fall back. . . . Don't get me wrong. It's like waking up and discovering you have a family.

THERAPIST: Well, relapse is always a worry.

JASON: Yeah, but now it's harder. I mean with the [Sosa and McGwire] home run contest on. All the guys at work are betting big time. Not only who will win, but by how much. All that money. It's just something so amazing. I feel bad that I can't watch baseball without betting. I really do.

THERAPIST: Can you or Crystal think of any ways that you can—you can enjoy the rest of the baseball season without gambling?

JASON: I don't know, it's kind of like drinking beer without getting drunk. I mean, like, why bother? I mean, like getting a hangover without getting drunk, you know?

CRYSTAL: You used to like baseball. Just to watch. He really did. When I met him, he even played softball at church.

JASON: It's not the same. I'd rather go outside and work on the yard or something. At least, when you work on the yard, you have something to show for it. I don't know, though, I still—I guess it's like an alcoholic. I want to be able to watch TV socially, you know, without feeling my wallet's got to have a lock on it.

THERAPIST: You're right. It is like an alcoholic. . . . Well, what can you two do to make it better—or to help follow sports without gambling? Both of you. I want you to think about it for a second.

JASON: Well, one thing, I mean, it gets harder when I just sit there. I have to keep up now, with whatever's on, you know, or I won't have anything to talk about at work. But just watching TV, it's just hard. You start thinking of all the money you're missing. Just sitting. . . .

CRYSTAL: That's where he gets a problem. When he just sits there. Then he gets on the phone, maybe starts drinking. It's despicable from there on. He'd sell his kids out just to make a bet.

THERAPIST: So you think that when Jason drinks, maybe he is more likely to gamble? What do you think, Jason?

JASON: You got that! Give me a six-pack and a TV and I'm gone. Goodbye! I don't like it. But it's hard this year, because the Saints are winning and the baseball's interesting. And now there's college football going on all the time. How come I have to quit the year things are happening? [Laughs] Aw, I'm just pickin' on you.

THERAPIST: Well, I'm a Saints fan, too. I wonder if there is any way you could keep up without betting?

JASON: I guess. I mean, during hunting season I watch the reruns (of daily sports) at night. As long as I am not sitting there watching and drinking, I'll be okay. I think I will be.

CRYSTAL: It's like we go over to my mother's house and watch TV because she has a satellite and can get all the games. And before I know it, he's off on the phones, fixing to lose his paycheck. Bam! Like that! We can't even go to my mother's house for dinner without me worrying.

THERAPIST: So you agree that Jason is at risk when he just sits and watches TV?

CRYSTAL: That's right. Just like that.

JASON: I wouldn't have to sit and watch TV if we didn't go to your mother's house every weekend—I swear. . . .

CRYSTAL: How can I keep my eyes on you if you don't go to my mother's? I mean, it's not like—

THERAPIST (interrupting to avoid conflict): Okay, let me get a pattern clear. Jason, you don't feel like gambling until you watch sports in progress, right?

JASON: Right.

THERAPIST: And you watch TV mostly at your mother-in-law's, because it's— let me guess—something to do over there?

JASON: Yeah. I go there and I just feel like I'm intruding, you know. Like they hand me the baby and go off. Like the front of the trailer is okay, but the back is off limits. There's nothing to do over there. I mean, it's country out there!

CRYSTAL: Jason, that's not right. You—

THERAPIST (interrupting again): Okay, don't worry, this is normal. Most people don't find their in-laws all that interesting. We just have to figure how to get you through Saturday and Sunday without gambling.

JASON: Well, during hunting season, I'm sure I'm okay. That's coming up. I just have to get there. I guess I could watch videos or something.

THERAPIST: Crystal, what do you think?

CRYSTAL: I don't know. If this were last year, he'd be betting on where that hurricane's going to hit.

JASON: When it is going to hit. That's what we'd bet on. Or how many will hit. You know, I won a lot of money a couple years ago betting on hurricanes.

THERAPIST: Well, this is this year and you have two beautiful children. Another on the way. As much fun as gambling might be, it just doesn't work for a family man.

JASON: You're right about that. Let me tell you. I know I can't gamble and raise a family. Crystal will kick my butt. And it's just not right.

THERAPIST: Well, until hunting season starts, what can you do?

CRYSTAL: I know it's stupid, but I have an idea. We take the beer out of mother's house.

JASON: Or don't buy any for Sunday [alcohol sales are illegal on Sunday in this area]. I don't ever drink unless I'm over there. I just don't like to have beer around the house. My folks don't like it. They're Pentecostals.

CRYSTAL: Or if I really wanted to be mean—[laughs]—what I would do is take the satellite box and program it, just like you do with the kids. You know, lock out the bad stuff.

THERAPIST: You mean, lock out sports? The sports shows? That's really brilliant!

CRYSTAL: Yeah, something like that. You know, you set the thing so it—it lets you keep certain shows from coming on. Like you can keep your kids from seeing something. The same thing here.

THERAPIST: Jason, how would you feel about that?

JASON: Okay, I guess. I mean, I'm not going to video poker. I'm staying out of bars. I don't mind one more thing. [pause] Maybe I feel like a kid or something. I don't know. All I know is, I don't want to have to face those bills, to do all that overtime. I'm just tired.

THERAPIST: Is there something else you could watch? On TV, while you're there?

JASON: Hmmm. Maybe that country music channel we don't get. What's the name of it?

CRYSTAL: She got [sic] two of them on her satellite.

JASON: Okay, and sometimes they show NASCAR. I don't bet on that. Nobody does. It's just to watch. Car racing takes too long. I mean, you might have somebody betting on who would be ahead each lap, but I won't go there. I don't know anybody's so stupid to bet [sic] on racecars.

THERAPIST: So let's get this all down. When you go over to your mother-in-law's, you will make sure that anything you usually bet on will be locked out, right? And you'll watch the highlights at night, instead of during the actual game? How about hunting? I know some people who bet on what they'll shoot. You know, a buck, a five-point buck, whatever? Is that a problem for you, too?

JASON: No. I get outside, I just forget about betting on anything. Hunting and gambling? It's like oil and water. Fishing, too. Give me a fishing pole and you can forget about video poker being a problem. I don't even think about what I catch, as long as it's legal and you can eat it.

This family continues in treatment. Their prognosis is uncertain. Optimally, Jason's chances of preventing a relapse would be greatly improved if there was an available GA. However, his probability of abstinence is furthered since his wife is working with him to prevent relapse. Skillful therapists will be able to find an often-unwilling ally among other members of the family system.

FAMILY CONFRONTATION AND CONJOINT INTERVENTIONS

Heineman (1994), a leading clinician at South Oaks Hospital, describes how the concept of a structured family intervention, which has been an effective procedure for getting alcoholics into treatment during the past 20 years, is now being used with compulsive gamblers. She cogently notes that because the gambling disorder is so easy to hide, the patient seems to be deep into the illness by the time the family seeks help. Furthermore, because the gambling offers intermittent rewards, the denial in both the patient and family can be stronger than with most alcoholics. She also notes that, during the intervention, it is important to tell the compulsive gambler why the help of a professional was sought, what changes have been observed by family members and friends as a result of his or her gambling, how family relationships have been hindered, what the family fears will happen if the gambler doesn't get help, and what each family member hopes will happen once the gambler is in a period of sustained recovery.

At this time, we do not have any data regarding the efficacies of such procedures, or any suggestions for how to perform them effectively.

Although they have been employed routinely for many years by addictions counselors, a "bottomed out" gambler rarely has enough intact social affiliations, including family members, to support family group confrontations and interventions. When such interventions are attempted, care needs to be taken to perform them with as much dignity as is possible for all family members, including those "in denial." Unbridled confrontation can too often become an excuse for venting anger that has accumulated over the years. In our opinion, this is rarely a productive strategy.

CHAPTER 11

Epilogue: Considerations for Future Research and Interventions

There is no such thing as an addiction to a nonpharmacological agent. It is physically impossible to be addicted to something unless a specific neurotransmitter and ligand exist to make the addiction possible. In the future, we will know that there is no such thing as "addictions" to shopping, gambling, sex, or any of these other concepts that we throw around so loosely.

—Addictions Researcher, 1997

Future? Gamblers live for the moment.

—A person seeking treatment, placed on a waiting list

Once we have widespread gambling, we don't foresee any increase in problem gambling. In fact, we anticipate it will lose its novelty, its "forbiddenness" as it becomes mainstream. When that happens, the so called "gambling disorders" will vanish.

—Industry consultant, state regulatory meeting, Louisiana, 1998

THROUGHOUT THIS book, we have emphasized reporting empirical findings and extending these findings to interventions for problem gamblers. Gambling has been discussed from a variety of perspectives, and future promising directions for research have been presented. Thus, this volume represents a systematic effort to present and integrate often-disparate areas, highlighted by our clinical experiences.

One of the book's limitations is that, *at best,* the authors have been frequently forced to draw tentative conclusions by using studies that have substantial methodological limitations. This is a common problem in any new field of psychological or behavioral science research; exploratory studies often predominate over theory-driven efforts that are part of a systematic program of research. Much of this book has been based on what we have referred to as "informed clinical decisions" and "clinical wisdom." Although this is a source of concern, we are not optimistic that this difficulty will soon be rectified.

Currently, there is no lack of interest or talent among researchers and clinicians. As the outstanding achievements of the researchers cited within this volume indicate, methodological sophistication is rapidly increasing among gambling researchers and is now beginning to rival that of many other areas of the behavioral sciences. However, access to patients or clients for research purposes is difficult. Funding opportunities are scarce. Even opportunities for peer-reviewed publications to find outlets are much fewer than in traditional behavioral research. Apart from dedicated journals for gambling studies, few journal editors give much credence to the notion that problem gambling behaviors are a serious enough problem to warrant valuable journal space. This is a clinical impression, but it has been derived from conversations with some of the leading journal editors in psychology, social work, and psychiatry.

Gambling interventions now lack a strong empirical basis. Consequently, many of the counseling and clinical strategies advocated as appropriate for treatment of gambling are based on modest empirical grounding. As we have noted, some interventions have simply been grounded in a rational–theoretical approach combined with clinical experience. Counselors and therapists should take note of these limitations. Many of the problems that plague attempts to generalize applied research to different settings may also be relevant to the work presented here. Therefore, results from the relatively small amount of outcome data regarding interventions may not generalize across different populations or settings. In other words, even where we have data, great care needs to be taken in their application from one population to another.

SPECIFIC AREAS OF FUTURE INTEREST

Works such as this often conclude with a unifying chapter that spells out future areas where resources can be meaningfully directed. Such a chapter often seems presumptuous because it includes suggestions from researchers in one field telling people in other areas how, where, and why their research should be undertaken. Occasionally, the purpose of such a chapter is less than forthright. Too often, authors use an epilogue as a springboard for advancing their specific research, clinical, or even moral agendas, and hence, they hope, their status in the scientific, academic, or political community. Perhaps the effect on readers occurs outside of the authors' awareness, or at least is unintentional because the authors are not aware of the impact that their jargon and specific terminologies have on readers outside of their immediate fields. In some books, a more systematic formulation of existing data is deliberately designed to support the authors' biases. The epilogue chapter may even be used as a forum for suggesting research that is already planned but has encountered no success for funding.

Because minimal prestige has been attached to gambling research, we needn't worry about these problems and can devote ourselves to attempting to instill enthusiasm about the topic in various subfields of psychology and the behavioral sciences. Our purpose is to increase interest, research, and theory in a variety of areas. It is impertinent to tell other researchers, who have specialized expertise, about the needs of their field. Therefore, we limit this chapter to a discussion of areas where present research suggests a natural interface that may be fruitfully explored by those with greater expertise than the authors.

SERVICE PROVISION: PRIORITY 1

One of the major concerns throughout this volume is the need for more services for gamblers. We do not endorse the idea of pouring money into a problem without adequately planning more program evaluation. The thinking that money alone solves problems is magical thinking—the kind found in chronic gamblers. Yet somehow society needs to come to grips with the fact that additional treatment resources are needed for gamblers, but gamblers are least likely to be able to pay for such services.

We would also like to see an emphasis on providing *innovative* services. These may include treatment through employee assistance programs, pastoral counseling, primary-care physicians' interventions, and many other techniques that have not been applied or perhaps even conceived. Traditional fee-for-services modalities do not appear to have met the needs of chronic problem gamblers, and our present third-party payer structure is unlikely to furnish economic incentive for people to specialize in gambling disorders. If this situation remains unchanged, only the least successful and least marketable clinicians will tend to relegate themselves to the treatment of gamblers.

Furthermore, although there will always be a need for "upscale" inpatient services to handle the "needs" of those who can pay for services out of pocket, the market for these types of facilities will soon be saturated. By the time most gamblers seek treatment, they have used up all of their assets. This segment of the service delivery market probably does not need expansion, unless provisions are made for integrating these patients into treatment modalities that less financially solvent clients can afford. In other words, we don't need any more high-roller hospitals. What we need are services for the rest of us.

We would also hope that any increase in funding for treatment would not be at the expense of adequate research dollars for understanding basic, as well as applied, processes that cause chronic gambling problems. Unfortunately, the tendency in the United States, once a problem is identified, is to pour vast sums of money into it, often without a logical rationale. Too frequently, the groups that "yell the loudest" receive the most service and research dollars. This is especially true in mental health. There is also a tendency to "overbiologicalize" psychological problems, perhaps because of honest misunderstandings about the potential causes and developments of psychobehavioral disorders.

If this is the reality for gambling disorders, we are pessimistic about the possibility of ever seeing adequate research and treatment funding. Unlike the well-organized lobbies for more "genteel" disorders, such as mental retardation or even schizophrenia, gambling continues to have such a negative moral stigma that it is unlikely that strong, indigenous lobbying efforts will emerge to attract adequate funding and treatment resources. Furthermore, although the biological substrates of gambling remain exceedingly important, they are not the only components of the puzzle worth understanding.

ENDING THE STIGMA ASSOCIATED WITH GAMBLING AND GAMBLING DISORDERS

Throughout this book, we have maintained the pragmatic stance that gambling is here to stay. Chapter 1 indicates that gambling has a long history, perhaps predating even humans. The rapid expansion of gambling since the 1970s may or may not have been wise, but it occurred and cannot be undone. Gambling will return underground if restricted. This is especially true in the present electronic information age. Society needs to examine its ability to recognize this fact, and, simultaneously, to set out on a research course designed to discourage the development of problem gambling.

In other words, we must get beyond the moral model. We need to stop condemning persons with gambling disorders as evil persons and recognize them for what they are: people with problems in behavior that can potentially be treated successfully. As for stigmas, our present evaluations of gambling are not dissimilar to the sentiments toward problem drinking in the 1930s! Something must change if we are going to deal with this increasing problem.

It is incumbent on practitioners to attempt to educate the public regarding the reality of the disease concept of problem gambling. If we do not do so, we will face during the next century a greater epidemic than we could imagine.

TREATING SPECIAL POPULATIONS

In an initial draft of this book, we included a chapter on people with special needs. These were defined as people who were "outside of the mainstream of society, or were somehow 'different.'" We defined these people as "special high-risk populations." A reviewer gently rebuked us. Every problem gambler or addicted gambler is special. One of our fears in retaining such a chapter was that people would single it out for evidence that there is a vast underserved array of people in need of gambling services, and they include people of color, elderly gays and lesbians, the dually diagnosed, and the poor. True enough. However, because there are so few services for anyone, it may be premature to speak of populations with "special needs."

On the other hand, it appears from clinical experience that "one type of treatment will not fit everyone." We attempted to summarize clinical experience regarding people with "exceptional needs." Unfortunately, this chapter was probably 20 years too premature. As disgraceful as the situation would be, if certain groups were systematically denied treatment, compared with others, it would mean that at least someone is being treated. There is no evidence of systematic discrimination against any group, except people with gambling disorders. They simply are not receiving services.

This does not discount the fact that we need to know much more about gender, culture, and ethnicity, and their roles in the development and maintenance of problem gambling behaviors. For example, there may be major differences between problematic gambling rates and different ethnic groups. Zitzow (1996) found that a variety of factors, including economic status, personal stress, lack of employment, alcohol abuse, depression, historical trauma, and the sociocultural lack of social alternatives may predispose Native American adults to greater problematic and pathological gambling behaviors. In Zitzow's study, females and males were at equal risk for gambling.

Zitzow (1996) also found higher rates of adolescent gambling in Native American populations than in whites. No data that we have been able to find compare the rates of black and white gambling in America. More desirable would be data examining gender and ethnic differences, as well as racial variables.

There also may be different problematic gambling rates among various socioeconomic groups within the same community. For example, in Louisiana, problematic gambling is more common among middle- and lower-class persons, regardless of gender or race. In other words, it is a function of class, not race. This makes intuitive sense, inasmuch as people with fewer economic resources are probably more vulnerable to notions of obtaining sudden wealth. Moreover, they have fewer resources to tap when they get into financial trouble.

Like those of the homeless, the demographics of pathological gamblers represent a heterogeneous group. Because of this variety, it is clear that one style, area, or manner of service provision will prove ineffective. (Perhaps some day we will even see gambling treatment services located across the street from casinos and other "high risk" areas.)

In early 1999, we finished conducting a survey of 234 practitioners who have special training or experience in the treatment of gambling. We asked them how critical it was to have more knowledge generated about the following populations, which are traditionally "underserved." The results are both comforting (clinicians appear to be interested) and disheartening (clinicians readily identify gaps in the literature).

Table 11.1 illustrates how much effort should be expended by researchers to enhance treatment knowledge and clinical understanding of the idiographic factors relevant to specific "high-risk" populations. These populations were defined by reference to traditional psychiatric and mental health literature of persons who have been understudied and

Table 11.1
Areas Identified by Practitioners as Needing More Services (Ratings per a Likert 1–7 Scale, with 7 Representing "Urgent Need")

- Native Americans (6.4)
- People with major psychiatric disorders who also gamble (6.2)
- Hispanics (6.1)
- African Americans (6.0)
- Women (5.93)
- Children (5.92)
- Families that exhibit a substantial degree of denial or impact (5.92)
- Elderly (5.91)
- People with personality disorder who also gamble (5.96)
- Persons with substance abuse addiction as well as gambling problems (5.65)
- Young people (5.54)
- Gamblers who have not "bottomed out" (5.45)
- Gay and lesbian problem and addicted gamblers (5.21)
- College students (5.20)
- Methods to enhance GA attendance (5.11)

traditionally underserved. The response was sobering. On a seven-point Likert scale, with five being "greatly need more research and methods of intervention," Table 11.1 indicates the groups of persons that scored higher than 5.0.

Lest we think this survey was skewed by a "yea-saying" response to every question, treatment providers were much more sanguine about our knowledge regarding denial, group therapy, rehabilitation, reducing shame, reducing impulsive behaviors, and research on partial hospital programs. The clinical community feels that its colleagues in research and academic realms have let them down. Either this is true or we are failing to disseminate what little knowledge we have. Probably both hypotheses are correct.

RECOGNIZING THE HETEROGENEITY OF FACTORS MAINTAINING PROBLEM AND ADDICTIVE GAMBLING BEHAVIORS

Gambling disorders vary in severity across individuals. There is nothing surprising about this. However, factors related to maintaining abusive gambling also vary according to populations. A model appropriate for college students' gambling does not fit a model for middle-aged gamblers' problems. Specifically, our research shows that college students are motivated more by a desire for disinhibitory experiences and the thrill of winning; older adults are motivated more by the necessity to chase and the fact that they have acquired gambling debts. Older adults also appear motivated, in part, to gamble to avoid negative affect. Younger, less experienced gamblers seem more primed to experience positive affect without "withdrawal" symptoms. These data indicate the obvious fact that what causes gambling in one age group or cohort may not cause it in another, at least not in the same manner. Gambling disorders may represent different "disease processes" at diverse points in the gamblers' spectrum. Whether this type of finding has treatment or prevention implications is not yet clear.

NEUROSCIENCE AND BIOPSYCHOLOGY: THE NEED FOR EXPANDING OUR FRONTIERS

Although we have some fear of the "over-biologicalizing" of gambling disorders, there are biobehavioral substrates that are clearly worthy of considerable attention. This discussion highlights just a few. Earlier in this book, we presented data suggesting that a lack of conscientiousness, along with the related construct of sensation seeking, may categorize one subtype of gamblers. Sensation seeking appears to possess moderately high heritability and to be related to specific neurophysiological processes that are just beginning to be understood (Zuckerman, 1999). This suggests that at least some of the variance in gambling may be related to genetically mediated physiological variables, such as activity involving the serotonergic system. Similar genetic mediation may occur for anxious task avoidance—the so-called "neurotic gambler" or "high-arousal gambler" discussed earlier—possibly through noradrenergic projections linked to the locus coeruleus. Dopamine, acting primarily at the nucleus accumbens, is also a prime area of interest.

At this point, we can only theorize regarding the distinct role played by neurotransmitters and receptor complexes. However, more recent advances in neuroscience have strongly suggested that the key to behavior will not be found in the "one neurotransmitter–one symptom" method that was popular during the first decades of this new, hybrid discipline. For example, Gray's (1987) biopsychological analyses of behavioral inhibition and activation systems provide a much more comprehensive framework for understanding behavior than attempting to link specific behavioral syndromes to single types of neurotransmitters, including neurohormones. Gray's model may serve as an appropriate anchor to describe typologies of persons who habitually gamble for distraction, for self-medication, or because they do not sufficiently discriminate appropriately relevant task cues.

A greater understanding of physiological variables may also encourage pharmacological treatment. The judicious use of medications may help to boost the effectiveness of clinical interventions. The relatively newer selective serotonergic reuptake inhibitors (SSRIs) appear to have a promising efficacy profile, insofar as they may reduce depression, decrease impulsive behaviors, and inhibit display of obsessive-compulsive symptoms. (Their effects on anxiety, however, are less clear, and probably more dependent on unique profiles.)

In theory, these agents may act to strengthen purposeful behavior, helping patients to remain goal-oriented. This would make them more amenable to psychosocial interventions. However, these questions can only be answered with appropriate clinical research and double-blind trials. In the meantime, the gambling practitioner does his or her best to handle very difficult patients and hope that any medications that are used can be of assistance.

DEVELOPMENTAL AND
EDUCATIONAL RESEARCH

Almost nothing is known about the severity of gambling in children and adolescents. Although teachers, parents, and school psychologists have reported anecdotal accounts of gambling in children as young as early elementary school age (M. Shure, personal communications, August 1998), no set of studies has demonstrated the existence or significance of this behavioral syndrome in people this young. More systematized efforts may direct attention to a class of dysfunctional behavior in this age range that has previously not been recognized. Early recognition may then greatly assist the student or adult later in life.

One goal of developmental research is to provide levels of prevention that are appropriate to the severity of the problem (L'Abate, 1994). Ideally, the developmental researcher wishes to learn about methods to *prevent* as many adult behavioral problems as possible, through either *primary* (i.e., general and broad-focused) or *secondary* (i.e., for persons at high risk) strategies. Presently, applied developmental research has produced outstanding methodologies to help parents treat children's behavioral problems. However, most of these interventions fall under the category of *tertiary* prevention, or treating persons who already demonstrate behavioral problems. Increasing effort is now being directed toward primary and secondary prevention of a variety of childhood disorders (Shure, 1993).

Of special interest are strategies designed to prevent anxiety and impulsiveness in children, because these are probably closely related to gambling. Most of these strategies are classroom-based and are very economically implemented. It is hoped that classroom-based interventions designed for primary prevention of gambling will soon begin in elementary school. Clinical experience suggests that nine- and ten-year-old children can benefit from such training. Abundant data clearly indicate that adolescents can benefit from a variety of decision-making skills. The teaching of similar skills relevant to leisure planning could be invaluable in the primary prevention of gambling disorders.

Another goal is broader secondary school prevention, prior to the college years, when gambling definitely becomes more likely to be problematic and may even increase throughout the college years. Successful secondary intervention would involve early identification of high-risk children and adolescents, either through specific behaviors, or through other methods, such as self-reports. However, the hope of secondary prevention presumes several applications of psychological knowledge that are not presently available. It will be necessary to: (1) develop methods to identify such children at high risk before their gambling becomes more problematic; (2) construct and test appropriate intervention strategies; (3) identify appropriate persons who could benefit from these early interventions; and (4) identify precisely the negative and positive reinforcers in the maintenance of gambling. Implementation of steps to meet the goal of secondary prevention lags far behind available strategies for other behavioral disorders. It is, we believe, a promising field for applied developmental, community, and, perhaps most of all, school psychologists.

INDUSTRIAL/ORGANIZATIONAL
LEVELS OF INTERVENTION

A major omission in this book has been an in-depth discussion of the possible importance of gambling in the workplace. Individuals who have difficulty completing work-related tasks are not typically viewed as outstanding employees. In fact, persons demonstrating elevated degrees of gambling probably do not find employment appropriate for their education and ability (although this remains an empirical question). Employers seem to recognize this. Consequently, it is not uncommon for potential employees to be screened for suitability in part by use of one of several nebulous measures of "job time usage," none of which appears to have been developed with respect to predictive criterion validity.

It may be of interest to organizational psychologists or consultants to develop accurate measures of gambling at the workplace in the belief that these measures may be successfully used in employee selection and promotion decisions. However, prior to the use of such instruments, careful longitudinal validation must occur, with close examination of the effects of work-related trait gambling on a variety of employee outcome measures with behavioral referents. It is important to note that *none* of the existing measures for trait gambling discussed in this book is directly applicable to work-related behavior. *It would be both unethical and probably legally indefensible to attempt to use any of the present measures for employee selection or promotion.*

Despite screening mechanisms such as interview processes, questionnaires, and evaluations of previous work history, many workers apparently do exhibit job-related gambling problems. Programs designed to reduce work-related gambling conceivably would contribute to increased productivity. Because the implications of gambling include decreased revenues and less opportunity for advancement, we believe this area may be of substantial interest to industrial and organizational psychologists and consultants.

It may further be hypothesized that individuals with a dispositional tendency to gamble excessively may be more vulnerable to displaying this behavior within their employment settings, depending on particular management patterns. Gamblers lacking in conscientiousness may require additional structure and a lack of options for "excuse making." Finally, it may be hypothesized that appropriately targeted counseling in Employee Assistance Programs (EAPs) may contribute to increased worker productivity and also decrease the subjective stress associated with gambling within employment settings and in other spheres of life.

PERSONALITY PSYCHOLOGY

Throughout this volume, we have used the term "personality" with some trepidation, preferring terms less associated with the many connotations commonly associated with dispositions or personologic variables. Our position is that gambling behavior is normally distributed and may be accelerated by fairly well understood personality traits. Traits associated with gambling are explainable within a variety of contemporary models of personality. These include the factor-analytic theories of Eysenck (1983) and the "Big Five" approach, which is enjoying increasing popularity (cf. Costa & McCrae, 1998). A trait theory of dysfunctional or problem gambling is also congruent with explanations of personality furnished by cognitive and social learning theorists or based on psychoanalytic and psychodynamic models.

One concern is that a construct fitting into any disparate theoretical schema may avoid the necessary scientific scrutiny and criticism. Perhaps the most appropriate test of the usefulness of the construct of trait propensities for gambling is whether it can generate *a priori* novel predictions, which could then be validated in subsequent investigations. If it can, then its further use is assured. If not, then Occam's razor and the scientific rule of parsimony suggest that it is best forgotten.

Finally, it is important to realize that available data suggest that problematic or addictive gambling is not a unitary construct; that is, gambling problems may have significant overlap within various orthogonal personality factors that may also exhibit different situational correlates. Using Cattell's (1990) distinction, problem gambling may best be conceived of as a "surface trait," a common behavioral syndrome due to two or more "source traits" or more fundamental constructs. Mathematically, this is expressed by the existence of two or more principal components, which may be related to successful classifications of typologies. Existing data strongly suggest that at least two "source traits" contribute to gambling: (1) a lack of conscientiousness, and (2) some form of anxiety or neuroticism. This means that people may have elevated levels of trait gambling for entirely different reasons—a fact that should not be overlooked by clinicians.

COGNITIVE AND SOCIAL PSYCHOLOGY

Social psychology constitutes one of the most vigorous areas of psychology in recent years, and this trend shows no evidence of abating. There are many ways in which recent theoretical developments in social psychology can be applied to explain and predict the behavior of gamblers. However, research in this area should now begin investigating the *mutual causal processes* that social psychological factors and problem or addictive gamblers exert on each other. Extreme social behavior is modified by its environmental milieu and also exerts reciprocal influences that change the milieu. Unidirectional hypotheses, although convenient for the researcher, are probably inappropriate models for the complex manner in which reality operates. Consequently, appropriate methodology will most certainly involve greater use of multivariate models designed to measure change, especially models such as confirmatory factor analyses with repeated observations (Miller, 1998).

Social psychology has also applied its methodologically rigorous technology to the understanding of the relation between cognitive processes and social variables. Again, there are numerous areas of inquiry or hypotheses that come to mind regarding gambling. However, one foreseeable problem is that problematic or addictive gambling remains somewhat of an ill-defined trait, especially in naturalistic settings. Measurement error is likely to substantially distort findings, unless models are chosen that can successfully address this problem. Fortunately, the popular confirmatory factor-analysis models were designed for these situations. Latent trait models of change can successfully be modeled despite measurement error. This minimizes our need for dependence on univariate and unidirectional social psychological research regarding gambling, which has been the standard to date. Future research will therefore require multiple measures of gambling (such as multiple behavioral indexes, family and peer ratings, and teacher or employer evaluations) to augment simple self-reports via questionnaire methodology.

Fortunately, extensive knowledge regarding the mathematics of latent trait models is no longer necessary with the development of newer, "user-friendly" computer packages. All that is required is an understanding of matrix algebra, which is not beyond the ability of most current graduate students in the behavioral sciences. The other major obstacle to the use of latent trait or confirmatory factor models is now practically irrelevant. Such models used to consume hours of mainframe computer time and were beyond the means of researchers who lacked both a substantial budget and a friendly and tolerant computer center staff. Now, however, the availability of popular computer programs and powerful desktop computers makes it possible to analyze very complex, interactive relationships with many parameters that would have been prohibitively time-consuming to model even a decade ago. What took several hours of dedicated cpu (central processing unit) time on a mainframe computer may now be done in just minutes, using a single desktop unit.

The suggestion that researchers should make greater use of multivariate causal methodology should not be taken as suggesting that traditional laboratory studies should be abandoned. Far from it! The recent history of cognitive social psychology has shown that there is a substantial benefit from developments that occur in tandem with well-controlled laboratory studies. Research from our laboratory has humbly followed in this direction. Results from correlational studies, however, are inherently limited, unless they are confined to well-defined and theoretically derived hypotheses. Progress regarding gambling is evident in the fact that hypothetical-deductive experimentation and theory building, rather than a mere "cast net approach," is now necessary (Zuckerman, Joireman, Kraft, & Kuhlman, 1999).

CLINICAL/COUNSELING PSYCHOLOGY, COUNSELING, AND PSYCHIATRY

Data presented in this volume suggest a relation between gambling and several different types of psychopathology. However, because studies regarding psychopathology have been primarily correctional and conducted at a single point in time, conclusions are limited. Longitudinal research is needed to solidify a claim of any causal relation. This is true for both Axis I and Axis II disorders. A promising line of inquiry involves research that evaluates gambling as a symptom *and* a risk factor for future problems. Along similar lines, more research is needed to ascertain the extent to which gambling contributes to internal distress and interpersonal difficulties. In other words, why doesn't gambling simply extinguish itself? Again, more sophisticated research designs are necessary to address complex clinical difficulties associated with gambling.

Regardless of the role of gambling in major psychopathology, this behavior is a source of concern for many people, including college students. Individuals will continue to seek treatment for it, and counselors, therapists, and clinicians will continue to struggle with finding appropriate methods of intervention. We are far from developing satisfactorily effective treatment strategies. Because we know so little about modifying this apparently distressing behavioral pattern, it is incumbent on practitioners to conduct outcome research regarding interventions designed to modify gambling. It is doubtful that individual clinician/researchers will be able to establish definitive patterns from their interventions, simply because they do not treat sufficient numbers of clients to draw valid conclusions. But there is no reason why research teams across sites—for example, within college counseling centers or private group practice—could not pool data in collaborative research efforts. In the absence of substantial grant funding, collaborative research might be the only feasible financial mechanism for expanding gambling outcome research.

EXPERIMENTAL PSYCHOLOGY AND EXPERIMENTAL PSYCHOPATHOLOGY: DON'T FORGET THE NEED FOR BASIC RESEARCH

A common complaint of practicing mental health clinicians is that research, whether "basic" or of the "applied clinical" variety, is irrelevant to their needs. This complaint is certainly reciprocated by experimental psychologists and other "basic researchers" who believe that clinicians (and funding agencies) frequently ignore the potential contributions that their efforts can make to the goal of enhancing well-being.

In this age of widespread funding cuts for behavioral science research, the debate about the relevance of basic versus applied research is likely to become more acrimonious. We hope researchers in the area of gambling can avoid these controversies. However, if forced to choose between conflicting funding priorities, our position and financial resources would now side with the neglected experimentalist. Basic experimental and laboratory research regarding gambling should be developed at an accelerated pace. Educational, epidemiological, personality, social psychological, outcome, and other fields of research are important, but findings generated from true or quasi-experimental designs are equally important and more neglected.

One mistake that we hope laboratory-based gambling researchers avoid is the belief that they are operating in a theoretical vacuum. Many observers have expressed concerns that the behavioral sciences, especially psychology, are now much too splintered to be considered a single, integrated discipline. An increasing tendency toward specialization is regarded by many as impeding any sense of unity or any opportunity for either researchers or practitioners to learn from areas outside of their own narrow fields. Basic research needs to include the integration of theories from cognitive, social, personality, clinical, and physiological behavioral sciences.

One example, taken from a broad array of possibilities, is the area of attention, where there is a rich scientific tradition potentially applicable to gambling. For example, M.W. Eysenck (1997) has argued that individuals who are high in trait anxiety differ from those low in this trait in several aspects of attentional functioning. Those high in trait anxiety show greater attentional selectivity and have smaller available attentional capacity and greater distractibility than people who are low in trait anxiety. Additionally, Eysenck proposes that the degree to which this tendency is demonstrated is a function of specific stimulus attributes.

Given what we know to be true about the behaviors of gamblers, a legitimate question is: Can attentional aspects to stimulus cues help explain aspects of aberrant and costly behavior? For example, problem gamblers may have a greater susceptibility to distraction than nonproblem gamblers. If this is demonstrated, further questions would regard the contributory role of various stimuli, arousal states, and situational contexts. Questions such as these may seem endless, perhaps because they have not been examined in a systematic fashion. They certainly could generate very fruitful careers for aspiring researchers!

In some ways, the lack of laboratory-based research is surprising. Apart from the outstanding efforts of Griffith and his colleagues, and many of the Australian researchers, consistent participants in this domain of research have been relatively absent. Gambling is an area in which subjects are not hard to find and college students are appropriate for drawing valid conclusions for many questions. (It is difficult to argue that the use of undergraduates in laboratory-based gambling research will lead to limited generalizability of findings.) Because of this, and because of the comparative novelty of the topic, individual researchers who lack sophisticated equipment and elaborate budgets can still make important contributions. Graduate students, working in conjunction with interested and mentoring faculty, can also make major advances. Few fields in the applied behavioral sciences are as potentially promising for young researchers. All that is needed is intellectual curiosity, which we hope this volume has helped to foster.

DESTIGMATIZING RESEARCH AND CLINICAL CAREERS REGARDING GAMBLING

One final obstacle for successful research and treatment is the stigma attached to working with a gambling-based population. Thirty years ago, it was not uncommon for bright, inquisitive graduate students to be told, "Don't waste your time with schizophrenics . . . they never change." Twenty years ago, similar advice was given to compassionate, potentially outstanding counselors or therapists interested in working with alcohol abusers or persons involved in domestic violence. Today, this type of "advice" is most commonly given to people who want to work with antisocial personality disordered persons and gamblers.

Researchers are often told to "steer clear" of developing an interest in gambling behaviors. For too many academic researchers, tenure is awarded primarily after securing major grant funding. Comparatively few such funds are available for persons who are interested in basic research or treatment applications regarding gambling disorders. Hence, well-meaning mentors quite realistically discourage very bright minds from "getting trapped with those types"—developing a research career with persons seeking treatment for gambling disorders. As long as we discourage interested clinicians and researchers from involving themselves with the perplexing problems associated with gambling disorders, we will never make substantial headway into an empirical understanding of their etiologies and maintenance. Moreover, gambling is expanding at an unprecedented rate. More and commercial forces are interlocked in an essentially illogical discussion regarding the desirability of this pattern. The cynical researcher begins to believe that no one wants to find out answers, out of fear of what they might be. The cynical clinician realizes that gambling proponents want to pretend problem gambling doesn't exist, and some enemies of gambling want patients to remain destitute. They seem to enjoy the "ammunition" found in the wrecked lives of people whose families, careers, and futures were ruined by excessive gambling. As one of our clients stated recently, "I don't want to be anybody's poster child. I just want you to help me to get better and leave it at that."

Why don't we know more about gambling disorders? Why don't we provide adequate treatment? We have no one to blame but ourselves. Too often, gambling stirs up primitive emotions—some connected with our evolutionary past, and some connected with our basic sense of fair play and of how the universe should behave. Parts of us identify with the gambler, seeing him or her as the free-spirited embodiment of something distinctively New World, a person whose life is graced by Providence. Other parts of us are revolted by an apparent moral lassitude and want to punish the abusive gambler for his or her moral lapses. Both views come from a simpler time and apply an inappropriate model.

The truth is that, for the present day, excessive gambling behaviors are probably best viewed from a disease perspective. As in all chronic diseases, there should be no stigma placed on the victim. The stigma should rest in a society that refuses compassionate treatment to all but a very small handful of those most able to afford care. Our best, brightest, most compassionate clinicians and researchers should be applauded for working in an area so murky and fraught with difficulties. Perhaps 100 years from now, people will look back on the treatment of excessive gamblers in much the same way that we now look back at the treatment of the chronically mentally ill in the seventeenth century and of alcoholics at the beginning of the twentieth century. In both instances, compassionate treatment technologies had to fight to become normal standards of care. Someday, even the most unlucky gambler will be afforded the dignity of receiving competent, empirically based treatments that may maximize the promise of success. However, for those of us in the trenches, this day seems like a distant, almost unthinkable horizon.

References

Abbott, M., & Volberg, M. (1994). Gambling and pathological gambling: Growth industry and growth pathology of the 1990s. *Community Mental Health in New Zealand, 9*(2), 22–31.

Abraham, F.D., Abraham, R.H., & Shaw, C.D. (1991). *A visual introduction to dynamical systems theory for psychology.* Santa Cruz, CA: Aerial Press.

Abraham, R.H., & Shaw, C.D. (1992). *Dynamics: The geometry of behavior* (2nd ed.). Redwood City, CA: Addison-Wesley.

Allcock, C.C. (1986). Pathological gambling. *Australian and New Zealand Journal of Psychiatry, 20,* 259–265.

American Psychiatric Association. (1980). *Diagnostic and statistical manual of mental disorders* (3rd ed.). Washington, DC: Author.

American Psychiatric Association. (1994). *Diagnostic and statistical manual of mental disorders* (4th ed.). Washington, DC: Author.

Amsel, A. (1958). The role of frustration non-reward in non-continuous reward situations. *Psychological Bulletin, 55,* 102–119.

Anderson, G., & Brown, R.I.F. (1984). Real and laboratory gambling, sensation-seeking and arousal. *British Journal of Psychology, 75,* 401–410.

Anderson, R. (1994). *Practitioner's guide to clinical neuropsychology.* New York: Plenum Press.

Antonello, S.J. (1996). *Social skills development: Practical strategies for adolescents and adults with developmental disabilities.* Needham Heights, MA: Allyn & Bacon.

Arkes, H.R., Joyner, C.A., Pezzo, M.V., & Nash, J.G. (1994). The psychology of windfall gains. *Organizational Behavior and Human Decision Processes, 59*(3), 331–347.

Ashton, J. (1969). *The history of gambling in England.* London: Patterson Smith.

Atkinson, J.W. (1958). *Motives in fantasy action and society.* Princeton, NJ: Van Nostrand.

Atlas, G.D., & Peterson, C. (1990). Explanatory style and gambling: How pessimists respond to losing wagers. *Behaviour Research and Therapy, 28,* 523–529.

Baars, B.J. (1986). *The cognitive evolution in psychology.* New York: Guilford Press.

Barkley, R.A. (1998). *Attention-deficit hyperactivity disorder: A handbook for diagnosis and treatment* (2nd ed.). New York: Guilford Press.

Barlow, C.A., Blythe, J.A., & Edmonds, M. (1999). *A handbook of interactive exercises for groups.* Needham Heights, MA: Allyn & Bacon.

Barlow, D.H. (1988). *Anxiety and its disorders: The nature of treatment of anxiety and panic.* New York: Guilford Press.

Bartussek, D., Diedrich, O., Naumann, E., & Collet, W. (1993). Introversion-extraversion and event-related potential (ERP): A test of J.A. Gray's theory. *Personality and Individual Differences, 14*(4), 565–574.

Baumeister, R.F., Heatherton, T.F., & Tice, D.M. (1994). *How and why people fail at self-regulation.* San Diego, CA: Academic Press.

Beck, A.T., Wright, F.D., Newman, C.F., & Liese, B.S. (1993). *Cognitive therapy of substance abuse.* New York: Guilford Press.

Beck, J.S. (1995). *Cognitive therapy.* New York: Guilford Press.

Becona, E., Lorenzo, V.C., Del Carmen, M., & Fuentes, M.J. (1996). Pathological gambling and depression. *Psychological Reports, 78*(2), 635–640.

Beltrami, E. (1993). *Mathematical models in the social and biological sciences.* Boston: Jones and Bartlett.

Benard, H.S., & MacKenzie, K.R. (1994). *Basics of group psychotherapy.* New York: Guilford Press.

Benjamin, L.S. (1996). *Interpersonal diagnosis and treatment of personality disorders* (2nd ed.). New York: Guilford Press.

Ben-Zeev, T. (1998). Rational errors and the mathematical mind. *Review of General Psychology, 2*(4), 366–383.

Bergh, C., & Kuehlhorn, E. (1994). Social, psychological and physical consequences of pathological gambling in Sweden. *Journal of Gambling Studies, 10*(3), 275–285.

Bergler, E. (1957). *The psychology of gambling.* New York: Hill & Wang.

Betcher, R.W., & Pollack, W.S. (1993). *In a time of fallen heroes: The re-creation of masculinity.* New York: Guilford Press.

Beyond the odds newsletter. (1996). *Chemical dependency and pathological gambling.* Anoka, MN: Gambling Problems Resource Center.

Binkel, R. (1999). *A quick casino guide.* Las Vegas, NV: Winners Press.

Black, D.W., Goldstein, R.B., Noyes, R., & Blum, N. (1994). Compulsive behaviors and obsessive-compulsive disorder (OCD): Lack of a relationship between OCD, eating disorders, and gambling. *Comprehensive Psychiatry, 35*(2), 145–148.

Blackman, S. (1987, April). *A preliminary study of outpatient treatment program for gamblers.* Paper presented at the annual meeting of the Eastern Psychological Association, Arlington, VA.

Blaszczynski, A.P., & McConaghy, N. (1994). Antisocial personality disorder and pathological gambling. *Journal of Gambling Studies, 10*(2), 129–145.

Blaszczynski, A.P., & Silove, D. (1995). Cognitive and behavioral therapies for pathological gambling. *Journal of Gambling Studies, 11*(2), 195–220.

Blaszczynski, A.P., & Silove, D. (1996). Pathological gambling: Forensic issues. *Australian and New Zealand Journal of Psychiatry, 30*(3), 358–369.

Blaszczynski, A.P., & Steel, Z. (1998). Personality disorders among pathological gamblers. *Journal of Gambling Studies, 14*(1), 51–71.

Blaszczynski, A.P., Steel, Z., & McConaghy, N. (1997). Impulsivity in pathological gambling: The antisocial impulsivist. *Addiction, 92*(1), 75–87.

Blum, K., Noble, E.P., Sparkes, R.S., Chen, T.H.J., & Cull, J.G. (Eds.). (1997). *Handbook of psychiatric genetics.* Boca Raton, FL: CRC Press.

Bohart, A.C., & Tallman, K. (1999). *How clients make therapy work: The process of active self-healing.* Washington DC: American Psychological Association.

Book, H.E. (1998). *How to practice brief psychodynamic psychotherapy: The core conflictual relationship theme method.* Washington DC: American Psychological Association.

Bornstein, R.F. (1993). *The dependent personality.* New York: Guilford Press.

Boyd-Franklin, N. (1989). *Black families in therapy.* New York: Guilford Press.

Brammer, L.M., & MacDonald, G. (1999). *The helping relationship: Process and skills* (7th ed.). Needham Heights, MA: Allyn & Bacon.

Brehm, S.S., & Brehm, J.W. (1981). *Psychological reactance: A theory of freedom and control.* New York: Academic Press.

Brenner, R. (1990). *Gambling and speculation: A Theory, a history, and the future of some human decisions.* Cambridge, England: Cambridge University Press.

Brick, J., & Erickson, C.K. (1998). *Drugs, the brain, and behavior.* New York: Haworth Press.

Brickman, P., Rabinowitz, V., Karuza, J., Coates, D., Cohen, E., & Kidder, L. (1982). Models of Helping and Coping. *American Psychologist, 37,* 368–384.

Briere, J. (1997). *Psychological assessment of adult post traumatic states.* Washington DC: American Psychological Association.

Brister, P., & Brister, D. (1987). *The vicious cycle phenomenon: Our battle for self-control: How to win the war.* Birmingham, AL: Diadem.

Broucek, F.J. (1991). *Shame and the self.* New York: Guilford Press.

Brown, B.A., & Brown, D.J. (1993). Predictors of lottery gambling among American college students. *The Journal of Social Psychology, 134*(3), 339–347.

Brown, B.R. (1994). Really not God: Secularization and pragmatism in gamblers anonymous. *Journal of Gambling Studies, 10*(3), 247–260.

Brown, R.I.F. (1984). *The effectiveness of Gambler's Anonymous.* Paper presented at the sixth National Conference on Gambling, Atlantic City, NJ.

Brown, R.I.F. (1986). Arousal and sensation-seeking components in the general explanation of gambling and gambling addictions. *The International Journal of the Addictions, 21,* 1001–1016.

Brown, R.I.F. (1987). Gambling addictions, arousal, and an effective/decision making explanation of behavioral reversions or relapses. *The International Journal of Addictions, 22*(11), 1053–1067.

Brown, R.I.F. (1987). Pathological gambling and associated patterns in crime: Comparisons with alcohol and other drug addictions. *Journal of Gambling Behavior, 3,* 98–114.

Brown, R.I.F., & Stewart, R.M. (1988). An outcome study of Gamblers Anonymous. *British Journal of Psychiatry, 152,* 284–288.

Buckley, K.W. (1989). *Mechanical man: John Broadus Watson and the beginnings of behaviorism.* New York: Guilford Press.

Bujold, A., Ladouceur, R., Sylvain, C., & Boisvert, J.M. (1994). Treatment of pathological gamblers: An experimental study. *Journal of Behavioral and Experimental Psychiatry, 25*(4), 275–282.

Burger, J.M. (1992). *Desire for control: Personality, social, and clinical perspectives.* New York: Plenum Press.

Burnham, J.C. (1994). *Bad Habits: Drinking, smoking, taking drugs, gambling, sexual misbehavior, and swearing in American history*. New York: University Press.

Bütz, M.R. (1992). Chaos, an omen on transcendence in the psychotherapeutic process. *Psychological Reports, 71*, 827–843.

Bütz, M.R. (1997). *Chaos and complexity: Implications for psychological theory and practice*. Washington, DC: Taylor & Francis.

Bütz, M.R., Chamberlain, L.L., & McCown, W.G. (1997). *Strange attractors: Chaos, complexity, and the art of family therapy*. New York: Wiley.

Byrne, B.M. (1996). *Measuring self-concept across the life span: Issues and instrumentation*. Washington DC: American Psychological Association.

Cambridge international dictionary. (1996). Cambridge, England: Cambridge University Press.

Carlson, A.B. (1997). *Trauma assessments: A clinician's guide*. New York: Guilford Press.

Carlton, P.L., & Goldstein, L. (1987). Physiological determinants of pathological gambling. In T. Glaski (Ed.), *A handbook of pathological gambling*. Springfield, IL: Thomas.

Carrasco, J.L., Saiz-Ruiz, J., Hollander, E., Cesar, J., & et al. (1994). Low platelet monoamine oxidise activity in pathological gambling. *Acta Psychiatrica Scandinavica, 90*(6), 427–431.

Castellani, B., & Rugle, L. (1995). A comparison of pathological gamblers to alcoholics and cocaine misusers on impulsivity, sensation seeking, and craving. *International Journal of the Addictions, 30*(3), 275–289.

Casti, J. (1990). *Searching for certainty: What scientists can know about the future*. New York: Morrow.

Casti, J. (1992). *Reality rules* New York: Pergamon Press.

Cattell, R.B. (1972). *Measurement of mood and personality by questionnaire* New York: Random House.

Cattell, R.B. (1982). *Psychotherapy by structured learning*. New York: Springer.

Cattell, R.B. (1990). Advances in Cattellian personality theory. In L.A. Pervin (Ed.), *Handbook of personality: Theory and research* (pp. 101–110). New York: Guilford Press.

Chamberlain, L., & Bütz, M. (Eds.). (1998). *Clinical chaos: A therapist's guide to nonlinear dynamics and therapeutic change*. Philadelphia: Brunner/Mazel.

Chamberlain, L., & McCown, W. (1998). Systems theory and chaos dynamics. In L. Chamberlain & M. Bütz, (Eds.), *Clinical chaos: A therapist's guide to nonlinear dynamics and therapeutic change*. Philadelphia: Brunner/Mazel.

Chantal, Y., Vallerand, R.J., & Vallieres, E.F. (1995). Motivation and gambling involvement. *Journal of Social Psychology, 135*(6), 755–763.

Chinn, S. (1991). *Better betting with a decent feller: Bookmaking, betting, and the British working class*. Oxford, England: Oxford University Press.

Chubb, H. (1990). Looking at systems as process. *Family Process, 29*(2), 169–175.

Ciarrocchi, J.W. (1993). Rates of pathological gambling in publicly funded outpatient substance abuse treatment. *Journal of Gambling Studies, 9*(3), 289–293.

Ciarrocchi, J.W., & Hohmann, A.A. (1989). The family environment of married male pathological gamblers, alcoholics, and dually addicted gamblers. *Journal of Gambling Behavior, 5*(4), 283–291.

Cocco, N., Sharpe, L., & Blaszczynski, A.P. (1995). Differences in preferred level of arousal in two sub-groups of problem gamblers: A preliminary report. *Journal of Gambling Studies, 11*(2), 221–229.

Collin, L., & Horn, J. (Eds.). (1991). *Best methods for the analysis of change: Recent advances, unanswered questions, future directions.* Washington, DC: American Psychological Association.

Comer, R.J. (1992). *Abnormal psychology.* New York: Freeman.

Comings, D.E. (1990). *Tourette syndrome and human behavior.* Duarte, CA: Hope Press.

Cooper, J.R. (1983). *Research on the treatment of narcotic addiction: State of the art.* Rockville, MD: U.S. Department of Health and Human Service, Alcohol, and Drug Abuse, and Mental Health Administration, National Institute of Drug Abuse.

Cormier, S., & Hackney, H. (1999). *Counseling strategies and interventions* (5th ed.). Needham Heights, MA: Allyn & Bacon.

Costa, P.T., Jr., & McCrae, R.R. (1989). *The NEO-PI/NEO-FFI manual supplement.* Odessa, FL: Psychological Assessments Resources.

Costa, P.T., Jr., & McCrae, R.R. (1998). Trait theories of personality. In D.F. Barone & M. Hersen (Eds.), *Advanced personality. The Plenum series in social/ clinical psychology* (pp. 103–121). New York: Plenum Press.

Costello, C.G. (1993). Cognitive causes of psychopathology. In C.G. Costello (Ed.), *Basic issues in psychopathology* (pp. 320–355). New York: Guilford Press.

Coulombe, A., Ladouceur, R., Desharnais, R., & Jobin, J. (1992). Erroneous perceptions and arousal among regular and occasional video poker players. *Journal of Gambling Studies, 8*(3), 235–244.

Coventry, K.R., & Brown, R.I.F. (1993). Sensation seeking, gambling, and gambling addictions. *Addiction, 88*(4), 541–554.

Cramer, P. (1996). *Storytelling, narrative, and the thematic apperception test.* New York: Guilford Press.

Cullari, S. (1996). *Treatment resistance: A guide for practitioners.* Needham Heights, MA: Allyn & Bacon.

Curtain, L., & Bernardo, K. (1997). *The history of sweepstakes.* Law Vegas: Sweepstakes News.

Custer, R., & Milt, H. (1985). *When luck runs out: Help for compulsive gamblers and their families.* New York: Facts on File.

Cvitanovic, C. (1984). *Introduction to universality in chaos.* Bristol, England: Adam Hilger.

Damasio, A.R. (1995). On some functions of the human prefrontal cortex. 241–251. In J. Grofman & K.J. Itolyock (Eds.), *Structural functions of the human prefontal cortex* (pp. 241–251). New York: New York University of Sciences.

Dana, R.H. (1993). *Multicultural assessment perspectives for professional psychology.* Needham Heights, MA: Allyn & Bacon.

Daniels, P. (1994). Will the good times go on rolling? *Economist, 331*, 30.

David, F.N. (1998). *Games, gods, and gambling: A history of probability and statistical ideas.* New York: Dover.

Denes-Raj, V., & Epstein, S. (1994). Conflict between intuitive and rational processing: When people behave against their better judgment. *Journal of Personality and Social Psychology, 66*(5), 819–829.

Derevensky, J.L., Gupta, R., & Cioppa, G.D. (1996). A developmental perspective of gambling behavior in children and adolescents. *Journal of Gambling Studies, 12*(1), 49–66.

Devaney, R. (1992). *A first course in chaotic dynamical systems: Theory and experiment.* Redwood City, CA: Addison-Wesley.

Dickerson, M. (1993). Internal and external determinants of persistent gambling: Problems in generalizing from one form of gambling to another. *Journal of Gambling Studies, 9*(3), 225–245.

Dickerson, M., & Adcock, S. (1987). Mood, arousal, and cognitions in persistent gambling: Preliminary investigation of a theoretical model. *Journal of Gambling Behavior, 3,* 3–15.

Dickman, S. (1993). A cognitive theory of impulsivity. In W. McCown, J. Johnson, & M. Shure (Eds.), *The impulsive client: Theory, research and treatment.* Washington, DC: American Psychological Association Press.

Digman, J.M. (1989). Five robust trait dimensions: Development, stability, and utility. *Journal of Personality, 57,* 195–214.

Digman, J.M. (1990). Personality structure: Emergence of the five-factor model. *Annual Review of Psychology, 41,* 417–440.

Domjan, M. (1998). *The principles of learning and behavior* (4th ed.). Pacific Grove, CA: Brooks/Cole.

Dumont, M., & Ladouceur, R. (1990). Evaluation of the motivation among videopoker players. *Behavior and Personality, 4,* 411–420.

Dusenbury, R., & Fennema, M.G. (1996). Linguistic-numeric presentation mode effects on risky option preferences. *Organizational Behavior and Human Decision Processes, 68*(2), 109–122.

Earn, B.M., & Kroger, R.O. (1976). The subject in psychological experiments: Effects of experimentally induced subject roles on laboratory performance. *Personality and Social Psychology Bulletin, 2*(4), 466–469.

Egan, G. (1975). *The skilled helper.* Monterey, CA: Brooks/Cole.

Eisenbuch, A.J. (1977). *The addictive gambler: An existential-phenomenological study.* New York: Compton Press.

Elkaim, M., Goldbeter, A., & Goldbeter-Merinfeld, E. (1987). Analysis of the dynamics of a family system in terms of bifurcations. *Journal of Social and Biological Structures, 10,* 21–36.

Emrick, C.D., & Hansen, J. (1983). Assertions regarding the effectiveness of treatment of alcoholism: Fact or fantasy? *American Psychologist, 38,* 1078–1088.

Epstein, S., Lipson, A., Holstein, C., & Huh, E. (1992). Irrational reactions to negative outcomes: Evidence for two conceptual systems. *Journal of Personality and Social Psychology, 62*(2), 328–339.

Eysenck, H.J. (1952). The effects of psychotherapy: An evaluation. *Journal of Consulting Psychology, 16,* 319–324.

Eysenck, H.J. (1967). *The biological basis of personality.* Springfield, IL: Thomas.

Eysenck, H.J. (1983). Drugs as research tools in psychology: Experiments with drugs in personality research. *Neuropsychobiology, 10,* 29–43.

Eysenck, H.J. (1985). Incubation theory of fear/anxiety. In S. Reiss & R.R. Bootzin (Eds.), *Theoretical issues in behavior therapy* (pp. 83–102). New York: Academic Press.

Eysenck, H.J. (1993). Cicero and the state-trait theory of anxiety: Another case of delayed recognition. *American Psychologist, 48,* 114–115.

Eysenck, H.J., & Eysenck, M.W. (1985). *Personality and individual differences: A natural science approach.* New York: Plenum Press.

Eysenck, M.W. (1988). Anxiety and attention. *Anxiety Research, 1*(1), 9–15.

Eysenck, M.W. (1997). *Anxiety and cognition: A unified theory.* Hove, England: Psychology Press/Erlbaum.

Fabian, T. (1995). Pathological gambling: A comparison of gambling at German style slot machines and "classical" gambling [Special Issue: Slot machine gambling]. *Journal of Gambling Studies, 11,* 249–263.

Fenster, J.M. (1994). Nation of gamblers. *American Heritage, 45,* 34–60.

Ferrari, J.R., Johnson, J.L., & McCown, W.G. (1995). *Procrastination and task avoidance: Theory, research, and treatment.* New York: Plenum Press.

Ferrari, J.R., Johnson, J.L., & McCown, W.G. (1996). *Procrastination and task avoidance: Theoretical and clinical perspectives.* New York: Plenum Press.

Finn, J. (1996). Computer-based self-help groups: On-line recovery for addictions. *Computers in Human Services, 13*(1), 21–41.

Fisher, G.L., & Harrison, T.C. (1997). *Substance abuse: Information for school counselors, social workers, therapists, and counselors.* Needham Heights, MA: Allyn & Bacon.

Fishman, D.B. (1999). *The case of pragmatic psychology.* New York: University Press.

Foy, D.W. (Ed.). (1992). *Treating PTSD.* New York: Guilford Press.

Franken, R.E. (1998). *Human motivation* (4th ed.). Pacific Grove, CA: Brooks/Cole.

Freud, S. (1950). Dostoyevsky and Parricide. In *Collected works* (Vol 5, pp. 222–242). London: Hogart Press. (Original work published 1929)

Friedland, N., Keinan, G., & Regev, Y. (1992). Controlling the uncontrollable: Effects of stress on illusory perceptions of controllability. *Journal of Personality and Social Psychology, 63*(6), 923–931.

Fromm, E., & Kahn, S. (1990). *Self-hypnosis.* New York: Guilford Press.

Gaboury, A., & Ladouceur, R. (1988). Irrational thinking and gambling. In W.R. Eadington (Ed.), *Gambling Research: Proceeding of the Seventh International Conference on Gambling and Risk Taking* (Vol. 3, pp. 142–163). Reno: University of Nevada-Reno.

Gaboury, A., & Ladouceur, R. (1993). Evaluation of a prevention program for pathological gambling among adolescents. *Journal of Primary Prevention, 14*(1), 21–28.

Galdston, I. (1968). The gambler and his love. *American Journal of Psychiatry, 117,* 553–555.

Gallo, N. (1994). The new addictions. *Better Homes and Gardens, 72,* 42–43.

Galston, W.A., & Wasserman, D. (1996). Gambling away our moral capital. *The Public Interest, 123,* 58–71.

Gambino, B., & Cummings, T. (1989). *Treatment for compulsive gambling: Where are we now?* Lexington, MA: Lexington Books.

Gamblers Anonymous. (n.d.). *Twenty questions.* Los Angeles: Author.

Garb, H.N. (1998). *Studying the clinician: Judgment research and psychological assessment.* Washington DC: American Psychological Association.

Garcia, J.G., & Zea, M.C. (1997). *Psychological interventions and research with latino populations.* Needham Heights, MA: Allyn & Bacon.

Garfinkel, A. (1983). A mathematics for physiology. *American Journal of Physiology, 245*, 455–466.

Geary, D.C. (1998). *Male, female: The evolution of human sex differences.* Washington DC: American Psychological Association.

Geha, R. (1970). Dostoyevsky and "the gambler": A contribution of the psychogenesis of gambling: I. *Psychoanalytic Review, 57*(1), 593–597.

George, E.M., & Schroeder, J.A. (n.d.). *Parental awareness of youth gambling: Results of a telephone survey of Minnesota parents.* Duluth: Minnesota Council on Compulsive Gambling.

Gilbert, P. (1992). *Depression: The evolution of powerlessness.* New York: Guilford Press.

Gilgen, A., & Abraham, F. (Eds.). (1993). *Chaos theory in psychology.* New York: Greenwood Press.

Gilovich, J. (1983). Biased evaluation and persistence in gambling. *Journal of Personality and Social Psychology, 44*, 110–126.

Glass, L., & Mackey, M.C. (1988). *From clocks to chaos: The rhythms of life.* Princeton, NJ: Princeton University Press.

Gleick, J. (1987). *Chaos: Making of a new science.* New York: Viking.

Goerner, S. (1993). *Chaos and the evolving ecological universe: A study in the science and human implications of a new world hypothesis.* New York: Gordon and Breech.

Goldberger, A.L., Rigeny, D.R., & West, B.J. (1990). Chaos and fractals in human physiology. *Scientific American, 262*(2), 42–49.

Goldfried, M.R. (1980). Toward the delineation of therapeutic change principles. *American Psychologist, 35*, 991–999.

Goodman, R. (1995). Grand illusions. *The Wilson Quarterly, 19*, 24–70.

Gossop, M. (1989). *Relapse and addictive behaviour.* London: Routledge & Kegan Paul.

Gottman, J.M., Katz, L.F., & Hooven, C. (1997). *Meta-emotion: How families communicate emotionally.* Mahwah, NJ: Erlbaum.

Gowen, D., & Speyerer, J.B. (1995). Compulsive gambling and the criminal offender: A treatment and supervision approach. *Federal Probation, 59*(3), 36–39.

Gray, J.A. (1988). Behavioural and neural-system analyses of the actions of anxiolytic drugs. *Pharmacology, Biochemistry and Behavior, 29*(4), 767–769.

Greenberg, L.S., & Safran, J.D. (1987). *Emotion in psychotherapy.* New York: Guilford Press.

Greenberger, D., & Padesky, C.A. (1995). *Mind over mood: Change how you feel by changing the way you think.* New York: Guilford Press.

Greenson, R.R. (1978). *Explorations in psychoanalysis.* New York: International Universities Press.

Griffiths, M. (1993). Fruit machine addiction in adolescence: A case study. *Journal of Gambling Studies, 9*(4), 387–399.

Griffiths, M. (1994). An exploratory study of gambling cross addictions. *Journal of Gambling Studies, 10*(4), 371–384.

Griffiths, M. (1995). The role of subjective mood states in the maintenance of fruit machine gambling behaviour. *Journal of Gambling Studies, 11*(2), 123–135.

Griffiths, M. (1996a). Pathological gambling: A review of the literature. *Journal of Psychiatry and Mental Health Nursing, 3*(6), 347–353.

Griffiths, M. (1996b). Pathological gambling and treatment. *British Journal of Clinical Psychology, 35*(3), 477–479.

Griffiths, M. (1998a). Fruit machine addiction: An issue for educational psychologists? *Educational and Child Psychology, 15*(4), 33–44.

Griffiths, M. (1998b). Why I study . . . behavioural addiction. *Psychologist, 11*(11), 543.

Griffiths, M., & Sutherland, I. (1998). Adolescent gambling and drug use. *Journal of Community and Applied Social Psychology, 8*(6), 423–427.

Gross, M.L. (1978). *The psychological society: A critical analysis of psychiatry, psychotherapy, psychoanalysis, and the psychological revolution.* New York: Simon & Schuster.

Grunbaum, A. (1966). Causality and the science of human behavior. In R. Ulrichm, T. Stachnick, & J. Maybry (Eds.), *Control of human behavior* (pp. 3–10). Glenview, IL: Scott, Foresman.

Guidano, V.F. (1987). *Complexity of the self.* New York: Guilford Press.

Haley, J. (1973). *Uncommon therapy: The psychiatric techniques of Milton H. Erickson, M.D.* New York: Norton.

Hall, N. (1991). *Exploring chaos: A guide to the new science of disorder.* New York: Norton.

Haller, R., & Hinterhuber, H. (1994). Treatment of pathological gambling with carbamazepine. *Pharmacopsychiatry, 27*(3), 129.

Halpern, D.F. (1995). *Thinking critically about critical thinking.* Mahwah, NJ: Erlbaum.

Hamburg, S.R. (1998). Inherited hypohedonia leads to learned helplessness: A conjecture updated. *Review of General Psychology, 2*(4), 384–403.

Harmon, P., & King, D. (1985). *Expert systems: Artificial intelligence in business.* New York: Wiley.

Harris, M., & Rosenthal, R. (1985). Mediation of interpersonal expectancy effects: 31 meta-analyses. *Psychological Bulletin, 97*, 363–386.

Harvey, J.H. (1996). *Embracing their memory: Loss and the social psychology of storytelling.* Needham Heights, MA: Allyn & Bacon.

Haubrich-Casperson, J., & Van Niespen, D. (1993). *Coping with teen gambling.* New York: Rosen.

Haustein, J., & Schurgers, G. (1992). Therapy with male pathological gamblers: Between self help group and group therapy: Report of a developmental process. *Journal of Gambling Studies, 8*(2), 131–142.

Hawkins, R., & Hawkins, C. (1998). Dynamics of substance abuse: Implications of chaos theory for clinical research. In L. Chamberlain & M. Bütz (Eds.), *Clinical chaos: A therapist's guide to nonlinear dynamics and therapeutic change.* Ann Arbor, MI: Brunner/Mazel.

Heineman, M. (1992). *Losing your shirt.* Minneapolis, MN: CompCare.

Heineman, M. (1994). Compulsive gambling: Structured family intervention. *Journal of Gambling Studies, 10*(1), 67–76.

Helms, J.E., & Cook, D.A. (1999). *Using race and culture in counseling and psychotherapy: Theory and process.* Needham Heights, MA: Allyn & Bacon.

Herman, R.D. (1967). *Gambling,* New York: Harper & Row.

Hermans, H.J.M., & Hermans-Jansen, E. (1995). *Self-narratives.* New York: Guilford Press.

Herron, W.G., & Welt, S.R. (1992). *Money matters*. New York: Guilford Press.

Hester, R.K., & Miller, W.R. (1995). *Handbook of alcoholism treatment approaches: Effective alternatives* (2nd ed.). Needham Heights, MA: Allyn & Bacon.

Higgins, R.L., & Marlatt, G.A. (1973). Effects of anxiety arousal on the consumption of alcohol by alcoholics and social drinkers. *Journal of Consulting and Clinical Psychology, 41,* 426–433.

Hill, C.E., & O'Brien, K.M. (1999). *Helping skills: Facilitating exploration, insight, and action*. Washington DC: American Psychological Association.

Hirsey, G. (1994, July 17). Gambling nation. *New York Times,* pp. 34–44.

Hollander, E., & Wong, C. (1995). Body dymorphic disorder, pathological gambling and sexual compulsions. *Journal of Clinical Psychiatry, 56*(4), 7–12.

Holtgraves, T.M. (1988). Gambling as self-presentation. *Journal of Gambling Behavior, 4,* 78–91.

Horowitz, M.J. (1998). *Introduction in psychodynamics: A new synthesis*. New York: Basic Books.

Horvath, A.T. (1998). *Sex, drugs, gambling, & chocolate: A workbook for overcoming addictions*. San Luis Obispo, CA: Impact.

Howard, G.S., & Conway, C.G. (1986). Can there be an empirical science of volitional action? *American Psychologist, 41,* 1231–1251.

Howard, G.S., & Myers, P.R. (1990). Predicting human behavior: Comparing idiographic, nomothetic, and egentic methodologies. *Journal of Counseling Psychology, 37,* 227–233.

Hoyert, M. (1992). Order and chaos in fixed-interval schedules of reinforcement. *Journal of Experimental Analysis of Behavior, 57,* 339–363.

Hraba, J., & Lee, G. (1995). Problem gambling and policy advice: The mutability and relative effects of structural, associational and attitudinal variables. *Journal of Gambling Studies, 11*(2), 105–121.

Hull, C.L. (1943). *Principles of behavior*. New York: Appleton-Century-Crofts.

Hurlburt, R.T. (1998). *Comprehending behavioral statistics* (2nd ed.). Pacific Grove, CA: Brooks/Cole.

Hutton, D. (1998). *Computerized version of the College Student Gambling Inventory*. Monroe: Northeast Louisiana University.

Hyland, M.E. (1987). Control theory interpretation of psychological mechanisms of depression: Comparison and integration of several theories. *Psychological Bulletin, 102,* 109–121.

Hyler, S.E., Skodol, A.E., Kellman, H.D., Oldham, J.M., et al. (1990). Validity of the Personality Diagnostic Questionnaire—Revised: Comparison with two structured interviews. *American Journal of Psychiatry, 147*(8), 1043–1048.

Impco, J. (1996). Laying bets on the internet. *People Weekly, 120,* 60.

Ingram, R.E., Miranda, J., & Segal, Z.V. (1998). *Cognitive vulnerability to depression*. New York: Guilford Press.

Janda, L.H. (1998). *Psychological testing: Theory and applications*. Needham Heights, MA: Allyn & Bacon.

Jausovec, N. (1998). Are gifted individuals less chaotic thinkers? *Personality and Individual Differences, 25*(2), 253–267.

Johnson, E., & Hamer, R. (1997). The lie/bet questionnaire for screening pathological gamblers. *Psychological Reports, 80,* 83–88.

Johnson, G. (1996). Indians take on the U.S. in a 90's battle for control. *New York Times, 4,* p. 6.

Johnson, J. (1994). *SS 77* (Version 3.1). New Orleans: NorthShore Press.

Johnson, J.L., & McCown, W.G. (1993). Addictive behaviors and substance abuse: An overview. In P.B. Sutker & H.E. Adams (Eds.), *Comprehensive handbook of psychopathology* (2nd ed., pp. 437–450). New York: Plenum Press.

Johnson, J.L., & McCown, W.G. (1997). *Family therapy of neurobehavioral disorders.* New York: Haworth Press.

Kahneman, D., & Tversky, A. (1972). Subjective probability: A judgment of representativeness. *Cognitive Psychology, 3,* 430–454.

Kahneman, D., & Tversky, A. (1979). Intuitive prediction: Biases and corrective procedures. *Management Science, 12,* 313–327.

Kahneman, D., & Tversky, A. (1982). The psychology of preferences. *Scientific American,* 136–142.

Kalat, J.W. (1998). *Biological psychology* (6th ed.). Pacific Grove, CA: Brooks/Cole.

Kalichman, S.C. (1998). *Understanding AIDS: Advances in research and treatment* (2nd ed.). Washington DC: American Psychological Association.

Kandel, D.B. (1984). Patterns of drug use from adolescence to young adulthood: Periods of risk for initiation, continued use, and discontinuation. *American Journal of Public Health, 74,* 660–666.

Kauffmann, S. (1993). *The origins of order: Self-organization and selection in evolution.* New York: Oxford University Press.

Kaufman, E. (1994). *Psychotherapy of addictive persons.* New York: Guilford Press.

Keeney, B.P., & Ross, J.M. (1985). The dance of duality: A stereoscopic view of change. *Family Therapy Networker, 9*(3), 46–50.

Kendall, P.C. (1998). Empirically supported psychological therapies. *Journal of Consulting and Clinical Psychology, 66*(1), 3–6.

Keren, G., & Lewis, C. (1994). The two fallacies of gamblers: Type I and Type II. *Organizational Behavior and Human Decision Processes, 60*(1), 75–89.

Kilpatrick, L.A., & Epstein, S. (1992). Cognitive-experiential self-theory and subjective probability: Further evidence for two conceptual systems. *Journal of Personality and Social Psychology, 63*(4), 534–544.

King, R. (1969). *Gambling and organized crime.* Washington, DC: Public Affairs Press.

King, R., Barchas, J., & Huberman, B. (1984). Chaotic behavior in dopamine neurodynamics. *Proceedings of the National Academy of Sciences USA (Neurobiology), 81,* 1244–1247.

Kofoed, L., Morgan, T.J., Buchkowski, J., & Carr, R. (1997). Dissociative Experiences Scale and MMPI-2 scores in video poker gamblers, other gamblers, and alcoholic controls. *Journal of Nervous and Mental Disease, 185*(1), 58–60.

Kuhn, T. (1963). *The structure of scientific revolutions.* Chicago: University of Chicago Press.

Kusyszyn, I. (1972). Psychology of gambling, risk-taking, and subjective probability: A bibliography. *Catalog of Selected Documents in Psychology, 2,* 7.

Kusyszyn, I. (1973). Risk taking and personality: A bibliography. *International Journal of the Addictions, 8*(1), 173–190.

Kusyszyn, I. (1977). How gambling saved me from a misspent sabbatical. *Journal of Humanistic Psychology, 17*(3), 19–34.

Kusyszyn, I. (1980). Compulsive gambling: The problem of definition. *International Journal of the Addictions, 13*(7), 1095–1101.

Kusyszyn, I., & Bettridge, L. (1973). *No postdecision dissonace at post time* (Vol. 8, pp. 273–274). Presented at American Psychological Association, Montreal, Canada.

L'Abate, L. (1994). *A theory of personality development.* New York: Wiley.

L'Abate, L. (1999). Increasing intimacy in couples through distance writing and face-to-face approaches. In J. Carlson & L. Sperry (Eds.), *The intimate couple* (pp. 328–340). Philadelphia: Brunner/Mazel.

L'Abate, L., & Baggett, M.S. (1997). *The self in the family: A classification of personality, criminality, and psychopathology.* New York: Wiley.

L'Abate, L., & Bryson, C.H. (1994). *A theory of personality development.* New York: Wiley.

L'Abate, L., & Cox, J. (1992). *Programmed writing: A self-administered approach for interventions with individuals, couples, and families.* Pacific Grove, CA: Brooks/Cole.

Ladouceur, R. (1996). The prevalence of pathological gambling in Canada. *Journal of Gambling Studies, 12*(2), 129–142.

Ladouceur, R., & Dube, D. (1997). Monetary incentive and erroneous perceptions in American roulette. *Psychology: A Journal of Human Behavior, 34*(3–4), 27–32.

Ladouceur, R., Dube, D., & Bujold, A. (1994). Gambling among primary school students. *Journal Gambling Studies, 10*(4), 363–370.

Ladouceur, R., & Gaboury, A. (1988a). Effects of limited and unlimited stakes on gambling behavior. *Journal of Gambling Behavior, 4,* 119.

Ladouceur, R., & Gaboury, A. (1988b). Risk-taking behaviors in gamblers and non-gamblers during prolonged exposure. *Journal of Gambling Behavior, 3,* 115–122.

Ladouceur, R., Gaboury, A., Dumont, M., & Rochette, P. (1988). Gambling: The relation between the frequency of wins and irrational thinking. *Journal of Psychology, 122,* 409–414.

Ladouceur, R., Giroux, I., & Jacques, C. (1998). Winning on the horses: How much strategy and knowledge are needed? *Journal of Psychology, 132*(2), 133–142.

Ladouceur, R., Paquet, C., & Dube, D. (1996). Erroneous perceptions in generating sequences of random events. *Journal of Applied Social Psychology, 26*(24), 2157–2166.

Ladouceur, R., Sylvain, C., Letarte, H., Giroux, I., & Jacques, C. (1998). Cognitive treatment of pathological gamblers. *Behaviour Research and Therapy, 36*(12), 1111–1119.

Langer, E.J. (1975). The illusion of control. *Journal of Personality and Social Psychology, 32,* 311–328.

Langer, E.J., & Roth, J. (1975). Heads I win tails it's chance: The illusion of control as a function of the sequence of outcomes in a purely chance task. *Journal of Personality and Social Psychology, 32*(6), 951–955.

Layden, T. (1995). You bet your life. *Sports Illustrated, 82,* 46–80.

Leary, K., & Dickerson, M. (1985). Levels of arousal in high and low frequency gamblers. *Behavioral Research and Therapy, 23*(6), 635–640.

Leary, M.R., & Kowalski, R.M. (1995). *Social anxiety.* New York: Guilford Press.

Lee, E. (1997). *Working with asian americans: A guide for clinicians.* New York: Guilford Press.

Lee, W. (1971). *Decision theory and human behavior.* New York: Wiley.

Lesieur, H.R. (1986). *Understanding compulsive gambling.* City Center, MN: Hazelden Foundation.

Lesieur, H.R. (1989). Current research into pathological gambling and gaps in the literature. In H.J. Shaffer & S.A. Stein (Eds.), *Compulsive gambling: Theory, research, and practice* (pp. 225–248). Lexington, MA: Lexington Books.

Lesieur, H.R. (1990). *Working with and understanding gamblers anonymous.* Silver Spring, MD: National Association of Social Workers.

Lesieur, H.R. (1994). Epidemiological surveys of pathological gambling: Critique and suggestions for modification. *Journal of Gambling Studies, 10*(4), 385–398.

Lesieur, H.R., & Blume, S.B. (1987). The South Oaks Gambling Screen (SOGS): A new instrument for the identification of pathological gamblers. *American Journal of Psychiatry, 144,* 1184–1188.

Lesieur, H.R., & Blume, S.B. (1993). Revising the South Oaks Gambling Screen in different settings. *Journal of Gambling Studies, 9*(3), 213–223.

Lester, D. (1994). Access to gambling opportunities and compulsive gambling. *International Journal of the addictions, 29*(12), 1611–1616.

Letarte, A., Ladouceur, R., & Mayrand, M. (1986). Primary and secondary illusory control and risk taking in gambling (roulette). *Psychological Reports, 84,* 231–259.

Lightfoot, C. (1997). *The culture of adolescent risk-taking.* New York: Guilford Press.

Linden, W. (1991). *Autogenic training: A clinical guide.* New York: Guilford Press.

Linnoila, M., Virkkunen, M., Roy, A., & Potter, W.Z. (1990). Monoamines, glucose metabolism and impulse control. In H.M. van Praag & R. Plutchik (Eds.), *Violence and suicidality: Perspectives in clinical and psychobiological research. Clinical and experimental psychiatry* (Vol. 3, pp. 218–241). New York: Brunner/Mazel.

Livingston, J. (1974). Compulsive gamblers: A culture of losers. *Psychology Today, 7*(10), 51–55.

London, P. (1964a). *The modes and morals in psychotherapy.* New York: Holt, Rinehart, and Winston.

London, P. (1964b). *The modes and morals in psychotherapy* (2nd ed.). New York: Hemisphere.

Lorenz, V.C. (1989). Some treatment approaches for family members who jeopardize the compulsive gambler's recovery. *Journal of Gambling Behavior, 5*(4), 303–312.

Lorenz, V.C. (n.d.). An annotated bibliography on pathological gambling with a profile of gambling behavior of students from the university of nevada at las vegas. *Dissertation Abstracts International, 44,* 747.

Louisiana Compulsive Gambling Study Committee. (1996). Report to the legislature of the state of Louisiana by Drs. Wesphal and Miller.

Loye, D. (1995). How predictable is the future? The conflict between traditional chaos theory and the psychology of prediction, and the challenge for chaos psychology. In R. Robertson & A. Combs (Eds.), *Chaos theory in psychology and the life sciences*. Mahwah, NJ: Erlbaum.

Loye, D., & Eisler, R. (1987). Chaos and transformation: Implications of non-equilibrium theory for social science and society. *Behavioral Science, 32,* 53–65.

Luborsky, L., & Crits-Christoph, P. (1998). *Understanding transference: The core conflictual relationship theme method* (2nd ed.). Washington DC: American Psychological Association.

Lumley, M.A., & Roby, K.J. (1995). Alexithymia and pathological gambling. *Psychotherapy and Psychosomatics, 63*(3/4), 201–206.

Lykken, D.T. (1995). *The antisocial personalities.* Mahwah, NJ: Erlbaum.

Magnavita, J.J. (1997). *Restructuring personality disorders: A short-term dynamic approach.* New York: Guilford Press.

Mandelbrot, B.B. (1977). *Fractals: Form, chance, and dimension.* San Francisco: Freeman.

Margolis, R.D., & Zweben, J.E. (1998). *Treating patients with alcohol and other drug problems: An integrated approach.* Washington DC: American Psychological Association.

Marlatt, G.A. (1985). Relapse prevention: Theoretical rationale and overview of the model. In *Relapse prevention: Maintenance strategies in the treatment of addictive behaviors* (pp. 3–70). New York: Guilford Press.

Marlatt, G.A. (1998). Basic principles and strategies of harm reduction. In G.A. Marlatt (Ed.), *Harm reduction: Pragmatic strategies for managing high risk behaviors* (pp. 49–66). New York: Guilford Press.

Marlatt, G.A., Baer, J.S., Donovan, D.M., & Kivlahan, D.R. (1988). Addictive behaviors: Etiology and treatment. In M.R. Rosenweig & L.W. Porter (Eds.), *Annual review of psychology* (Vol. 39, pp. 223–252). Pal Alto, CA: Annual Reviews.

Marlatt, G.A., Demming, B., & Reid, J.B. (1973). Loss of control drinking in alcoholics: An experimental analogue. *Journal of Abnormal Psychology, 81,* 233–241.

Martin, R.P. (1988). *Assessment of personality and behavior problems: Infancy through adolescence.* New York: Guilford Press.

Marvel, M. (1994). Gambling on the reservations: What's really at stake? *Interview, 24,* 114.

Marx, H. (1952). *Gambling in America.* New York: Wilson.

Maurer, C.D. (1994). Practical issues and the assessment of pathological gamblers in a private practice setting: Special issue: Pathological gambling: Clinical Issues: I. *Journal of Gambling Studies, 10*(1), 5–20.

May, R.M. (1976). Simple mathematical models with very complicated dynamics. *Nature, 261,* 459–462.

McAuliffe, W.E., & Alber, J. (1992). *Clean start: An outpatient program for initiating cocaine recovery.* New York: Guilford Press.

McBrady, B.S. (1985). Alcoholism. In D. Barlow (Ed.), *Clinical handbook of psychological disorders* (pp. 245–298). New York: Guilford Press.

McCabe, M.H. (1992). *Gambling fever: Odds are you've got it: A report of the midwestern legislative conference.* Lexington, KY: Council of State Governments.

McClelland, D.C. (1987). *Human Motivation.* New York: Cambridge University Press.

McClelland, D.C. (1993). Motives and health. In G.G. Brannigan & M.R. Merrens (Eds.), *The undaunted psychologist: Adventures in research* (pp. 129–141). Philadelphia: Temple University Press.

McClelland, D.C., & Watson, R.L. (1973). Power motivation and risk-taking behavior. *Journal of Personality, 41*(1), 121–129.

McCormick, R.A. (1993). Disinhibition and negative affectivity in substance abusers with and without a gambling problem. *Addictive Behaviors, 18*(3), 331–336.

McCormick, R.A. (1994). *Pathological gambling.* New York: Plenum Press.

McCown, W.G. (1997). *College Student Gambling Inventory.* Monroe: Northeast Louisiana University, Department of Psychology.

McCown, W.G., Fink, A.D., Galina, H., & Johnson, J.L. (1992). Effects of laboratory-induced controllable and uncontrollable stress on Rorschach variables m and Y. *Journal of Personality Assessment, 59*(3), 564–573.

McCown, W.G., & Johnson, J.L. (1993). *Therapy with treatment resistant families: A consultation-crisis intervention model.* New York: Haworth Press.

McCown, W.G., Johnson, J.L., & Shure, M.B. (Eds.). (1993). *The impulsive client: Theory, research and treatment.* Washington DC: American Psychological Association.

McCown, W.G., & Keiser, R. (2000). *Addiction, fantasy and perception: The role of protective techniques in assessment and treatment planning of addicted individuals.* Mahwah, NJ: Erlbaum.

McGowan, R. (1994). Lotteries and sin taxes: Painless revenue or painful mirage? *America, 170,* 4–5.

McGurrin, M.C. (1992). *Pathological gambling: Conceptual, diagnostic, and treatment issues.* Sarasota, FL: Professional Resource Press.

McKeever, B.C. (1998). *Hidden addictions: a pastoral response to the abuse of legal drugs.* New York: Haworth Press.

McMurran, M. (1994). *The psychology of addiction.* London: Taylor & Francis.

McNally, R.J. (1994). *Panic disorder: A critical analysis.* New York: Guilford Press.

Meier, B. (1994, August 8). A confusion of competition cools Florida's casino fever. *New York Times,* p. B6.

Mello, N.K., & Mendelson, J.H. (1978). Alcohol and human behavior. In L.L. Iverson, S.D. Iverson, & S.H. Snyder (Eds.), *Handbook of psychopharmocology, 12,* New York: Plenum Press.

Messer, S.B., & Warren, C.S. (1995). *Models of brief psychodynamic therapy.* New York: Guilford Press.

Meth, R.L., & Pasick, R.S. (1990). *Men in therapy: The challenge of change.* New York: Guilford Press.

Meyer, R.G., & Deitsch, S.E. (1996). *The clinician's handbook: Integrated diagnostics, assessment, and intervention in adult and adolescent psychopathology* (4th ed.). Needham Heights, MA: Allyn & Bacon.

Mickel, E., & Liddie Hamilton, B. (1997). Addiction, choice theory and violence: A systems approach. *International Journal of Reality Therapy, 17*(1), 24–28.

Miller, S.A. (1998). *Developmental research methods* (2nd ed.). Upper Saddle River, NJ: Prentice-Hall.

Miller, W. (1986). Individual outpatient treatment of pathological gambling. *Journal of Gambling Behavior, 2,* 95–107.

Miller, W.R., & Rollnick, S. (1991). *Motivational interviewing: Preparing people to change addictive behavior.* New York: Guilford Press.

Minnesota Council on Compulsive Gambling. (1995). *Counseling the compulsive gambler.* Minneapolis: Author.

Mobilia, P. (1993). Gambling as a rational addiction. *Journal of Gambling Studies, 9*(2), 121–151.

Moody, G. (1995). The roots, significance, value, and legislation of gambling. *Journal of Gambling Studies, 11*(1), 35–59.

Moon, F. (1992). *Chaotic and fractal dynamics: An introduction for applied scientist and engineers.* New York: Wiley.

Morrison, J. (1997). *When psychological problems mask medical disorders: A guide for psychotherapists.* New York: Guilford Press.

Munting, R. (1996). *An economic and social history of gambling in Britain and the USA.* Cambridge, England: Cambridge University Press.

Murray, J.B. (1993). Review of research on pathological gambling. *Psychological Reports, 72,* 791–810.

Nelson, J. (1998). *Compulsive.* New York: Cheshire Moon.

Newell, A., & Simon, H. (1972). *Human problem solving.* Upper Saddle River, NJ: Prentice-Hall.

Nisbett, R.E., & Wilson, T.D. (1977). Telling more than we know: Verbal reports on mental processes. *Psychological Review, 84,* 231–259.

Nolan, M.J., & Ostrovsky, D.S. (1996). A gambler's model of natural selection. *American Biology Teacher, 58*(5), 300–302.

O'Brien, T.L. (1998). *Bad bet: The inside story of the glamor, glitz and danger of America's gambling industry.* New York: Times Books.

O'Connell, D.F. (1997). *Dual disorders: Essentials for assessment and treatment.* New York: Haworth Press.

Ogles, B.M., Lambert, M.J., & Masters, K.S. (1996). *Assessing outcome in clinical practice.* Needham Heights, MA: Allyn & Bacon.

Oxford Dictionary of English Etymology. (1966). Oxford, England: Oxford University Press.

Padaskey, C.A., & Greenberger, D. (1995). *Clinician's guide to mind over mood.* New York: Guilford Press.

Palmer, J., & Palmer, L. (2000). *An introduction to evolutionary psychology.* Englewood Cliffs, NJ: Prentice-Hall.

Pargament, K.I. (1986). *The psychology of religion and coping: Theory, research, and practice.* New York: Guilford Press.

Paris, J. (1998). *Working with traits: Psychotherapy of personality disorders.* Northvale, NJ: Aronson.

Parsons, T., & Bales, R. (1955). *Family socialization and interaction processes.* Glenco, IL: Free Press.

Pavalko, R.M. (1999). *Risky business: America's fascination with gambling.* New York: Burnham.

Peele, S. (1990). Behavior in a vacuum: Social-psychological theories of addiction that deny the social and psychological meanings of behavior. *Journal of Mind and Behavior, 11*(3/4), 513–529.

Peele, S. (1993). The conflict between public health goals and the temperance mentality. *American Journal of Public Health, 83*(6), 805–810.

Peniston, E.G., & Kulkosky, P.J. (1989). Brain wave training and B endorphin levels in alcoholics. *Alcoholism: Clinical and Experimental Research, 13*(2), 271–279.

Pennebaker, J.W. (1990). *Opening up: The healing power of expressing emotions.* New York: Guilford Press.

Pinsker, H. (1997). *The primer of supportive psychotherapy.* Mahwah, NJ: Erlbaum.

Piper, W.E., McCallum, M., & Azim, H.F.A. (1992). *Adaptation to loss through short-term group psychotherapy.* New York: Guilford Press.

Popper, K. (1935). *Logik der Forschung.* Vienna, Austria: Springer.

Posthuma, B.W. (1999). *Small groups in counseling and therapy: Process and leadership* (3rd ed.). Needham Heights, MA: Allyn & Bacon.

Prager, K.J. (1995). *The psychology of intimacy.* New York: Guilford Press.

Pre du, A. (1997). *Humor and the healing arts.* Mahwah, NJ: Erlbaum.

Pribram, K.H. (1991). *Brain and perception: Holonomy and structure in figural processing.* Mahwah, NJ: Erlbaum.

Price, J.A. (1996). *Power and compassion: Working with difficult adolescents and abused parents.* New York: Guilford Press.

Prigogine, I., & Stengers, I. (1984). *Order out of chaos.* New York: Bantam Books.

Quinn, J. (1987). *The best of thoroughbred handicapping.* New York: Morrow.

Ramirez, M., III. (1991). *Psychotherapy and counseling with minorities: A cognitive approach to individual and cultural differences.* Needham Heights, MA: Allyn & Bacon.

Ramirez, M., III. (1999). *Multicultural psychotherapy: An approach to individual and cultural differences* (2nd ed.). Needham Heights, MA: Allyn & Bacon.

Rapp, P.E. (1995). Is there evidence for chaos in the human central nervous system? In R. Roberson & A. Combs (Eds.), *Chaos theory in psychology and the life sciences* (pp. 89–100). Mahwah, NJ: Erlbaum.

Reid, R.L. (1986). The psychology of the near miss. *Journal of Gambling Behavior, 2,* 32–39.

Retzlaff, P.D. (1995). *Tactical psychotherapy of the personality disorders: The MCMI-III-based approach.* Needham Heights, MA: Allyn & Bacon.

Richards, P.S., & Bergin, A.E. (1997). *A spiritual strategy for counseling and psychotherapy.* Washington DC: American Psychological Association.

Rickels, K., Schweizer, E., Case, W., & Greenblatt, D. (1991). Longterm therapeutic use of benzodizepines: I. Effects of abrupt discontinuation. *Archives of General Psychiatry, 47,* 899–907.

Robins, L.N. (1985). *Age of onset of drug use as a factor in drug and other disorders.* Rockwell, MD: National Institute of Drug Addictions.

Rockland, L.H. (1992). *Supportive therapy for borderline patients: A psychodynamic approach.* New York: Guilford Press.

Room, R. (1968). Cultural contingencies of alcoholism: Variations between and within nineteenth century urban ethnic groups in alcohol related death rates. *Journal of Health and Social Behavior, 9,* 99–113.

Room, R., & Greenfield, T. (1993). Alcoholics anonymous, other step movements and psychotherapy in the U.S. population, 1990. *Addiction, 88*, 555–562.

Rosenthal, F. (1997). *Gambling in Islam.* Oxford, England: Oxford University Press.

Rosenthal, R.J. (1995). The phenomenonology of "bad beats": Some clinical observations. *Journal of Gambling Studies, 11*(4), 367–372.

Rosenthal, R.J., & Jacobson, L. (1968). *Pygmalion in the classroom: teacher expectations and pupil's intellectual development.* New York: Holt, Rinehart, and Winston.

Rosenthal, R.J., & Lesieur, H.R. (1992). Self-reported withdrawal symptoms and pathological gambling. *American Journal on Addictions, 1*(2), 150–154.

Rosenthal, R.J., & Lesieur, H.R. (1996). Pathological gambling and criminal behavior. In L.B. Schlesinger (Ed.), *Explorations in criminal psychopathology: Clinical syndromes with forensic implications* (pp. 149–169). Springfield, IL: Thomas.

Roth, A., & Fonagy, P. (1996). *What works for whom: A critical review of psychotherapy research.* New York: Guilford Press.

Rowe, D.C. (1993). *The limits of family influence: Genes, influence, and behavior.* New York: Guilford Press.

Roy, A. (1994). Suicide. In L. Grunhaus & J.F. Greden (Eds.), *Severe depressive disorders. Progress in psychiatry* (No. 44, pp. 223–241). Washington, DC: American Psychiatric Press.

Roy, A., Custer, R., Lorenz, V.C., & Linnoila, M. (1989). Personality factors and pathological gambling. *Acta Psychiatrica Scandinavica, 80*(1), 37–39.

Roy, A., de Jong, J., Ferraro, T., Adinoff, B., & et al. (1989). CSF GABA and neuropeptides in pathological gamblers and normal controls. *Psychiatry Research, 30*(2), 137–144.

Roy, A., de Jong, J., & Linnoila, M. (1989). Extraversion in pathological gamblers: Correlates with indexes of noradrenergic function. *Archives of General Psychiatry, 46*(8), 679–681.

Roy, A., Virkkunen, M., & Linnoila, M. (1990). Serotonin in suicide, violence, and alcoholism. In E.F. Coccaro & D.L. Murphy (Eds.), *Serotonin in major psychiatric disorders. Progress in psychiatry* (No. 21, pp. 187–208). Washington, DC: American Psychiatric Press.

Roy, M.B., Adinoff, B., & Roehrich, L. (1998). Pathological gambling. *Archives of General Psychiatry, 45*, 369–373.

Rozin, P., & Stoess, C. (1993). Is there a general tendency to become addicted? *Addictive Behaviors, 18*, 81–87.

Ruelle, D. (1991). *Chance and chaos.* Princeton, NJ: Princeton University Press.

Rutan, J.S., & Stone, W.N. (1993). *Psychodynamic group psychotherapy.* New York: Guilford Press.

Schartz, M.S. (1995). *Biofeedback: A practitioner's guide* (2nd ed.). New York: Guilford Press.

Scheff, T. (1981). The labeling theory paradigm. In C. Eisdorfer, D. Cohen, A. Kleinman, & P. Maxim (Eds.), *Models of clinical psychopathology* (pp. 27–41). New York: SP Medical & Scientific Books.

Schlichter, A., & Valente, J. (1996). A long road to daylight. *People Weekly, 45,* 18–20.

Schon, D.A. (1983). *The reflective practitioner: How professionals think in action.* New York: Basic Books.

Schore, A.N. (1994). *Affect regulation and the origin of the self: The neurobiology of emotional development.* Mahwah, NJ: Erlbaum.

Selekman, M.D. (1997). *Solution-focused therapy with children: Harnessing family strengths for systemic change.* New York: Guilford Press.

Shaffer, H., & Hall, M.N. (1996). Estimating the prevalence of adolescent gambling disorders: A quantitative synthesis and guide toward standard gambling nomenclature. *Journal of Gambling Studies, 12*(2), 193–214.

Shaffer, H., Hall, M.N., & Bilt, J. (1997). Estimating the prevalence of disordered gambling behavior in the United States and Canada: A meta-analysis. *Cambridge, MA: Harvard Medical School, Division of Addictions.*

Shaffer, H., LaBrie, R., Scanlan, K., & Cummings, T. (1994). Psychological gambling among adolescents: MA gambling screen (MAGS). *Journal of Gambling Studies,* 353–358.

Shaffer, H., Stein, S.A., Gambino, B., & Cummings, T.N. (Eds.). (1989). *Compulsive gambling: Theory, research, and practice.* Lexington, MA: Lexington Books.

Shapiro, D.H., Jr., Schwartz, C.E., & Astin, J.A. (1996). Controlling ourselves, controlling our world: Psychology's role in understanding positive and negative consequences of seeking and gaining control. *American Psychologist, 51*(12), 1213–1230.

Sharpe, L., & Tarrier, N. (1992). A cognitive-behavioral treatment approach for problem gambling. *Journal of Cognitive Psychotherapy, 6*(3), 193–203.

Sharpe, L., & Tarrier, N. (1993). Towards a cognitive-behavioural theory of problem gambling. *British Journal of Psychiatry, 162,* 407–412.

Sharpe, L., Tarrier, N., Schotte, D., & Spence, S.H. (1995). The role of autonomic gambling arousal in problem gambling. *Addiction, 90*(11), 1529–1540.

Shure, M.B. (1993). *I can problem solve: An interpersonal problem-solving program for children.* Champaign, IL: Research Press.

Simon, H.A. (1969). *The sciences of the artificial.* Cambridge, MA: MIT Press.

Simurda, S.J. (1994). When gambling comes to town. *Columbia Journalism Review, 32,* 36–38.

Singleton, T. (1999). *Winning in Las Vegas.* Las Vegas, NV: Decktrick Press.

Skarda, A., & Freeman, W.J. (1987). How brains make chaos into order to make sense of the world. *Behavioral and Brain Sciences, 10,* 161–195.

Skinner, B.F. (1953). *Science and human behavior.* New York: Free Press.

Sloan, S.Z., & L'Abate, L. (1985). Intimacy. In L. L'Abate (Ed.), *Handbook of family psychology and therapy* (pp. 405–427). Pacific Grove, CA: Sage.

Smith, P.F., & Darlington, C.L. (1996). *Clinical psychopharmocology.* Mahwah, NJ: Erlbaum.

Snyder, W. (1978). Decision-making with risk and uncertainty: The case of horse racing. *American Journal of Psychology, 91*(2), 201–209.

Sobell, M.B., & Sobell, L.C. (1993). *Problem drinkers.* New York: Guilford Press.

Solomon, R.L. (1980). The opponent-process theory of acquired motivation: The costs of pleasure and the benefits of pain. *American Psychologist, 35*(8), 691–712.

Spanier, D. (1995). The joy of gambling. *Wilson Quarterly, 19,* 34–40.

Specker, S.M., Carlson, G.A., Christenson, G.A., & Marcotte, M. (1995). Impulse control disorders and attention deficit disorder in pathological gamblers. *Clinical Psychiatry, 7*(4), 175–179.

Sprott, J., & Rowlands, G. (1992). *Chaos data analyzer.* New York: American Institute of Physics.

Spunt, B., Dupont, I., Lesieur, H.R., Liberty, H.J., & Hunt, D. (1998). Pathological gambling and substance misuse: A review of the literature. *Substance Use and Misuse, 33*(13), 2535–2560.

Steel, Z., & Blaszczynski, A.P. (1996). The factorial structure of pathological gambling. *Journal of Gambling Studies, 12*(1), 3–20.

Stein, D.J., Hollander, E., & Liebowitz, M.R. (1993). Neurobiology of impulsivity and the impulse control disorders. *Journal of Neuropsychiatry and Clinical Neurosciences, 5*(1), 9–17.

Stellway, R.J. (1990). Christiantown, USA. *Church and Synagogue Libraries, 25*(3).

Sternberg, R.J. (1998). A balance theory of wisdom. *Review of General Psychology, 2*(4), 347–365.

Sternlieb, G., & Hughes, J.W. (1985). *The Atlantic City gamble.* Cambridge, MA: Harvard University Press.

Sutherland, E. (1947). *Principles of criminology.* Chicago: Aldine.

Swinson, R.P., Antony, M.M., Rachman, S., & Richter, M.A. (Eds.). (1998). *Obsessive-compulsive disorder: Theory, research, and treatment.* New York: Guilford Press.

Taber, J., & McCormick, R.A. (1987). Follow-up of pathological gamblers in treatment. *American Journal of Psychiatry, 144,* 757–761.

Tarlow, G., & Maxwell, A. (1989). *Clinical handbook of behavior therapy: Adult psychological disorders.* Cambridge, MA: Brooklyn Books.

Thompson, C.P., Skowronski, J.J., Larsen, S.F., & Betz, A. (1996). *Autobiographical memory: Remembering what and remembering when.* Mahwah, NJ: Erlbaum.

Tufillaro, N., Abott, T., & Reilly, J. (1992). *An experimental approach to nonlinear dynamics and chaos.* Redwood City, CA: Addison-Wesley.

Tversky, A., & Kahneman, D. (1993). Probabilistic reasoning. In A.I. Goldman (Ed.), *Readings in philosophy and cognitive science* (pp. 43–68). Cambridge, MA: MIT Press.

Valverde, M. (1998). *Diseases of the will: Alcohol and the dilemmas of freedom.* New York: Cambridge University Press.

Vannicelli, M. (1992). *Removing the roadblocks: Group psychotherapy with substance abusers and family members.* New York: Guilford Press.

Vitaro, F., Ferland, F., Jacques, C., & Ladouceur, R. (1998). Gambling, substance use, and impulsivity during adolescence. *Psychology of Addictive Behaviors, 12*(3), 185–194.

Volberg, R.A. (1995). *Wagering and problem wagering in Louisiana.* A report to the Louisiana Economic Development and Gaming Corporation (pp. 1–41).

Volberg, R.A. (1996). Prevalence studies of problem gambling in the united states. *Journal of Gambling Studies, 12*(2), 111–128.

Volberg, R.A., Dickerson, M.G., Ladouceur, R., & Abbott, M.W. (1996). Problem gamblers and their families. *Journal of Gambling Studies, 12*(2), 215–231.

Wachtel, P.L. (1997). *Psychoanalysis, behavior therapy, and the relational world.* Washington DC: American Psychological Association.

Wadle, C., & Owens, J. (1996). Pathological gambling. *Iowa Medicine, 86*(8), 323–324.

Wakefield, P.J., Williams, R.E., Yost, E.B., & Patterson, K.M. (1996). *Couple therapy for alcoholism.* New York: Guilford Press.

Waldop, M. (1992). *Complexity: The emerging science at the edge of order and chaos.* New York: Simon & Schuster.

Walker, M.B. (1985). Explanations of gambling. In G. Caldwell, B. Haig, M.G. Dickerson & L. Sylvan (Eds.), *Gambling in Australia* (pp. 146–162). Sydney: Croom Helm.

Walker, M.B. (1988). A comparison of gambling in TAB shops and clubs. In W.R. Walker (Ed.), *Gambling Research: Proceedings of the Seventh International Conference on Gambling and Risk Taking,* (Vol. 3, pp. 65–82). Reno: University of Nevada-Reno.

Walker, M.B. (1996). *The psychology of gambling.* New York: Butterworth Architecture.

Walker, M.B., & Phil, D. (1992). Irrational thinking among slot machine players. *Journal of Gambling Studies, 8*(3), 245–261.

Walsh, B.W., & Rosen, P.M. (1988). *Self-mutilation: Theory, research, and treatment.* New York: Guilford Press.

Walters, G.D. (1994). The gambling lifestyle: I: Theory. *Journal of Gambling Studies, 10*(2), 159–182.

Walters, G.D. (1999). *The addiction concept: Working hypothesis or self-fulfilling prophecy?* Needham Heights, MA: Allyn & Bacon.

Welt, S.R., & Herron, W.G. (1990). *Narcissism and the psychotherapist.* New York: Guilford Press.

Westphal, J.R., & Rush, J.A. (1996). Pathological gambling in Louisiana: An epidemiological perspective. *Journal of the Louisiana State Medical Society,* 353–358.

Wexler, A., & Wexler, S. (1992). *Facts on compulsive gambling and addiction.* Rutgers, NJ: Counseling and Personnel Services, Center of Alcohol Studies.

Wexler, A., & Wexler, S. (1993). *The counselor and compulsive gambling: The hidden addiction. Facts on compulsive gambling and addiction. Clearinghouse fact sheet.* Piscataway, NJ: Rutgers' University.

White, W.L. (1998). *Slaying the dragon: The history of addiction treatment and recovery in America.* Bloomington, IL: Chestnut Health Systems.

Wiener, D.J. (1999). *Beyond talk therapy: Using movement and expressive techniques in clinical practice.* Washington DC: American Psychological Association.

Wiesenhutter, E. (1974). Compulsive gambling. *Zeitschrift-fur-Klinische-Psychologie-und-Psychotherapie, 22*(2), 147–160.

Wildman, R.W. (1989). Pathological gambling: Marital-familial factors, implications, and treatments. *Journal of Gambling Behavior, 5*(4), 293–301.

Williams, M.E. (1999). *Legalized gambling.* New York: Greenhaven Press.

Willis, T.A. (1996). Escalated substance use: A longitudinal grouping analysis from early to middle adolescence. *Journal of Abnormal Psychology, 105*(2), 166–180.

Wilson, A.W. (1972). Magic in contemporary life and in psychoanalysis. *Psychoanalytic Review, 59*(1), 5–18.

Wilson, J.R. (1992). *Addictionary: A primer of recovery terms and concepts from a abstinence to withdrawal.* New York: Simon & Schuster.

Winters, K.C., Stinchfield, R.D., & Fulkerson, J. (1993). Toward the development of an adolescent gambling problem severity scale. *Journal of Gambling Studies, 9*(1), 63–84.

Winters, K.C., Stinchfield, R.D., & Kim, L.G. (1995). Monitoring adolescent gambling in Minnesota. *Journal of Gambling Studies, 11*(2), 165–183.

Wong, P.T.P., & Weiner, B. (1981). When people ask "why" questions, and the heuristics of attributional search. *Journal of Personality and Social Psychology, 40,* 650–663.

Wood, G. (1992). Predicting outcomes: Sports and stocks. *Journal of Gambling Studies, 8*(2), 201–222.

Wray, I., & Dickerson, M.G. (1981). Cessation of high frequency gambling and withdrawal symptoms. *British Journal of Addiction, 76,* 401–405.

Zillman, D. (1998). *Connections between sexuality and aggression* (2nd ed.). Mahwah, NJ: Erlbaum.

Zinberg, N.E., & Shaffer, H.J. (1985). The social psychology of intoxicant use: The interaction of personality and social setting. In H.B. Milkman & H.J. Shaffer (Eds.), *The addictions: Multidisplinary perspectives and treatments* (pp. 57–74). Lexington, MA: Lexington Books.

Zitzow, D. (1996). Comparative study of problematic gambling behaviors between American Indian and non-Indian adults in a northern plains reservation. *American Indian and Alaska Native Mental Health Research, 7*(2), 27–41.

Zucker, R.A. (1987). The four alcoholisms: A developmental account of the etiologic process, In P.C. Rivers (Ed.), *Nebraska Symposium on motivation, 1986: Vol. 34, Alcohol and addictive behaviors,* Lincoln: University of Nebraska Press.

Zucker, R.A., & Gomberg, E.S.L. (1986). Etiology of alcoholism reconsidered: The case for biopsychosocial processes. *American Psychologist, 41,* 783–793.

Zuckerman, M. (1979). *Sensation seeking: Beyond the optimal level of arousal.* Hillsdale, NJ: Erlbaum.

Zuckerman, M. (1984). Sensation seeking: A comparative approach to a human trait. *Behavioral and Brain Sciences, 7,* 413–471.

Zuckerman, M. (1999). *Vulnerability to psychopathology: A biosocial model.* Washington DC: American Psychological Association.

Zuckerman, M., Joireman, J., Kraft, M., & Kuhlman, D.M. (1999). Where do motivational and emotional traits fit within three factor models of personality? *Personality and Individual Differences, 26*(3), 487–504.

Author Index

Subject Index

Printed in the United States
141632LV00004B/20/A

9 780471 189695